D0898193

JEWISH THOUGHT AND THE SCIENTIFIC
REVOLUTION OF THE SIXTEENTH CENTURY

THE LITTMAN LIBRARY OF
JEWISH CIVILIZATION

FOUNDER
L. T. S. Littman

EDITORS
David Goldstein
Louis Jacobs
Vivian D. Lipman

For the love of God
and in memory of
JOSEPH AARON LITTMAN

'Get wisdom, get understanding:
Forsake her not and she shall preserve thee'

Jewish Thought and the Scientific Revolution of the Sixteenth Century

David Gans (1541–1613) and his Times

ANDRÉ NEHER

TRANSLATED FROM THE FRENCH
BY DAVID MAISEL

PUBLISHED FOR
THE LITTMAN LIBRARY
BY
OXFORD UNIVERSITY PRESS
1986

Oxford University Press, Walton Street, Oxford OX2 6DP
Oxford New York Toronto
Delhi Bombay Calcutta Madras Karachi
Petaling Jaya Singapore Hong Kong Tokyo
Nairobi Dar es Salaam Cape Town
Melbourne Auckland
and associated companies in
Beirut Berlin Ibadan Nicosia

Oxford is a trade mark of Oxford University Press

Published in the United States
by Oxford University Press, New York

British Library Cataloguing in Publication Data
Neher, André
Jewish thought and the scientific revolution of
the sixteenth century: David Gans (1541–1613) —
(The Littman Library of Jewish civilization)
1. Gans, David   2. Intellectuals —
Czechoslovakia—Biography
I. Title   II. Series
943.7'092'4   DB2151.G/
ISBN *0–19–710057–0*

Library of Congress Cataloging in Publication Data
Neher, André.
Jewish thought and the scientific revolution
of the sixteenth century.
(The Littman library of Jewish civilization)
Translation of: David Gans, 1541–1613.
Bibliography: p.
Includes index.
1. Gans, David ben Solomon, 1541–1613.   2. Judaism—
History—Medieval and early modern period, 425–1789.
3. Astronomy—History.   4. Cosmography—History.
5. Astronomers—Czechoslovakia—Biography.
I. Title   II. Series.
QC36.G36N4413 1986   520'.92'4   85–21797
ISBN *0–19–710057–0*

Set by Hope Services, Abingdon
Printed in Great Britain by
The Alden Press, Oxford

Preface to the English Edition

THE original French edition of this book, published in 1974, was the first comprehensive study of the work of David Gans and his intellectual environment, both in its Jewish aspect and with regard to the great spiritual revolutions of the sixteenth century (the discovery of America, the round-the-world voyages, the Renaissance, the Reformation, the astronomical discoveries from Copernicus to Galileo).

As far as possible, all previous works were carefully consulted. These, although numerous, were so dissimilar one from the other, and, above all, so unequal in quality that I decided to leave it to the reader to separate the wheat from the chaff. At the same time, I pointed out the omissions, the errors, and very often the absurdities that even the most serious authors sometimes passed on over the decades and centuries without troubling to check their sources.

Among the errors I exposed was the notion that David Gans was the first Jew in the Ashkenazi world to devote himself to profane studies—history, astronomy, mathematics. To make such an assertion would mean overlooking the Rema, the Maharal, Mordecai Jaffe, and a great many other Ashkenazi Jews who were the formative influences on Gans and his predecessors.

I also disproved the stereotype of an obscurantist Ashkenazi Judaism shut up within an intellectual ghetto and incapable of opening itself up to the great currents of universal thought as did Italian and Dutch Judaism at the same period. I demonstrated the relationship of Jewish thought in Prague, Posen, Cracow, and Frankfurt to the general thinking of the Renaissance.

From 1974 onwards, my book with its meticulous bibliography helped to clear away this undergrowth and to shed light on that period, so important with regard to both Jewish and universal thinking. Mistakes were corrected; gaps were filled. Writers such as Joseph Delmedigo, Abraham Farissol, Meir Ibn Gabbai, and, of course, David Gans himself, all of whom I was the first to bring to the attention of the specialists, became the subjects of serious, substantial monographs themselves provided with instructive bibliographies.

I am therefore able to look back with satisfaction, knowing myself to have been the pioneer, as I hoped, of a new area of research whose exploration is still in progress.

It is in this perspective that the English translation of my book is now being offered. It will bring the reader and researcher much new and, I believe, stimulating material which thus far cannot be found elsewhere.

I wish to express my gratitude to David Maisel, who has already translated my *Exile of the Word*, and who once again, in my opinion, has made an excellent translation.

Tishri 5746–October 1985   André Neher
Jerusalem

Contents

PART ONE
THE SPIRITUAL LANDSCAPE

The publication of Zemah David, David Gans's first work, a few weeks after the meeting of Rudolph II of Habsburg and the Maharal in the Hradschin palace.

The centenary of the discovery of the New World; St. Bartholomew's night; the introduction of the Gregorian calendar. Henry of Navarre, an example of tolerance. An example of intolerance: the martyrdom of Giordano Bruno.
   Padua, 1592
   Galileo's first lecture; his praise of Tycho Brahe, who settled in Prague in 1599 and had Johannes Kepler and David Gans among his assistants. David Gans's plan for Nehmad ve-Na'im.

The ingratitude of contemporaries and historians towards David Gans.
   A life in three stages. Westphalia, the Rhine, and the Main. The first vital encounter with science: the discovery of Euclid. A humanistic yeshiva: Cracow.
   A dazzling city: Prague, myth and reality. Prague: David Gans's account of the origins and of the beauty of Prague; Exile and Redemption.
   The unexpected epilogue: 'I have scanned the heavens in Tycho Brahe's observatory'.

The conflict of reason and mysticism. The awkward appropriation of reason by mysticism: Maimonides metamorphosed into a kabbalist.

PART TWO

DAVID GANS, COSMOGRAPHER

the Cartesian rearguard action. From the terror of Pascal to the wonder of David Gans.

Abbreviations

Alter	George (Jiri) Alter, *Two Renaissance Astronomers* (Prague, 1958)
BH	*Be'er Ha-Golah* (pagination according to the Pardes edition, Tel Aviv, 1956)
Cat. Bodl.	Moritz Steinschneider, *Catalogus Librorum Hebraeorum in Bibliotheca Bodleiana* (Berlin, 1852–60). This should be checked by reference to A. E. Cowley, *A Concise Catalogue of the Hebrew Printed Books in the Bodleian Library* (Oxford, 1929)
DG	David Gans
Dreyer, *TB*	J. L. E. Dreyer, *Tycho Brahe. A Picture of Scientific Life and Work in the XVI Century* (New York, 1890) (reprinted 1963)
Freedman	C. S. Freedman, *Introduction to David Gans: His Life, Background and Works*, (stencil, New York, 1937)
HJ	*Historia Judaica*
HUCA	*Hebrew Union College Annual*
Ix	See Index
JB	*Judaica Bohemiae*
JGGJC	*Jahrbuch der Gesellschaft für Geschichte der Juden in der Cechoslovakischen Republik*
JK, *Werke*	Johannes Kepler, *Gesammelte Werke*, ed. Max Caspar (Munich, 1949–59), 18 vols.
JQR	*Jewish Quarterly Review*
MGWJ	*Monatsschrift für Geschichte und Wissenschaft des Judenthums*
NI	*Nezah Israel* (pagination of Pardes edition, Tel Aviv, 1956)
NN	*Nehmad ve-Na'im* (pagination of edition printed Jessnitz, 1743)
NO	*Netivot Olam* (pagination of Pardes edition, Tel Aviv, 1956)
REJ	*Revue des Études Juives*
RHPR	*Revue d'Histoire et de Philosophie Religieuses*
TB, Op. Om.	*Tychonis Brahe Dani Opera Omnia*, ed. J. L. E. Dreyer (Copenhagen, 1913–29), 15 vols.
TH	*Torat ha-Olah* (pagination Prague edition, 1570)
ZD	*Zemah David* (pagination of the Huminer edition, Jerusalem, 1966)
ZGJT	*Zeitschrift für Geschichte der Juden in der Tschechoslovakei*

List of illustrations

Two Contemporary Judgements
on Nicholas Copernicus

A Jewish opinion: September 1612

About seventy years ago there lived a man named Nicholas Copernicus, a scholar of genius, surpassing all his contemporaries in his knowledge of astronomy. It is said of him that he has been unequalled by anyone since Ptolemy. He ascertained the positions and motions of the planets and stars with great precision, and, in order to solve the innumerable complex problems involved, and, above all, in order to discover the true causes of all these movements and their deviations, he decided, asserted and, with an extraordinary greatness of mind, endeavoured to demonstrate that the spheres are absolutely immobile and that it is the terrestrial globe which is in constant rotation around them. He devoted to this demonstration a great book of infinite depth and intelligence. A large number of the leading scholars of our time have declared themselves entirely in agreement with his theories. I mention this fact in order to make it absolutely clear that we by no means consider that everything relating to the movements of stars and planets is entirely in accordance with the opinions of the ancient astronomers on the matter. No, in this domain man is completely at liberty to discover the theory which seems to him to be most consistent with his sense of reason, providing only that the theory offers a reasonable explanation of the paradoxes of the movements of the heavenly bodies.

David Gans, Preface to *Magen David*, Prague 1612.
First explicit reference to Copernicus in a Hebrew text.

A Christian opinion: March 1616

Seeing that it has come to the notice of the General Congregation of the Index that the Pythagorean doctrine—which is false and entirely opposed to the Holy Scriptures—of the movement of the earth and the immobility of the sun is also taught by Nicholas Copernicus in *De Revolutionibus orbium coelestium* . . ., in order that this opinion should not be further propagated to the detriment of the Catholic truth, the Sacred Congregation has decreed that the said book should be suspended until it is corrected . . ., and that all similar works which contain these teachings should be prohibited, this present decree prohibiting, condemning, and suspending all of them respectively. In witness whereof this present decree has been signed and sealed by the hand and seal of the Very Reverend Monsignor the Cardinal of Santa Cecilia, Bishop of Albano.

Decree of the Holy Office, Rome, 5 March 1616.

PART ONE

THE SPIRITUAL LANDSCAPE

I

Spotlight: Prague 1592

EXACTLY a century had passed since the expulsion of the Jews from Spain, since that momentous event which Don Isaac Abravanel—its witness and victim—called the fall of the Third Temple.

It had been a century of Exile *par excellence* in which thousands of Jews had been scattered all over the world, including those new lands which Christopher Columbus had discovered in that same year 1492, one century before 1592. It had been a century, also, of Messianic stirrings, of intense and fervent preparation for the redemption which one hoped, one knew, must necessarily come to compensate for the dispersion. After the stormy episode of David Reubeni and Solomon Molcho in 1532, the most eminent Jewish sages had gathered together in Safed in Palestine, and the inspiration disseminated by Joseph Caro, Moses Cordovero, and Isaac Luria from the top of that rock in Galilee had flooded the second half of the sixteenth century with a Messianic light unknown till then in Israel.

A few rays of that light had already reached Prague, but in that city as in all Bohemia, Moravia, and as far as neighbouring Poland, an original light had begun to manifest itself, making that region of Central Europe a breeding-ground of Messianism, but not of a vertical Messianism like that of Safed. The Maharal, the founder of the Messianism of Prague, had turned it in a horizontal direction. More concerned with the world and humanity than with cosmic phenomena, the Maharal (Judah Loew 1525–1609) had founded a humanistic Messianism of which, in 1592, he had already given remarkable testimony through the publication of his first works: *Gur Aryeh* in 1578, *Gevurot ha-Shem* in 1582 and *Derekh Ḥayyim* in 1589. The main part of his work, however, still remained to be accomplished, and most of it was published around the period 1595 to 1600.

This dual centenary did not pass in Prague before certain key events had taken place, raising life on to another level. Three events of capital importance succeeded one another in the space of a few weeks, each one marking a new stage in the spiritual history of the School of Prague. First of all, on Sunday the third of Adar 5352 (15 February 1592), or, as another source has it, the following Sunday, the Maharal, the Chief Rabbi of Prague, was invited to the Hradschin Palace for a long meeting with the Emperor Rudolph II of Habsburg.

Then, on Thursday the fourth of Iyar (16 April), the Maharal left Prague for Posen, his native town, where he served as rabbi until his return to Prague in 1597. It was in the synagogue at Posen that, four weeks before taking up his appointment, on the feast of Shavuot (the sixth of Sivan or 17 May), he preached his great sermon on revelation, a kind of manifesto of what we have called the humanistic Messianism of the Maharal.

And finally, six days before the feast of Shavuot, at the beginning of the month of Sivan (Tuesday, the first of Sivan or the twelfth of May), a book of importance was published in Prague: a dual chronicle of Jewish and universal history, from the beginnings of mankind until that year 1592—the last item but one being the Maharal's audience with the Emperor and his departure from Prague. The title of the book was *Sefer Ẓemaḥ David* (The Book of the Messianic Shoot of the House of David), and its author was David Gans, a disciple of the Maharal of Prague who was already known for his piety and learning. This book was the first in a series he worked on parallel to the work of the Maharal between 1592 and the time of their deaths: the Maharal's in 1609 and Gans's in 1613.

Dedicated to his elder brother Joshua Seligmann Gans, this history book was the first work of David Gans to be published. From the point of view of the author, this first offering represented a promise of other works to come—notably two treatises on mathematics and geometry called *Migdal David* and *Magen David*, which already existed in manuscript, and also other books concerning other areas of science which he dreamt of writing eventually. The name *Ẓemaḥ* (shoot) was quite deliberately chosen for the chronicle: it was a shoot from which, in the fullness of time, would spring the future books of David Gans.

None of these future books—many of which remained unfinished and some of which were lost while still in manuscript—were published during the author's lifetime, and only one was published at all, under the title of *Neḥmad ve-Na'im*, but that was in 1743, a hundred and thirty years after David Gans's death.

This present work is devoted to a study of David Gans's *Neḥmad ve-Na'im*, which is far less well known than *Ẓemaḥ David*. The subject-matter of this book takes us back to the crucial year 1592 in which *Ẓemaḥ David* appeared, but here we must enlarge our field of vision, looking beyond the Jewish community of Prague and taking in the whole of human society in western Europe in order to discern the salient features of that fateful year.

2

Searchlight on the end of a century

IT is 1592. The sixteenth century is coming to an end. We must attempt to go back four centuries and to see things, for a moment, with the eyes of a western European of that year 1592, but only selecting, among the events which took place, those which concern us for the purposes of this book.

An event which already seems distant in time, but which is close to us in its importance, is the discovery of the New World by Christopher Columbus. It seems to have happened a long time ago, since the New World is already well known and the great powers have fought over its partition. Now, it is no longer a matter of the New World but of New Spain, New Portugal, New France, New England, and New Holland. The New World is greatly over-shadowed by the Old World.

It was in this year 1592 that the complete works of Petrus Nonius (1492–1577) were published in Basle. A cosmographer and map-maker, he played a large part in providing the scientific knowledge for this conquest of the New World by the armadas of western Europe. This purely bookish event has been mentioned because of its bearing on our present investigations. The Latinized name Petrus Nonius stands for that of Pedro Nunes, Professor of Philosophy, Mathematics, and Cosmography at the universities of Lisbon and Coimbra: a Marrano, one of the many Jews of the Iberian peninsula who accepted baptism in order to escape the Inquisition. He was born in the very year of the expulsion of the Jews from Spain and the discovery of America by Christopher Columbus. If he himself died unscathed by the Inquisition, several of his descendants died at the stake at the beginning of the seventeenth century. Here we see a connection between two things which will repeat itself frequently in the course of our study: between the Marranos and the discovery of America.

A closer event—marked by the great gash which its bloody axe-stroke made in the body of the Church—was the one which took place in Paris in August 1572, exactly twenty years ago, in the Louvre and in the neighbouring quarters. It had taken place at night, and that night of Saint Bartholomew had rent the Church more cruelly even than Martin Luther's rebellion in 1519. Catholics and Protestants lived henceforth in a state of armed schism which planted itself like an ulcer on the already-existing political and religious differences, gnawing at Europe until it broke apart in the following century in the terrible Thirty Years War.

Still closer in time, however, hardly ten years ago, the bells of nearly all the Western Churches—the Catholics enthusiastically, the Protestants with somewhat more reticence—had pealed for an event which might give one reason to suppose that inter-factional harmony was still possible. In 1582 the reform of the calendar proposed by Pope Gregory XIII had been adopted, and Western man suddenly grew older by eleven days.

Closer still, about this year 1592, a shrewd and generous king was also working for a religious truce. Henry IV had begun the siege of Paris in 1590. He had weighed up whether Paris was worth a mass and come to his decision in July 1593, passing from the Protestant to the Catholic Church and, at at the very end of the century, promulgating the Edict of Nantes in 1598 as a pledge of his good intentions.

As though to counterbalance the tolerance of Henry of Navarre, in that same year 1592 an Italian humanist who had fled to Padua was delivered by the Venetian Senate to the Inquisition, which imprisoned him and for eight years submitted him to the most terrible physical and mental tortures. This man was Giordano Bruno: his life and ideas will concern us on more than one account in this book. His many wanderings in France, Switzerland, England, and Germany brought him to Prague for a few months in 1588 and then to Padua in 1592. He was burnt alive in the Piazza della Fiore in Rome on 16 February 1600. All this constituted a kind of tragic footbridge leading from the end of one century to the beginning of another.

Among the accusations of heresy brought against him by the Inquisition, there were mystical ideas derived from the *Kabbalah*, but also the major crime of concurring with the absurd theories of a certain Copernicus who had died fifty years previously and whose name was beginning to emerge from the lava of a volcanic eruption which was at work underground in the second half of the sixteenth century in the field of astronomy. One of the things which went across this fragile and blood-laden footbridge together with Bruno, believe it or not, was astronomy.

We shall end this short sketch of the end of a century by directing the beams of our searchlight on Padua, one of the cradle-cities of that Renaissance humanism with which fifteenth-century Italy had endowed Europe, lighting a flame which from Rome, Florence, and Venice had spread to Paris, Amsterdam, Basle, Strasbourg, Nuremberg, and Prague through contacts and across wars, conflicts, migrations, and exiles, lighting up stakes and conflagrations, but also kindling torches of art and erudition which cast their challenge at eternity.

PADUA, 1592

The illustrious university of that city, long famous for its tolerance and broadmindedness from which many Jewish students had benefited as well as Christian scholars on the edge of heresy, had on its staff Galileo Galilei, a young mathematician of 28, who held the chair of mathematics and who thus entered for the first time into history. Galileo's courses in the University of Padua were outstanding for their originality and audacity, and were so popular that he had to wait nearly twenty years until, as well as being a lecturer and researcher, he could resolve to become a writer and so commit some of his discoveries to print.

Galileo's initial lesson has remained famous. It was given in an auditorium full to bursting-point on 7 December 1592 and, in addition to a discreet but clear reference to the amazing calculations published half a century previously by the Prussian astronomer Nicholas Copernicus, it contained an enthusiastic description of the instruments which the famous Danish astronomer Tycho Brahe had invented and installed in his observatory at Uraniborg near Copenhagen.

We know this lecture of Galileo's in detail through the magnificent album which Tycho Brahe later devoted to a description of Uraniborg. Dedicated to the Emperor Rudolph II of Habsburg, it was published in 1598, the year of the promulgation of the Edict of Nantes, and gave some prominence to Galileo's words of praise of six years before.

Tycho Brahe left Denmark in 1597, and in June 1599 made a

triumphal entry into Prague where he became the official mathematician of the Emperor Rudolph II until his premature death in October 1601. In a year and a half he was able to reinstall Uraniborg at Benatek near Prague, and to attract Johannes Kepler, who succeeded him as imperial mathematician until the death of the Emperor in 1612. We should recall that the Maharal died in 1609, David Gans in 1613.

So, for months and years, the Maharal, David Gans, Tycho Brahe, and Johannes Kepler were all to be found together in Prague. We should add that one of the first students at Galileo's lectures, Joseph Solomon Delmedigo, spent the last years of his life in Prague, where he was buried in 1655. His tomb can still be seen there in the old Jewish cemetery, a few feet away from those of the Maharal and David Gans and a short distance also from the Teynkirche which contains the sepulchral monument of Tycho Brahe; and it was the events which took place in Padua and Prague in 1592 which contained the seeds of these encounters which were prolonged into death.

In the very same year when Galileo spoke in praise of Tycho Brahe, David Gans published his historical chronicle and dreamt of other works, of which the only one to appear in print, a hundred and thirty years after his death, was *Neḥmad ve-Na'im*, a work of astronomy. We said that this book is devoted to a study of that work. Before beginning to examine it, we shall attempt to make a brief sketch of the author, as little known as the work itself.

3

A modest but enthusiastic worker

I KNOW few men who have been as ungratefully treated as David Gans.

He has given us the first reference to Nicholas Copernicus, Tycho Brahe, and Johannes Kepler in a Hebrew text, the first reference to the Maharal's audience with Rudolph of Habsburg, the first correct modern map of the world in a Jewish cosmography. All this would normally be enough to ensure him fame, if not glory.

I have to accept the bitter fact that, quite apart from contemporary scholars—so extraordinarily grudging towards a man who, although undoubtedly not a genius, was nevertheless an innovator in the world of science—not one of the great Jewish or non-Jewish contemporaries of whom David Gans spoke with such touching emotion and veneration deigned as much as to mention his name, his book, or the mere fact of his existence.[1]

I can no more claim to have read the colossal works of the Rema, the Maharal, Tycho Brahe, and Johannes Kepler from end to end than I can measure myself against the Himalayas, but I can say that I have attempted to study them carefully and methodically, using and checking indexes, works of reference, monographs crammed with details. I have searched for David Gans's name in its German form—Gans, in its Hebrew form—Avous, in its Latin forms—Avsi or Apsi—which the Bishop of Lodève used in his rabbinical bibliography of 1645,[2] and in other Latinized forms which were used in the sixteenth century—Anser, Anserius, what-have-you. I have searched for it under the name of the work for which he was known in his lifetime *Zemaḥ David*, or in the simple form of Rabbi David. . . There is nothing, not a thing. There is not a single reference, and I am sorry for his sake. Even the chronicles of the Prague Jewish community during his residence of more than half a century in that city are completely silent. It was not until the

---

[1] See bibliography.   [2] See p. 53.

fragmentary publication of his *Magen David* in 1612, one year before his death, that he received public recognition from men who, if not his mentors, were at least his equals; but, as we shall see later on,[3] the *Magen David* was ill-fated. And then, in 1613, David Gans died, and on his tomb are inscribed the modest symbols of his name: a goose (*Gans* in German) and a star of David, and then the traditional formula which would be quoted by future Jewish historians: 'Here is buried *he-Ḥasid Morenu David Gans, Ba'al Ẓemaḥ David*' ('The Righteous Rabbi David Gans, author of *Ẓemaḥ David*').

I am sorry for his sake: all the more so in that it is through him, through his chronicle, through his astronomical work, that we are acquainted with so many personalities, events, items, curiosities which enable us to reconstruct a whole universe throbbing with life—a universe from which he himself was excluded. No doubt, in some cases this was an inadvertent omission, as in that of Tycho Brahe, who drew up a comprehensive list of his collaborators in Denmark, but did not have the time to do the same for those in Bohemia. Perhaps, if such a list had existed, the name of David Gans would have figured in it.[4] In other cases, this neglect was probably due to carelessness, thoughtlessness, or forgetfulness, as with the Rema, for whom David Gans was one young pupil among many others, or with Kepler, surrounded by a crowd of avid listeners among whom David Gans did not in any way stand out. And, finally, I think the neglect was deliberate in the case of the Maharal, whose relationship with David Gans must have been ambiguous—a mixture of love and respect for a spirit akin to his own with a kind of disdainful pity for his essential incapacity to understand him and enter into his spiritual universe.

For, we have to admit, David Gans was not on the level of the geniuses with whom he was associated. In today's universities we would place him among the technical assistants—serious, hard-working, indispensable for the advancement of scholarship, but not involved in 'pure research'. Neither in Jewish studies nor in the general sciences was David Gans more than a modest workman, but it is nevertheless true that this honest worker deserved a less ungrateful treatment from the Doctors of the Law and the Doctors of Science whose daily concerns he shared.

This modest workman had one quality, at any rate, which intellectually was by no means negligible and was even more valuable in the sphere of human relations: enthusiasm. We shall soon come upon it in his work, making it warm, vital, and, finally, even significant from the scientific point of view.

And we sense its vibrancy also in his biography which, as we have just pointed out, we are only able to trace from what David Gans himself tells us. In the absence of other evidence, we have to rely on his own, given piecemeal, first in *Zemaḥ David* and later in *Neḥmad ve-Naʾim*. Before us, Freedman, Alter, and Huminer tried to reconstruct this biography from his evidence and, like us, they were enchanted by their encounter with this modest and affable, pure, naïve, and above all faithful and enthusiastic man who was David Gans.

A LIFE IN THREE STAGES

It is curious: one century before the Thirty Years War, the dates of the two ends of David Gans's life can be related to those of that murderous war which made Germany a devastated territory and completely transformed the demographic situation of Central European Jewry. But they correspond with it the other way round: David Gans was born in Westphalia a hundred and seven years before the Treaty of Westphalia put an end to the Thirty Years War, and he died in Prague five years before the Defenestration in that city gave the signal for that war to begin.

Having duly noted this fact and classed it, in accordance with the reader's preference, either with the providential signs of Leibniz or the absurd coincidences of Ionesco, two parts of David Gans's life must be distinguished: his youth in western Germany (Westphalia where he was born, Bonn, and Frankfurt-on-Main), and his adolescence and maturity in eastern Europe (Cracow) and Central Europe (Prague). There is a similar division in the lives of many of David Gans's contemporaries, for the young Jews in sixteenth-century western Germany who wished to pursue an intellectual career (which was generally a rabbinical one) had to study for a shorter or longer period in the brilliant *yeshivot* of Poland or Central Europe, which were more famous than those of the West. And this period of study easily became a permanent residence when the prestige of a great rabbi, such as existed in the sixteenth century in Lublin, Cracow, Posen, and Prague, kept the student rooted to the spot.

Between these two parts of David Gans's life, there was a brief episode at Nordheim, midway between western and eastern Europe. It was only a stop-over with a cultured relative but, as we shall see in a moment, crucial for David Gans's spiritual development.

Westphalia, the Rhine, and the Main

We first come upon him in Westphalia, where he was born in Lippstadt in 1541. He liked this province and came back to it often after he had left it, still young, but leaving his heart behind there. It is an interesting point that he liked it, not on account of what he received from its Jewish community in his childhood, but for certain characteristics of its climate and its secular institutions. He tells us how in 1556, when he was 15, he drank the salt waters at the source at Hommel, which sprang up only for a few months but attracted thousands of invalids, blind people, and paralytics who were helped or cured by these marvellous waters (*ZD* 196b). He describes with great admiration the *Freischöffen* (or Holy *Vehme*), that secret confraternity of magistrates who recognized one another by certain signs and possessed the right of jurisdiction in what might be said to be cases involving moral law: slander, calumny, etc. Penal or criminal cases were merely investigated by them and then transferred to the official law-courts. Gans claimed that the institution dated from the time of Charlemagne, but, corrupted in the course of time, it fell into a state of disorganization to which the Emperor Frederick III put an end in 1439, retaining it only in Westphalia to which he thus accorded a great ethical privilege which existed nowhere else. (*ZD* 140b.)

Gans's family must have been in Westphalia for generations, for he tells us that his grandfather Seligmann Gans had lived there. Concerning this grandfather, he relates a picturesque tradition: in 1500, when Rabbi Lämmlen's Messianic preaching was spreading like wildfire all over western Europe, Seligmann was so convinced of Lämmlen's Messiahship that he broke his oven for baking *matzot* in a thousand pieces, firmly believing that the following year the *matzot* would be baked in Jerusalem (*ZD* 73b).

The first *yeshiva* where Gans began his advanced rabbinical studies was not far from Westphalia. It was at Bonn on the Rhine,

and was directed by Rabbi Reuben Fulda, who miraculously
escaped the sack of Bonn by the bands of Martin Schenk in 1588
(*ZD* 202a). From Bonn, Gans went to Frankfurt-on-Main, where
he studied in the *yeshiva* of Rabbi Eliezer Treves (who died there in
1573, at the age of 82). Eliezer Treves was known as a Kabbalist.
When Gans told him the story about his grandfather Seligmann,
Treves, far from condemning his gesture of breaking up his oven,
thoroughly approved of it. He, too, thought the episode of Rabbi
Lämmlen was not without significance, but believed that Israel's
sins had probably prevented Lämmlen from being revealed as the
hoped-for Messiah (*ZD* 73b).

The first encounter with science: Euclid

After his period of study in Bonn and Frankfurt, David Gans made
his great migration (quite usual at that period, as we said) to eastern
Europe. From among the great *yeshivot* of Poland which shone like
beacons, Gans chose that of Cracow.

On his way, at Nordheim in Saxony, Gans stopped at the home of
one of his relatives, Rabbi Mann, and in Mann's library he came
upon Moses Ibn Tibbon's translation from Arabic into Hebrew of
Euclid's 'Elements'. Once he had found this book, he was not
satisfied, as he said, with merely leafing through it: he really studied
it: '*Ve-ani ha-kotev ra'iti hetek sefer Eklides ve-lamadtiv*' (*ZD* 70b).

Judging from the way he spoke of Euclid later on, one can
imagine that David Gans, who was still very young (he was 19 when
he left Cracow), had passed through a real experience:

Euclid is the name of the celebrated genius whose intelligence and mighty
spirit surpassed all that the nations had known hitherto. No other non-Jewish
scholar, moreover, has equalled him until today. He is the author of the
famous book which bears his name: 'The Book of Euclid', a work of
incalculable depth. The most eminent scholars, ancient and modern, are all
agreed in declaring that, among the nations, no book surpasses his beneath the
heavens, nor can be compared to it, so great is his penetration and intelligence
and the content of his teaching. Although he did not say much on the subject
of astronomy, we should be completely at a loss in this science and unable to
find our way without his book, for Euclid's book is like a ladder thrown
between earth and heaven, and its top reaches heaven. Take away the book,
and it will be impossible for you to mount heavenwards. (*NN* 8c,d.)

It was the beginning of a passion—for mathematics, the exact
sciences, astronomy—which was never to leave him. It was also the

beginning of a taste for reading, for plunging into the ocean of books which submerged the sixteenth century; or, in other words, it exemplified the vibrant enthusiasm of a young Ashkenazi Jew who, without leaving the Talmudic universe, had discovered humanism in the broadest sense of the term. It is to Nordheim that one must trace the starting-point of his will to creativity, of the constant projects, which kept his mind in a perpetual ferment, for books concerning the most varied aspects of sixteenth-century humanism.

One should not imagine that at the *yeshiva* at Cracow this passion would be momentarily set aside, or that the young Talmudist could only cultivate it secretly. David Gans was fortunate enough to find at the head of the great *yeshiva* at Cracow one of the two great thinkers of contemporary Judaism: Rabbi Moses Isserles, known to history as the Rema (the acronym of his initials). The second thinker, the Maharal, Gans later met in Prague, where he went to complete his studies, and which he did not leave (except for some brief visits to his native Westphalia) until his death in 1613.

A humanistic Yeshiva*: Cracow*

The *yeshiva* of Rabbi Moses Isserles was wide open, first of all, to astronomy, whose attraction David Gans had recently felt when studying Euclid, for at that period geometry and astronomy were synonymous. There exist, in fact, two major works by the Rema on astronomy. One, to which we shall return at some length because Gans read it carefully and assiduously, appeared in Prague in 1570 under the title *Torat ha-Olah*. The other, entitled *Mehallekh ha-Kokhavim* (The Course of the Stars), consisted of glosses by the Rema to the Hebrew translation of the *Theorica Planetarium* by Georg Peurbach. These have remained unpublished,[5] and pose a problem which has already been raised by Alter:[6] namely, the fact that David Gans never mentions them and that the very name Peurbach appears to have been unknown to him.

[5] The Rema's commentary on Peurbach's *Theorica* is to be found in MS Op. 704 in the Bodleian Library, Oxford.

[6] Alter, p. 29. Georg Peurbach (1423–61) is regarded as one of the 'precursors' of Copernicus. Although one has to be careful in using the term 'precursor' in astronomy and in the sciences in general, it can be said that Peurbach had a strong influence on Regiomontanus and, through him, on Copernicus. The Rema's glosses are a very conservative interpretation of Peurbach's book, in which no hint of the 'Copernican revolution' is to be detected. He translates the title *Theorica Planetarium* as *Tohar rakia* (The Clarity of The Heavens).

Gans's attendance at the Rema's academy not only encouraged him in his taste for astronomy but directed him towards another discipline which was far from the ordinary preoccupations of a rabbinical *yeshiva*: history.

The Rema, in fact, had constructed a kind of bridge between astronomy and history by including a commentary on the eighteenth chapter of the fourth book of the treaty of astronomy *Yesod Olam* by Isaac Israeli in his glosses to the second edition of the chronicle *Yuḥasin* by Abraham Zacuto.[7] These two sciences were closely associated in these glosses which the Rema wrote in the style of his glosses to the *Shulḥan Arukh*. One feels him to be as much at home in humanism as in rabbinical studies. And what is particularly interesting is that he takes up the cudgels in defence of the study of history when reproached about it by colleagues who are less particular when it comes to astronomy. Astronomy is necessary in determining the Jewish calendar. But history? And profane history at that?

The Rema had already adopted an unequivocal position with regard to the study of profane philosophy. In answer to Solomon Luria (the Maharshal) who had strongly reproached him for allowing the reading of Aristotle in his *yeshiva*, the Rema invoked the authority of his illustrious predecessors, especially Maimonides, adding that he would not allow the rabbinical orthodoxy of his *yeshiva* to be questioned. The six days of the week were entirely devoted to the Talmud, but on the Sabbath and festivals when others went out walking, in his *yeshiva* they studied philosophy. What harm was there in that?[8]

He also regarded history as an intellectual distraction more suited to the Sabbath and festivals than purely physical forms of relaxation. The Rema also went further and gave history his official

[7] The first edition of Abraham Zacuto's *Yuḥasin* was published in Constantinople in 1566. The Rema's glosses appear in the second edition (Cracow, 1580), eight years after the Rema's death. On the chronicle *Yuḥasin* and its author Zacuto, see p. 42.

[8] Moses Isserles: *She'elot u-Teshuvot* (Asher Ziv, Jerusalem), part 7, p. 15. Cf. Israel Zinberg, *Die Geschichte der Literatur bei Yiden* (in Yiddish) (Vilna, 1935), vol. 3, pp. 416–17. The Maharshal reproached the Rema with disseminating in his *yeshiva* the 'prayer of Aristotle': an apocryphal letter of Aristotle to his pupil Alexander the Great in which the latter acknowledged, after a meeting with a Jewish sage, that knowledge cannot be gained from reason alone but also required revelation. This apocryphal letter gave Aristotle the status of a kind of *ba'al teshuvah* (penitent), thus opening the doors of the *yeshiva* to him.

sanction in the following note in his authoritative glosses to the
Shulḥan Arukh:

People for whom narratives and the communication of news is a form of
pleasure may indulge in it on the Sabbath as well as on weekdays. . .[9] As for
profane narratives and historical chronicles, we should point out that it is
forbidden to read them only if they are written in a foreign language, but it is
perfectly permissible to read them in Hebrew. I base myself on the opinion of
the Tosafists (Tractate *Shabbat* 115a), and, moreover, in this domain, custom
has long become a law.[10]

David Gans was to invoke these rulings when he embarked on
the profane part of his great historical work, *Zemaḥ David*. He
quoted the Rema twice: first, his glosses to the *Shulḥan Arukh* to
justify the reading of historical works in Hebrew such as *Zemaḥ
David*, and secondly, his glosses to the *Sefer Yuḥasin* allowing
explicit reference to the names of philosophers and 'great non-
Jews' in general.[11]

Thus, by the time he reached Prague, the rabbinical student
David Gans had gained from his *yeshiva* additional incentives to
study astronomy and fresh motivations for the study of history. The
yeshiva, far from stifling his humanism, had only rendered it
stronger.

AN ENCHANTING CITY: PRAGUE, MYTH AND REALITY

We do not know the exact date of the arrival of David Gans in
Prague. He was already there by 1559, when an unjust accusation
—neither the first nor the last of its kind—hit the Jewish
community, prohibiting it from using the *Sifrei Torah* (Scrolls of the

[9] *Shulḥan Arukh, Oraḥ Ḥayyim*, 307: 1.
[10] *Oraḥ Ḥayyim* 307:16. Interestingly enough, the Rema is in agreement with Joseph
Caro in forbidding the reading of 'love stories'. In the following paragraph (307: 17), the
two authors agree about permitting the use of the astrolabe on the Sabbath. It seems that
astronomy enjoyed certain privileges which were not granted to history.
[11] David Gans wrongly states that the Rema's comments refer to the eleventh chapter
of Isaac Israeli's *Yesod Olam*, without specifying which section that chapter belongs to. In
fact they refer to chapter 18 of the fourth part of Isaac Israeli's work in which he provides
a short biblical and Talmudic chronology. In the article on Isserles in the *Encyclopedia
Judaica*, his glosses on chapter 18 of *Yesod Olam* are mentioned, without specifying that it
is the eighteenth chapter of the fourth part of the book. We should point out that on this
question of referring to non-Jewish men of learning, David Gans is in total disagreement
with the Maharal, for whom it was one of the reasons for his violent attack on Azariah dei
Rossi (cf. below I. 4 and our *Puits de L'Exil*, pp. 104 ff.).

Law) in its synagogues. What a cruel piece of sadism! A Jewish community deprived of the apple of its eye! The *Sifrei Torah* were taken to Venice and the cantors of Prague had to officiate from memory until justice had been done and the sacred scrolls had been restored to their places in the many large and small synagogues of the ghetto.[12]

But if the date of David Gans's arrival cannot be established with certainty, one may easily gauge the impression which the city made on the young man from the many vibrant, picturesque, and lyrical pages which Gans devoted to Prague in his works. He succumbed to an enchantment, a permanent enchantment. No city is mentioned so often by David Gans, not only for the purpose of describing the events which took place there, the people who lived there; not only in order to evoke its triumphs and tragedies. In Gans's relationship with Prague, there was something mysterious—a predestination which linked the man to the city, of which Gans was fully aware. Over the reality of Prague, David Gans, like so many others after him (novelists, poets, dreamers: Max Brod, Rainer Maria Rilke, Franz Kafka) embroidered a myth. Here I would like to call attention to the salient features of this complex attachment.

First, there was the founding of Prague, and then the astonishing connection between David Gans's date of birth in Westphalia and a striking event in the history of the Jews of Prague. Then there was the coincidence with which we began this book between the date of the only book of David Gans to appear in his lifetime and that of the strange interview given by Rudolph of Habsburg to the Maharal in the Hradschin Palace. Finally, there was the setting up near Prague, as unexpected and as providential for David Gans as for Johannes Kepler, of Tycho Brahe's 'astronomical court'. All this constitutes a kind of symphony whose movements may easily be traced throughout the work of David Gans.

Prague: David Gans's account

First, there was the founding of Prague. For David Gans the would-be historian this immediately took on a mythical aspect. It is

[12] *Zemah David*, 75b. The publisher Solomon Cohen (Katz) adds the interesting observation that Gans failed to mention that the change in the situation was due to his father Mordecai Katz, who travelled to Rome to intercede with the Pope. Ferdinand I had apparently vowed never to allow the Jews to re-establish their community in Prague, but Mordecai Katz obtained a letter from Pope Pius IV releasing the Emperor from his vow.

true that Gans's informants all drew their information from Cosmas, whose *Chronica Boemorum*, written in the tenth century, is an ideal source for all those who like their history mixed with legend.[13]

Gans claimed that Prague and Bohemia had two periods of historical existence, separated by a gap of nearly two thousand years. The original founding of Prague, pre-dating that of Troy, took place in the year 2455 from the Creation, or 1305 before the Christian era. At that period, Boya conquered Bavaria and Bohemia, where he founded the city of Beinheim (later Prague) which subsequently disappeared, if not from history, then at least from the documents which reveal it. It was only in 639, in the middle of the seventh century of the Christian era, that the Czechs invaded this whole region, including Poland; and in 722, the legendary queen Libussa, who had been obliged to marry the first prince of the line of Przmysl, founded a new capital in the marshes of the former capital of Bohemia which bore the Czech name of Prague.

Gans said that this only confirmed the old Jewish tradition that Prague was already a metropolis at the time of the Second Temple, and that there were Jews who had settled there at that period.[14] However that may be, on his first mention of Prague in the mythical period of the Trojan War, Gans seized the opportunity of 'singing the praises' of the province of Bohemia and its capital.

A translation, insipidly rendering the warmth of the biblical and Talmudic expressions, can give only an approximate idea of David Gans's intention in the enchanting miniature which follows, in which he implies that Bohemia is a little Holy Land, blessed like the Land of Israel, in which Prague has the honoured central position just as Jerusalem is enthroned in majesty in the centre of the Land of Promise:

Prague, that great, splendid and populous city is the capital of this Land of Bohemia. It is situated exactly in the centre, for on each side a distance of about fifteen parasangs separates the city of Prague from the frontiers of the State. And, as for Bohemia, what an abundance of population, of unfortified towns, of villages, of great and splendid cities, of palaces, and of castles which out-rival one another in their beauty! This land is full of the blessings of God: wheat, wine and must exist there in such quantities that the neighbouring

[13] On David Gans's sources, see Sedinova and Breuer.
[14] *ZD* 95b, 134a, 136b.

countries draw their subsistence from it. It is also a land of rivers, great and
small—many majestic waterways: an abundance of fish, pastures, forests. It is a
land where the stones are iron and the mountains are brass. The tin-mines of
the Schalkwald region are of incalculable value, no less than the lead and silver
which are to be found in abundance around the Jochemstal and in many other
places. And all this is crowned by the gold-mines of Eule, three parasangs
from Prague, and grains of gold-dust and pearls are also gathered in the rivers.
One can also find the waters of Tiberias in Carlsbad and Teplitz: no traveller
has found any more beneficent throughout the entire world. Finally, precious
stones—diamonds, amethysts, garnets—abound in this land which indeed is
lacking in no conceivable good.[15]

Exile and Redemption

Over this land and capital city there reigned sovereigns who sought
to protect the Jews, but, ill-informed, they sometimes intervened
too late. Thus, in 1541, when fires broke out all over Bohemia, the
shepherds (probably nomads, possibly gypsies) and the Jews were
claimed to be responsible. Certain Jews, under torture, confessed
and perished at the stake. The others were expelled from the
realm: only ten men were permitted to remain in Prague, where the
Jews had been very active in saving the Hradschin palace from the
flames. That same year, however, an inquest instituted by the
Emperor Ferdinand I established the complete innocence of the
Jews who were recalled by the Emperor, and under his benevolent
authority regained their little Bohemian homeland.[16]

Now, 1541 was the very year when David Gans was born in
Westphalia. The celebrated Christian Kabbalist Guillaume Postel
had declared that 1541 would be the year of the apocalypse, but
less pretentiously it was the year of David Gans's birth. That year,
at any rate, provided a kind of miniature version of the Jewish
destiny in exile: false accusations, persecutions, expulsions, martyr-

---

[15] *ZD* 95b.

[16] The events of 1541 described by David Gans in *Zemaḥ David*, 194a are confirmed
by Joselmann of Rosheim in his Journal (*REJ*, xvi (1888), p. 93, §25). Joselmann relates
how he travelled to Prague in order to persuade the Emperor to relent. He had already
been called to Prague in 1533 in order to resolve a crisis in the Jewish community, and
he returned there in 1547 and was happy to observe that the community was fully re-
established. There is nothing surprising in the fact that Gans was not acquainted with
Joselmann's Journal, but it is astonishing that in *Zemaḥ David*, where the privileges
granted to the Jews by the emperors Maximilian and Charles V are several times alluded
to, Gans fails to mention Joselmann—who was the great intermediary between the
Emperor and the Jewish communities in Germany—in either the Jewish or in the
general part of his chronicle.

doms, but also the perseverance of a providential *minyan* (group of ten people) which carried in itself the promise of the Return.

Was it through some form of ideological rather than purely chronological association that 1540, the year preceding his birth, is described in David Gans's chronicle as the year in which Sultan Suleiman ordered the walls of Jerusalem to be rebuilt and the water-supply system inside the city to be renovated? That fact is repeated in the second, profane section of the chronicle, but it is also in the first, purely Jewish part, for the Jews saw this event, so beneficial to the Holy City and its Jewish population, as a Messianic symbol. David Gans implicitly suggests this in employing in connection with Suleiman a phrase which the Bible uses about Cyrus: 'The Lord stirred up his spirit.'[17]

Thus, the year of David Gans's birth was marked by the conjunction of two events representing the two contrary aspects of the eternal Jewish destiny: the tribulations of exile and the promise of Redemption.

Life in the Jewish community of Prague was continually subject to this Messianic polarity. In 1571, for instance, the Emperor Maximilian passed through the ghetto of Prague with great pomp,[18] but in 1582 the community was almost wiped out by a plague and survived only by the grace of God.[19] The last entries of *Zemah David*, those concerning the year 1592 when the book was published by Solomon and Moses Cohen in Prague, reveal a surprising mixture of joy and distress, both on the Jewish side and the non-Jewish.

On the non-Jewish side, he recorded that 'on the occasion of the marriage of King Sigismund of Poland to the niece of Emperor Rudolph, heir to the throne of Croatia, there was rejoicing such as had not been seen for centuries', but, on the other hand, there was 'an attack by the Turks on the principal fortress in this same kingdom of Croatia with the powerful aid of an artillery more lethal than had ever been known, forcing the brave defenders to surrender and delivering the city up to arson, looting, and massacre'.

Gans concludes these two entries by expressing the hope of seeing peace reign upon Israel, but with a picturesque variation of the traditional formula: 'May He who makes peace in the heavens

[17] *ZD* 74b, 193b.
[18] *ZD* 198b, cf. below I. 5 (Extracts from *Zemah David*).   [19] *ZD* 201a.

make peace *among the peoples* [the traditional text says: 'upon us'] and upon all Israel, Amen!'

On the Jewish side, there are three entries for that year: one relating to the Maharal, another to Rabbi Mordecai Jaffe, with whom we shall become more fully acquainted later on, and a third to a layman, Mordecai Meisel, whose generosity, like that of his two successive wives, was boundless. Not only did all the Jewish poor live off his charity, which was both liberally and judiciously bestowed, but the ghetto was restored thanks to him, and the magnificent synagogue he erected (it was just completed in that year 1592), was regarded as a little 'Temple of Jerusalem'. But, at the same time, if these events were flooded with light, others of that year were shrouded in shadow. There was the mystery—Messianic, no doubt—of the interview, unique of its kind in the annals of the exile, between the Maharal and the Emperor in the Hradschin Palace; there was the enigmatic nature of the fact that that same year in which the Meisel Synagogue was inaugurated in the Prague ghetto saw the arrival in Prague of the eminent Rabbi Mordecai Jaffe and the departure for Posen of the even more eminent Rabbi Loew (otherwise the Maharal), whose little old Klaus Synagogue seemed to defy the imposing Meisel Synagogue, although there was no obvious connection between the arrival and departure of these two rabbis. The account of Prague in the *Zemaḥ David* ends on the note of ambiguity: it provides the reader with the outlines of a reality upon which he is able to embroider the most fantastic and mysterious dreams. Such is the interweaving of history and mythology in the Prague of David Gans.

THE UNEXPECTED EPILOGUE: 'I HAVE SCANNED THE HEAVENS IN TYCHO BRAHE'S OBSERVATORY'

The last vision of this historico-mythical Prague is Tycho Brahe's observatory in the castle of Benatek, as described in the 'conclusion of conclusions' of *Neḥmad ve-Na'im*[20]

I have kept for the ending of this book something extraordinary: namely, that in the year 5360 [1600] our sovereign the noble Emperor Rudolph, may his glory be exalted, eminent in science, wisdom, and knowledge, learned in astronomy, a lover of wise men and a great patron of scholars, sent a mission to

[20] *NN* 82d.

the land of Denmark and invited the eminent scholar Tycho Brahe, one of the princes of his people, the greatest astronomer who has ever lived, and installed him in a castle called Benatek, five parasangs from the capital Prague. He lived there surrounded by his learned disciples, and received an allowance of three thousand crowns a year, together with a total provision of bread, wine, and liquor, not to speak of the various gifts and donations.

In this castle I have mentioned, Tycho Brahe lived with twelve people, all learned in the astronomical sciences. Their task was to manipulate instruments which were larger and more marvellous than any which had ever been seen.

The Emperor built him a series of twelve consecutive rooms. In each of these rooms was placed an instrument which enabled the position and movements of all the planets and most of the stars to be observed.

Uninterruptedly, throughout the whole year, they would carry on their observations from day to day, carefully noting the movement of the sun and its position in its orbit and in longitude, its height in the sky, and its distance from the earth. Each night they would observe each of the six planets in the same way, recording their position in longitude, in latitude, their height in the sky, and the approximate variations in their distance from the earth. The same applied to most of the stars whose movement and position was examined.

I should add that I, the author of this book, have had the privilege of being there three times, each time for a period of five consecutive days. Yes, I was there amongst them in the rooms used as an observatory, and I saw with my own eyes the marvellous work that was carried on there—great and marvellous undertakings, in connection not only with the planets but with most of the stars, each of which was known by its name. The procedure was as follows: three instruments, each operated by two scholars, took the astronomical determination of the star at the very moment it passed the line of midnight. These determinations were immediately transcribed into hours, minutes, and seconds at the very moment when the star stood on the line of midnight. For this purpose [Tycho Brahe] used a clock of a new and marvellous conception.[21]

I can testify in all sincerity that we have never seen or heard, that our ancestors have never revealed to us, that we have never read in any book, whether its author was a member of the Jewish people or—to differentiate—a

[21] On the contribution which this remark can make to our knowledge of the astronomical clock which Tycho Brahe used in his observatory, see E. Zinner, *Geschichte der Sternkunde* (Berlin, 1931), p. 427 and Alter, pp. 32–3. Tycho Brahe's clock on the island of Sveen as described by Brahe himself does not sound like the one so much admired by David Gans, but it is possible that in the meantime Tycho Brahe had improved his instruments and Gans witnessed one example of the progress achieved at 'Uraniborg' between the Danish period and the Prague period.

We should point out that both the printed book of 1743 and the Brno manuscript (cf. Alter) fail to mention that Tycho's clock not only indicated the hours and minutes but also the seconds, whereas this detail is mentioned in the Geneva manuscript which we have quoted here.

member of the other nations, anything which allows us to suppose that such a thing ever existed previously.

Thus ends David Gans's description of Prague: in a rapturous evocation of Tycho Brahe's observatory which was as close to legend as reality, such pains did he take to make it not only a centre of careful astronomical research but a palace of a thousand and one marvels. It is not surprising if David Gans, entering there, had the overwhelming sensation of having reached the culmination of all that Prague meant to him. Side by side with the Klaus of the Maharal and the Meisel Synagogue, it was as if the Holy of Holies had taken up residence in this city which in the year 1600, at the end of the sixteenth century, sheltered both the Torah and Wisdom at its highest level: the imperial abode of Rudolph of Habsburg, the Maharal, and Tycho Brahe; this city where David Gans had lived and where he was still to live the most vital years of his life, the city where he was to die and be buried on 22 August 1613[22]—the radiant city of Prague, the capital of Bohemia but also one of those 'Jerusalems' of the exile where the Jews of the medieval Diaspora found a provisional and providential resting-place.

[22] On the date of his death (the twenty-second rather than the twenty-fifth of August), see Freedman, p. 5, n. 1. See also: Guido Kisch: *In Search of Freedom: A History of American Jews from Czechoslovakia*, London, 1949.

4

David Gans and the internal problematics of Judaism at the end of the sixteenth century

IN Prague, the very place where the decisive battle of modern astronomy was fought out at the end of the century; in Prague where, one century after the revolution in man's knowledge of the earth brought about by the discovery of the New World, there was a revolution in man's knowledge of the heavens through the discovery of Kepler's laws, a Jewish rabbi entered fully, intensely into this combat. That rabbi was David Gans.

The second and third parts of this book will be devoted to a description of that struggle. We shall attempt to describe this fight carried on by a Jew within the unparalleled spiritual ferment of the end of the sixteenth century. We shall see that, in this combat, David Gans was neither a hero nor a Don Quixote but a humble servant of the truth: a truth which, where he was concerned, was universal and comprehensive, and involved him as much as a Jew as a member of the human race.

It was into this two-sided conflict that David Gans threw himself. Its outer aspect—the debate with the non-Jewish universe incarnated in Tycho Brahe and Kepler—cannot be dissociated from its inner aspect: David Gans's struggle within the Jewish community itself. It is to this second aspect that we shall first devote our attention.

As a man of faith, David Gans could not turn, like sixteenth-century men of all confessions, exclusively towards an outside world which was becoming increasingly profane and secular. He had to cope with the various, often opposing, and nearly always contradictory tendencies which clashed within his own religious community. Religion was not only challenged by secularism: it was divided from within. And just as within the Christian religion Catholics and Protestants were engaged in a tragic struggle, so in the Jewish religion a conflict was taking place which was less tragic but equally painful in its implications: that between philosophy and mysticism which reached its height at the end of the sixteenth century.

In this 'vertical' struggle David Gans also had his place. An uncomfortable place, certainly, because his two successive Masters whom he revered equally and of whom he spoke with the same degree of feeling were the Rema and the Maharal, who in this conflict between philosophy and mysticism took up positions which were completely contradictory and, seemingly, mutually exclusive.

Long before Tycho Brahe, the non-Jewish apostle of contradiction, crossed his path, he had desperately sought to reconcile Copernicus and Ptolemy, and long before Johannes Kepler, the non-Jewish representative of the conflict between reason and mysticism, made his appearance, David Gans was confronted with the spiritual dispute between his two successive Masters.

We shall attempt to demonstrate the difficulties which this timid disciple had to overcome in order to adapt his thinking to theirs in a way which lacked neither courage nor a basic respect for the opinions of others and a desire for the serene conciliation of irreconcilables. This desire, which is characteristic of David Gans, accounts for the ultimate contradiction of the constant alternation of his own thought between the extremes of timidity and audacity.

THE CONFLICT OF REASON AND MYSTICISM

It is known that rationalist philosophy dominated Jewish thinking from the tenth century (the period of Saadiah Gaon) until the thirteenth century, which began with the death of Maimonides and ended with the publication of the *Zohar*. Reason triumphed, despite all the savage blows administered by unreason. In his commentary on the *Sefer Yezirah*, Saadiah Gaon took up a rationalist position. Judah Halevi condemned philosophy, but he did so in the name of another philosophy which tended to rationalize mystical phenomena such as prophecy. Maimonides assigned limits to reason, but that, apparently, was only in order to strengthen its position and to give Aristotle his place in relation to the Bible.

It was the *Zohar* with its strong, pervasive influence, its power to persuade and convert, its penetration into the soul of the people (philosophy becoming more and more the prerogative of an intellectual élite) which produced, in the fourteenth and fifteenth centuries, an increasingly violent contradiction, the spiritual and sociological implications of which have recently been studied by a number of scholars.

In the sixteenth century, this conflict came out into the open, and it was mysticism which triumphed and philosophy which was eclipsed: so much so that, in his standard work, *The Philosophy of Judaism*, Julius Itzhak Guttmann ended his account at the beginning of the sixteenth century (when only a few stragglers remained), taking it up again with Mendelssohn in the second half of the eighteenth century. The gap of the two intervening centuries was filled entirely by mysticism, which Guttmann considered as not belonging to 'philosophy'.

In reality, however, things were not quite as simple as that. With the appearance of the great Kabbalist works of the sixteenth century—that of Meir Ibn Gabbai and those of the School of Safed (Moses Cordovero, Isaac Luria)—two characteristic tendencies in the conflict between philosophy and mysticism came to light. One might be called the appropriation of philosophy by mysticism. The other sought to widen the gap between the two and to render it unbridgeable, so that triumphant mysticism might the more easily throw philosophy on to the rubbish heap.

The first approach found its advocate in Isaac Abravanel at the beginning of the century; the second was expressed at the end of the century by the Maharal. To appreciate the difference of tone between them we should cite Meir Ibn Gabbai, who lived mid-way between Abravanel, of whom he was an enthusiastic reader, and the Maharal, whom his books inspired in founding his system.

THE APPROPRIATION OF REASON BY MYSTICISM: MAIMONIDES METAMORPHOSED INTO A KABBALIST

Among all the Jewish philosophers, is there a single one who can equal our great Rambam [Moses Maimonides], may his memory be blessed? Yet, when the Rambam discovered the pearl without price [the *Kabbalah*], he threw away philosophy, which he henceforth accounted a thing of no value!

Thus wrote Meir Ibn Gabbai in 1545, in the thirteenth chapter of the second part of his mystical work *Avodat ha-Kodesh*.[1] Moses Maimonides had died three centuries earlier, in 1204, leaving behind him a monumental, unequalled achievement of Jewish

[1] Meir Ibn Gabbai, *Sefer Avodat ha-Kodesh*, ed. Levin-Epstein (Jerusalem, 1954), p. 66a.

'philosophy'. For three centuries nothing was said about a 'conversion' of Maimonides to mysticism,[2] but at the beginning of the sixteenth century, the great philosopher Don Isaac Abravanel, reticent in his attitude to the *Kabbalah* which he claimed to admire without having been initiated, noted in his commentary on the 'Treatise on Principles' (*Naḥalat Avot*, III, end) that towards the end of his life Maimonides had passed through a traumatic spiritual experience. He had been initiated into the *Kabbalah* by an old man, and henceforth was convinced that it contained the truth. In his life's work he had followed the ways of philosophy, and it was too late now to refashion that work in the light of the *Kabbalah*.

Abravanel claimed to have seen in one of Maimonides' works the following passage: 'Towards the end of my days on earth an old man came to see me who enlightened my eyes concerning the wisdom of the *Kabbalah*. And if my books had not already been disseminated throughout the world, I would retract many things which I wrote and about which I am now sorry.'

Meir Ibn Gabbai, who did not fail to cite Isaac Abravanel as an authority, went further back in time to adduce additional proof of this story of the conversion of Maimonides; and in order to convince any foolish scholar who might still be in error, any backward rationalist 'philosophers' who still did not realize, in the middle of the sixteenth century, that philosophy was only a by-product of the *Kabbalah*, he recalled the text of a kabbalistic commentary on the mystical interpretation of the Torah by Naḥmanides (1194–1270). This text gave the name of the 'old man' who initiated Maimonides into the *Kabbalah*. It was a Rabbi Jacob: 'This Rabbi Jacob gained himself lasting fame, because he undertook the voyage to Egypt in order to transmit the *Kabbalah* to Maimonides. Maimonides received this initiation with so great a joy that he gloried in it on several occasions in front of his pupils, but that, alas, was late in his life. All the books of Maimonides that we possess today had already been written and published by him!'

For anyone who knew—and who did not then know?—to what an extent Maimonides' work, from start to finish, is imbued with a great respect for philosophy and reason; for anyone who knew the famous letter in which, precisely in the last years of his life, Maimonides discouraged his disciple and translator Samuel Ibn

---

[2] See G. Scholem, *Me-ḥoker li-mekubal: aggadot ha-mekubalim al ha-Rambam* (Tarbiz-Jerusalem, vi, 2, 1935), pp. 90–8.

Tibbon from making the perilous journey from Provence, where he lived, to Egypt, where the sage, overwhelmed by his responsibilities as physician to the Sultan, physician to Fostat (near Cairo), adviser to his own community, and guide of the Jewish communities the world over, was uncertain whether he was able to spare a few minutes from these many activities for a serious discussion with his pupil; for anyone who knew all this—and who did not know it in the middle of the sixteenth century?—the texts quoted by Meir Ibn Gabbai must have seemed particularly remarkable.

So Rabbi Jacob the Kabbalist made the journey which the timid rationalist Ibn Tibbon had decided against making. So the Eagle of the Synagogue, sought after and crushed by his superhuman responsibilities, was able to overcome his age and weariness in order to engage in a dialogue with Rabbi Jacob and experience the great joy of spiritual revelation, the discovery of a great truth of which he had hitherto been frustrated. But, if this was so, his frustration could not have been compensated in any visible or lasting manner. Maimonides would have to have re-written all his books, and how could he have done this when these had already gone out into the world and he was at death's door?

Death thus overtook Maimonides at the very moment when he was being torn apart by the tragic contradiction between the work by which he is remembered and the new spiritual understanding which it was no longer possible for him to express in writing.

We feel that this change of position in an intellectual conflict in the depths of human soul associated with Maimonides shows the pertinacity with which, in the first half of the sixteenth century (the period between the death of Abravanel and that of Ibn Gabbai is exactly this half-century), the Kabbalists attempted to prove that the greatest 'philosophers' in reality were, or wished to be, Kabbalists. One finds the same change of position associated with other sages such as Rabbi Isaac ben Sheshet or Abravanel himself who were reserved in their attitude to the *Kabbalah*, but whose authority was vigorously claimed by the Kabbalists as sanctioning their own school of thought.

Towards the end of the century, this way of thinking gradually led to a tendency to equate philosophy with the *Kabbalah*: an equation whose most authoritative representative was Rabbi Moses Isserles (the Rema) of Cracow.

The Maharal, in Prague, took up arms against precisely such an equation with a violence which we have described in *Le Puits de L'Exil* ('The Well of Exile'). In his polemic with Eliezer Ashkenazi, the Maharal was not only fighting against the retrograde philosopher of Cracow. Through the philosophy of Ashkenazi, it is also the equation of the Rema of Cracow which is quite explicitly aimed at, as we shall see, even if the Rema's name is not mentioned.[3] For the Maharal, there could be no identity, no compromise. Despite the fact that, in the Maharal, the *Kabbalah* borrows a philosophical language,[4] despite the Maharal's doctrinal relativism, on this point he was quite adamant: truth is exclusively on the side of the *Kabbalah*.

Once again, David Gans gained his initiation into Jewish thought first with the Rema, then with the Maharal. One could hardly imagine a more awkward and difficult situation in which to find oneself. We will now see how he found his way between them, and what position he took up.

DAVID GANS BETWEEN HIS TWO TEACHERS: ABOVE THE FRAY

Some miniatures: the entries in David Gans's chronicle on the Rema and the Maharal

Here are David Gans's accounts of his two successive teachers in Cracow and Prague respectively: Rabbi Moses Isserles (the Rema) and Rabbi Judah Loew ben Beẓalel (the Maharal). The features of these two men appear in these miniatures drawn from life which well express the esteem and admiration with which he never ceased to regard them.
Ẓemaḥ David, 1592 (pp. 76a, 77b):

1572 (Jewish year 5332). In that year Rabbi Moses Isserles passed away. He was a man of perfect piety whose books, including *Torat ha-Olah*, *Torat ha-Hattat*, and the *Shulḥan Arukh* lighten the eyes of the exiles. He had many

---

[3] As early as 1557 a kabbalistic rabbi, Joseph Ashkenazi (died in Safed in 1582; not to be confused with the rationalist Eliezer Ashkenazi) had attacked Maimonides violently in Posen. The question was debated in the *yeshiva* in Prague which condemned his opinions on the grounds that Maimonides and the *Kabbalah* are not irreconcilable. See B. Suler, 'Ein Maïmonides Streit in Prag im 16 Jahrhundert', *JGGJC*, 7 (1935), pp. 411–20.
[4] See the note of the Rav Abraham Isaac Kook quoted by the Rav ha-Nazir (David Cohen) in *Kol ha-Nevuah* (Jerusalem, 1970), p. 177, n. 113. Kook described the Maharal as 'a kabbalist with a literary style'.

disciples and expounded his teachings in the holy community of Cracow for some twenty years.

1563 (Jewish year 5323). The year of the deaths of Rabbi Eliezer Treves of Frankfurt and Rabbi Jacob of Worms. Rabbi Jacob was an eminent rabbi, recognized as an authority in the entire Ashkenazi diaspora.[5] He was also the paternal uncle of four brothers who at the present time are *Geonim* and heads of *yeshivot* of universal renown. These are Rabbi Hayyim of Friedberg, Rabbi Loew, Rabbi Sinai, and Rabbi Samson. All four are outstanding in our generation, the Heads of Ariel (the Holy 'Lions'), and I shall mention them again.

1592 (Jewish year 5352). Out of his beneficence and out of his desire to learn the truth, our sovereign, the Emperor Rudolph, a just ruler, the source of great and brilliant light, may his glory be exalted, called to him the *Gaon*, our teacher Rabbi Loew ben Bezalel, and received him most graciously, speaking to him face to face as a man speaks to his equal. As for the substance and purpose of this dialogue, it remains a secret which the two men decided not to disclose. This event took place in Prague on Sunday, the third of Adar 5352.

1592 (Jewish year 5352). Rabbi Loew is the greatest Master, the crown of the sages, and the wonder of our generation. His light illumines all our people, and the whole Jewish Diaspora drinks at his source. He is the author of *Gur Aryeh* (a commentary on Rashi), of *Gevurot ha-Shem*, of *Derekh Ḥayyim* (which is a commentary on the *Pirkei Avot*), and many other books which we have not yet the good fortune to possess in printed form. For twenty years he was the rabbi of the whole province of Moravia, then in the year 5333 (1573) he took up residence here in Prague. He had many disciples and founded a House of Study for the sages, the great *Bet Midrash* known by the name of *Klaus*. He disseminated knowledge for eleven years, and then, again, for four years more. And now, on Thursday the 4th of Iyar 5352 (1592) he has set out to take up a post in the holy community of Posen, having been nominated *Rosh Yeshivah* and Rabbi of the whole province of the Polish diaspora. And may our eyes (again) behold the king in his glory, judging the peoples with righteousness.

Neḥmad ve-Na'im (written *c.*1600) (p. 8a.)

My Master and Rabbi, who raised me and guided me as a father his son, the eminent Rabbi Moses Isserles, may his memory be blessed, also discussed astronomical problems in a brilliant manner in several passages of his book *Torat ha-Olah*. Thus, in the second chapter of the first part he wrote: 'If the objection is raised that the opinions of our sages are based on tradition, which may be the case, I do not see it as a reason to refute them. We hold fast to

---

[5] He was the 'Emperor's Rabbi', and enjoyed a spiritually privileged position comparable to the temporal position of Rabbi Joselmann of Rosheim under Charles V. See M. Ginsburger, 'Le Rabbin de l'Empereur, Jacob de Worms', *REJ*, lxxxii (1926), pp. 461–8.

tradition, even if that tradition seems to be at variance with reason. However, if there is any possibility of finding a compromise and interpreting the words of our sages in such a way that they do not contradict rationality and even come close to it, it is a good and desirable thing to utilize that possibility.' He added in that same passage that whoever desires to defend the honour of the Creator and the honour of our sages should study the writings of the latter, for he would certainly come to the conclusion that our sages had a better knowledge of astronomy than the wise amongst the Gentiles. In that same chapter, as in Chapter 8 and many other chapters, he gave quotations from the sages which, at first sight, seem to be in flagrant contradiction with scientific and experimental astronomy, but he succeeded in reconciling them with scientific fact by means of interpretations as attractive as oranges arranged in silver baskets.

In our time, my Master and Rabbi, the eminent Rabbi Loew—may he yet be granted many long years of life—has also excelled in this. In the sixth 'well' of his book, *Be'er ha-Golah* [Well of the Exile], there are many examples of quotations from our sages which at first sight seem strange and bewildering, remote from reason and truth, but which he is able to interpret in a satisfying and remarkably attractive manner.

THE REMA AND THE MAHARAL: A CONTRADICTORY PAIR

The Rema, apostle of conciliation

Rabbi Moses Isserles has entered into the history of Jewish thought through a work and a phrase. The work is the 'tablecloth' which he spread over Joseph Caro's 'Laid Table'—i.e., his glosses which adapted the *Shulḥan Arukh* of the Sephardi Joseph Caro to the usages of the Ashkenazi world. Even today, just as there is no edition of the Talmud without Rashi's commentary, so there is no current edition of the *Shulḥan Arukh* without the glosses of Moses Isserles. The two scholars were contemporaries: Caro lived in Safed, Isserles in Cracow. It was a fine example of a significant spiritual encounter between the Holy Land and the Diaspora, between the Sephardi world and the Ashkenazi.

The phrase which contributed to Rabbi Moses Isserles's celebrity is to be found in his *Torat ha-Olah*, one of the many other works written and published by the learned rabbi of Cracow, none of which became as popular and famous as the 'Spread Tablecloth'. It is a lapidary phrase which no encyclopaedia fails to mention: *Ki ḥokhmat ha-Kabbala hi ḥokhmat ha-filosopia, rak she be shnei leshonot yedaberu* ('*Kabbalah* and philosophy are one and the same.

The difference is that the two are expressed in different languages.')
(*TH*, III, 4, 75d.)

It is seldom pointed out, however, that the phrase is not the Rema's own, although he does use a slightly different version of it: *Ki darkhei ha-Kabbalah hen be-azman darkhei ha-filosopia* ('The methods of the *Kabbalah* are essentially the same as the methods of philosophy.) (*TH*, III, 4, 75a). The original phrase is a quotation from the commentary on the *Sefer Yezirah* written by Moses Botarel at the beginning of the fifteenth century and published in Mantua in 1562. In the last quarter of the sixteenth century, this phrase in the published work clearly had an explosive contemporary significance, since the conflict between philosophy and mysticism had then reached its climax. But at the beginning of the fifteenth century this conflict had only begun to develop, and did not yet trouble the major thinkers of the period. Moreover, Moses Botarel, known for his participation in the disputation of Tortosa in 1413, was not considered a sage but rather a miracle-worker for whom the *Kabbalah* had a 'practical' purpose rather than a theoretical significance.

Whatever the case, in repeating Botarel's striking formula in 1570, in calling attention to the inner identity of the *Kabbalah* and philosophy, the Rema was attempting to settle the conflict just when it posed its greatest challenge to the leading Jewish thinkers. There was no proof, of course, but what mattered to the Rema was not to prove his case but to state it, and by this means to play in the dramatic spiritual conflict at its height in that last quarter of the sixteenth century the role of arbiter and mediator which he had also assumed in the sphere of halachic legislation. Just as there should be no conflict between Sephardi and Ashkenazi codes of conduct, so there should be no rupture between philosophical and mystical thought.

It may be said that on these two principles which constitute the Rema's coat of arms, the Maharal of Prague was in complete disagreement with him.

The Maharal, apostle of confrontation

The Maharal had already protested against the *Shulhan Arukh*—against Joseph Caro and the makers of 'digests' who made things easy for the observant Jew by creating a sort of pocket-edition of the Law, whereas the Maharal, for his part, conceived and attempted to put into practice a pedagogical system whereby Jews would study the Law in progressive stages, starting with the Bible and the Mishna, and continuing to the Talmud, and only then, as the culmination of this course of study, proceeding to a straight-forward knowledge of the commandments. The Rema's comment-ary on the *Shulḥan Arukh*, adapting it to the requirements of the Ashkenazi Jew, seemed to him futile, useless, and even pernicious. It was an invitation to laziness—to that intellectual laziness against which the Chief Rabbi of Posen and Prague fulminated in his books and from the pulpits of synagogues.

As for the little phrase about the identity of philosophy and the *Kabbalah*, it was in total opposition to a position which the Maharal adopted rather late, but with a degree of passion of which we have no other examples in his work.

In my *Puits de L'Exil* (Well of Exile; pp. 129 ff.) I was one of the first to draw attention to the importance of the polemic between the Maharal and Eliezer Ashkenazi in *Derekh Ḥayyim*. It was the only moment in his spiritual career when he openly and uncompromis-ingly took up a position in favour of the *Kabbalah*, setting up a partition between *Kabbalah* and philosophy and deriding those who thought that philosophy and *Kabbalah* were identical, whereas in his view they were two contradictory and irreconcilable worlds which confronted one another. The problem at issue was the very one which had prompted the Rema to write his seemingly inoffensive little phrase: that of the essence of the divine attributes. And it was precisely because Eliezer Ashkenazi protested against the mystical interpretation of it given by the Maharal in his preface to *Gevurot ha-Shem* that the Maharal launched out with unparalleled violence against Eliezer Ashkenazi's philosophical interpretation of it. The Rema's ideas were so close to those of Ashkenazi that if Ashkenazi's book *Ma'asei ha-Shem* had not been specifically mentioned by the Maharal in his diatribe (where he does not, however, do Ashkenazi the honour of mentioning him by name), the reader might easily make the mistake of thinking that the 'gentleman from Poland' referred to by the Maharal who had the effrontery to put *Kabbalah* and philosophy in the same category was not Eliezer Ashkenazi but Moses Isserles, whose 'little phrase' was quoted by the Maharal, but without any mention either of the name of Rabbi Moses Isserles nor of his book *Torat ha-Olah* in which it occurs.

Yet, despite these essential differences between the Maharal and the Rema, there were certain points in common to which we should also draw attention.

The Rema's philosophical outlook

First of all, Rabbi Moses Isserles could have confined himself to the four cubits of *halakhah*, in which he was a Master. Like so many of his contemporaries, he could have left us glosses, *responsa*, juridical studies. And if, like the Maharal, he ventured into the realm of abstract thought, it was not that he deceived himself about the dangers. He was well aware of the drama that was taking place outside the walls of the *yeshivot*. He knew he had to take up a position in the contest between philosophy and *Kabbalah*, and if his position turned out to be a conciliatory one, that was more on account of his temperament than because of conviction. The Rema had a passion for harmonization which was no less strong and worthy of respect than the Maharal's passion for discord. At least the two men had the same courage in confronting problems. Just as in the case of the Maharal, one can speak of the Rema's humanism. His incursions into dogmatic theology, science, history, and, more generally, his determination to be present at the heart of the problems of his time, parallel those of the Maharal. We have already drawn attention to these, and shown how they exerted a decisive influence on the development of David Gans (see above: I, 3).

But the difference was that these incursions, which in the Maharal's case developed into a system and a *Weltanschauung*, had been made by the Rema some thirty years earlier in a schematic and incidental fashion. The vigorous assertion of a thesis by the Maharal had disrupted the established order and led to heated polemics; in the case of the Rema there were timid proposals made with an obvious concern to offend the extremists neither of the right nor the left so as to arrive at a consensus as quickly as possible. He dared to take up a position: that was the measure of the Rema's courage. His position, however, had to be as conciliatory as possible, and that was the reason for the timidity of his options. Despite this timidity, some of the Rema's ideas anticipated the system later developed by the Maharal.

In the Rema there is the intuition of an epistemology (theory of the method or grounds of knowledge), the elements of a theory of knowledge, and the statement of a logic of relativity: three ideas which, as we showed in our *Puits de L'Exil* were the corner-stones of the Maharal's doctrines.

With regard to the epistemology, the Rema did not allow himself to be easily drawn into the familiar pattern of Jewish thought since Philo and Maimonides. Like them, he accepted the idea that philosophy had originated in Israel with Moses and Solomon, and that the Greeks had only repeated what the Jews had already said. According to this view, Socrates imbibed wisdom from Ahitophel and Plato from the Hebrew prophets. Aristotle, whose authority was unquestioned, was fortunate enough to have been offered the use of Solomon's library by Alexander the Great who had discovered it during his conquest of Jerusalem, and after a meeting with a Jewish sage he had written a letter describing his conversion to a philosophy based on faith (cf. chapter 1, n. 8). But the Rema thought that there was nevertheless a great difference between Aristotle and Moses, Athens and Jerusalem, Greek philosophy and Jewish philosophy, and that that difference was of an epistemological kind. The content of these two philosophies was the same, but the means by which they arrived at the identical truth was based on different criteria. Aristotle did not copy Solomon: he acknowledged that there was a deep similarity between them. But Aristotle's criterion of knowledge, and that of the non-Jewish philosophers as a whole, was that of free enquiry, critical investigation (in Hebrew *ḥakirah*), while the criterion of Moses, Solomon, and their disciples the Jewish philosophers was tradition, the chain of divine revelation handed down from Sinai (in Hebrew, *Kabbalah*) (cf. *TH* III, 4, 75a).

Now, these, even in their very terminology, are also the criteria postulated by the Maharal, with this conception of the transmission of the revealed truth being paralleled by the very modern idea of research on a rational basis. And there is the same similarity with the Rema in the theory of knowledge in the Maharal, which appears in the Rema in a parenthetical phrase—also a quotation from Moses Botarel—in which the terminology employed by the Maharal as a key to open the doors most recalcitrant to reason is expressed by the words *be-ẓad mah, be-ẓad mah* (on the one hand, on the other hand): 'Although the ideas of certain Kabbalists sometimes appear contradictory, some believing that the divine attributes belong to the divine essence and others that they are its means of action, all in practice agree on the principle of the ambivalence of the attributes which on the one hand are inherent in the divine essence and on the other hand constitute its means of action'. (*TH* III, 3, 75d).

Thus, Botarel and the Rema, like the Maharal, are precursors of Kant and the dialectics of Hegel. In speaking of these ideas, the Rema employs a daring formula: 'unity based on contradiction'. This is once again a quotation, this time from one of the mystical prayers attributed to Rabbi Simeon bar-Yohai: 'Blessed is God who simultaneously creates a thing and its contrary' (*TH* III, 4, 73d). The Rema, however, reconciles the two with a famous Talmudic sentence permitting the reconciliation of irreconcilables (i.e., the School of Hillel and the School of Shammai): 'Both [the words of both schools] are the words of the living God' (*TH*, I. 2, 7c).

It should be pointed out, however, that the Rema was not the only sixteenth-century Jewish thinker who preceded the Maharal with statements of this kind. If we have drawn attention to him here, we should not forget that it is because it was with him that David Gans gained his first initiation into this world of ideas which he was later to rediscover with the Maharal, but far more systematized and on a far higher level.

With the Rema, David Gans could find only indications lacking any broad systematization, incorporation into a theory sufficiently far-reaching to illuminate the whole spiritual landscape. What David Gans found with the Rema in miniature, he found with the Maharal enlarged on an enormous scale. The Rema's thought is a sketch: that of the Maharal a finished painting.

We should state the fact quite clearly: in the difference of opinion between the Maharal and the Rema, David Gans was on the side of the Rema, not because his doctrine appeared to him to be truer, but because it was more flexible, more conciliatory, less profound, and less daring than that of the Maharal. The Maharal readopted some of the Rema's ideas, but only on the surface. He incorporated them into a system, and then raised that system onto an exalted level where few of those around him were able to follow him. Like Joshua and Aaron, Dans Gans remained with the Rema at the foot of the mountain, while the Maharal, like Moses, went up to the summit.

THE THIRD MAN: AZARIAH DEI ROSSI

When David Gans declared in *Zemaḥ David* (1592) that he intended to write books about geography, mathematics, and astronomy, he was dealing with subjects which were already well represented in his library, although hitherto he had consulted only the history books he needed for writing his chronicles. Euclid, Aristotle, and Ptolemy among the ancients, Isaac Israeli, Abraham bar Ḥiyya, Judah Halevi, Maimonides, and Isaac Abravanel among more recent writers were all authorities in these new areas he was about to enter.

Among the most recent writers it was naturally two close contemporaries, his teachers the Rema and the Maharal, who played the most important part. Gans had the difficult task of choosing between the different doctrines and approaches of these two figures with whom he had a Master-and-disciple relationship, when there appeared on the scene the two non-Jewish scholars, Tycho Brahe and Johannes Kepler, whose disciple he became from 1600, the very year when the Maharal ceased his literary activity.

The difficulty of the choice was further complicated by the emergence of another Jewish authority: one whom David Gans had not known personally, but whose book—*Me'or Einayim*, published in Mantua in 1575, five years after the Rema's *Torat ha-Olah* and seven years before the Maharal's *Gevurot ha-Shem*—had long been familiar to David Gans at the time of the appearance of *Zemaḥ David* in 1592. This 'third man' was essentially a historian, and his book, like *Zemaḥ David*, was a history book.

Azariah dei Rossi (1513–78) whom we are referring to here needs no introduction, since we spoke a great deal about him in *Le Puits de L'Exil* (pp. 98 ff.); *Me'or Einayim*, the work of this Italian Jewish humanist, is mentioned more than ten times in *Zemaḥ David*, for it was an important and accurate source of information concerning historical dates and events, especially with regard to the Second Temple and Hellenistic periods which were Azariah dei Rossi's special preserves. David Gans was also impressed by Azariah's account of the earthquake at Ferrara in 1571 with which he began his book. He gave it a place of importance in *Zemaḥ David* and, like Azariah, speculated about the moral and religious significance of catastrophes of this kind (*ZD* 198b, 203a).

It was precisely when Azariah dei Rossi raised problems such as these that he became for David Gans a serious spiritual rival to his two Teachers, the Rema and the Maharal, for Azariah's opinions were marked by a vigorous scepticism which clearly bewildered David Gans and put him off his balance.

First of all, there are the methodological chapters in *Me'or Einayim* in which (as we showed in *Le Puits de L'Exil*) Azariah raises the problem of the relationship of history and tradition, severely criticizing the traditional Talmudic approach and submitting it to a very modern form of analysis. David Gans does not relate to these chapters: his *Ẓemaḥ David* is not a history book but a chronicle. He never stops, like Azariah, to assess the facts, to compare the sources, to weigh them up and arrive at an approach. He draws up lists of events in chronological order, without ever discussing them or questioning them. Sometimes contradictions pile up, but the main thing, for David Gans, is to relate history and not, as for Azariah dei Rossi, to reconstruct it. The truth has not the same meaning for these two historians.

Did it have the same meaning for these two men when, leaving history, they confronted it in other spheres? For Azariah dei Rossi did not shrink from incursions into the areas which David Gans intended to study after the publication of *Ẓemaḥ David*. Mathematics, geography, astronomy were also subjected to methodological and critical analysis by Azariah, and *Me'or Einayim* remained a work of reference for Gans long after he had completed his chronicle. When David Gans became a cosmographer and astronomer, he still had to consult the *Me'or Einayim* of Azariah dei Rossi, which remained on his work-table, a rich source of information, side by side with the works of the Rema and the Maharal.

Because of this, David Gans found himself drawn, quite against his will, into a heated controversy which made even more difficult a choice already made difficult enough by the contrast between the Rema's universe and that of the Maharal.

Between the Rema and the Maharal, Azariah dei Rossi represents, we said, a 'third man', whose position is completely different from that of the two other writers, themselves opposed on so many important points. The intellectual aspects of this disagreement we shall discuss at some length in our study of David Gans's works following *Ẓemah David*. Here we shall simply point out the impasse in which David Gans found himself around the year 1600, when he began to plan his book of astronomy.

Azariah versus the Rema

Chronologically speaking, this impasse was reached in the most simple and straightforward manner imaginable. It was like a sort of ballet. David Gans's masters successively accused each other of ignorance and even heresy, each one taking up the cudgels when the previous one was dead.

In 1575, when the Rema had been dead for five years, Azariah dei Rossi, at the end of his most important methodological chapter, the eleventh of the *Imrei Binah* of *Me'or Einayim*, with an air of seeming innocence added an appendix introduced by the following words:

Having come with God's help to the end of this chapter, I cannot conceal from the reader that a book entitled *Torat ha-Olah*, printed in Prague in 1570, has just come to my notice. Its author was one of the Sovereigns of the Spirit who reigned in the city of Cracow, crowned with the seven qualities which our Sages attribute to genius. These are enumerated at the beginning of the book, and rightly so, for I have heard it said that in our generation he was a man of God, a *zaddik*, a Talmudist without equal. Leafing through the book, I have noticed that he broached the very questions I have raised in this chapter: namely, the confrontation of certain opinions of our ancient Sages with present-day doctrines. It was thus with a feeling of love that I pored over this book in pleasurable anticipation of the things that I ardently hoped to find there.

There follow some twenty lines in which Azariah dei Rossi 'demolishes' the book in the most perfidious pamphleteering manner. Basing his criticism on two or three examples from the book taken from the area of cosmography, Azariah reproached the Rema for having stated the problems correctly, exactly as he himself had done, but for having given such childish answers, both in form and content, that these conciliatory gymnastics can give only the most miserable and insulting idea of the intellectual level of the sages of the Talmud. Like Job's comforters, he thought, the *Torat ha-Olah* debases the truth of God, and, playing on the words which make up the title of the Rema's book, Azariah coined a phrase which has remained famous in the history of Jewish polemics: 'If you want to make an offering to God, offer it up to the Truth.' Although Azariah does not forget that he is an Italian and a Sephardi, and so one of a company of scholars of an intellectual level far higher than that of the Ashkenazi 'Talmudists' to whom Moses Isserles belongs, he nevertheless ends with the hope that some learned and enlightened men will be found among the Ashkenazim who will support his opinions and not stupidly oppose them with the arguments which the 'the Sovereign and Sustainer' of Cracow would have advanced against them: 'I have no doubt that his intentions were good and that he now shares the joys of eternity with the Sages, but I am quite certain that with his policy, however well-intentioned, of justifying our Sages' opinions at any cost, he has not invalidated my approach'—an approach which, as we saw in *Le Puits de L'Exil*, was to justify the truth against the opinion of the Talmud, whenever that truth appeared to be self-evident.

The Maharal versus Azariah

And in 1582, four years after Azariah's death, the Maharal began to publish the first of his series of great works, *Gevurot ha-Shem*. From the time of the appearance of this first book until he reached the climax of his achievement with *Be'er ha-Golah* in 1600, it was now the Maharal's turn to cross swords with Azariah dei Rossi, which he did, not in order to defend the honour of the Rema whom, as we said, he also attacked in *Derekh Hayyim* (1589), but in order to expound his own doctrine which was irreconcilable with that of the Rema and, even more, with that of Azariah. What is particularly amusing is that, in the *Be'er ha-Golah*, the scenario follows the same pattern as that of Azariah dei Rossi's criticism of the Rema. After expounding his ideas in the sixth well, the last but one of the seven 'wells' which constitute his 'Defence and Illustration of the Midrash', the Maharal concluded as follows:

> I ought to have ended here and concluded my expositions had a book by a member of our people not come into my hands. Those who presented me this book praised it and offered it to me as a work which gave one a completely new understanding of the problem. How great was my joy! I approached the book literally with the delight of a bridegroom receiving his bride! But when I had read only a few pages here and there, my heart gave way and my soul sank within me, and I cried: Woe unto the eyes which see such things, woe unto the ears which hear them. . .

There follows a polemic which we have described at some length in *Le Puits de L'Exil*. It was a polemic of extraordinary violence which, even going as far as to express regret that the author, the publisher, and the book itself had not been placed under a ban, sounds a jarring note in the work of the Maharal—a proud spirit, certainly, but normally open and tolerant.

Thus, finding himself placed between several different combatants, all of whom he held in equal veneration, the modest spectator David Gans chose the path of tolerance. He referred to the Rema respectfully, without taking Azariah's criticisms into consideration, and with the same degree of respectfulness referred to the book of Azariah dei Rossi, without paying attention to the fulminations of the Maharal. This moderation and tolerance of spirit are especially touching in this particular context. It is not impossible that David Gans was prominent among 'those who presented the book of Azariah dei Rossi to the Maharal 'and praised it'. The rabbi's violent reaction in no way prevented his pupil from including *Me'or Einayim* among his bedside books.

A BYSTANDER: ELIEZER ASHKENAZI

The same applies to that other target of the Maharal's fulminations: Eliezer Ashkenazi. Born in Asia Minor in 1513, Ashkenazi had wandered in various countries and directed the *Ḥevra Kaddisha* (burial society) in Prague in 1564, before finally settling in Poland, where he died in Cracow in 1586. In *Le Puits de L'Exil* we gave an account of the Maharal's controversy with Ashkenazi, to which too few scholars have given the attention it deserves in view of the fact that it represents one of the climaxes of the struggle between philosophy and the *Kabbalah* at the end of the sixteenth century. Until the present time, we have not had the opportunity to take our researches any further nor, above all, to decide which of the two, Ashkenazi or the Maharal, was the attacker and which was the attacked. Whatever the case, where David Gans was concerned, the facts are these: in 1589 David Gans must have become aware, through the publication of *Derekh Ḥayyim*, of the Maharal's violent opposition to Eliezer Ashkenazi's ideas in *Ma'asei ha-Shem* (1583), but that did not prevent him from mentioning this work of Ashkenazi's on several occasions in *Neḥmad ve-Na'im* and supporting some of his own ideas with interpretations taken from *Ma'asei ha-Shem*, just as if the book had never been attacked by the Maharal.

Thus, in an age when polemics were continuous, harsh, and pitiless, David Gans appears as a very innocent figure. In the triangular debate in which three of the thinkers who were closest to him were at loggerheads, and in the wider controversy in which the great minds of the period clashed with one another, David Gans remained a modest but effective servant of all forms of the truth, even when advanced in contradictory fashion by men of sometimes irreconcilable temperament. He was clearly animated by a passionate desire to place himself 'above the fray'.

But if, in these spiritual conflicts in which the Rema, Azariah dei Rossi, and the Maharal occupy the foreground, Eliezer Ashkenazi gives the impression in David Gans's work of being only a bystander, someone in the wings, we still have to turn our attention to a fifth person who was also important in the internal conflict of the Jewish people towards the end of the sixteenth century, but in David Gans's work played the enigmatic and unexpected role of a phantom. We are referring to Mordecai Jaffe whom we will now introduce before bringing down the curtain on this *comoedia spiritualis* which we are watching from David Gans's viewpoint.

A PHANTOM: MORDECAI JAFFE

The last entry but one in *Z̧emaḥ David* (1592), sandwiched between the one concerning the Maharal and the one in praise of Mordecai Meisel, introduces the eminent figure of Rabbi Mordecai Jaffe. This is David Gans's description of him, constituting the middle section of the trilogy which concludes the Jewish part of the chronicle:

Rabbi Mordecai Jaffe is a great scholar of outstanding knowledge and wisdom, standard-bearer of the camp of Israel. He is the author of the great work *Sefer Levush Malkhut* [The Book of the Royal Garment] which is a compendium of all the ordinances of the Talmud and the commentators, the author of a commentary on the Torah and a collection of sermons, and finally the author of a commentary on the *Guide to the Perplexed* and on ordinances concerning the Sanctification of the New Moon by Maimonides as well as a commentary on the Recanati. He was head of a *yeshiva* first for twenty years at Grodno, then at Lublin and Kremnitz. Everywhere he had many disciples, and he is considered the spiritual head of the great scholars of the *yeshivot* and of the judges of the Three Provinces.

He came here in the month of Iyar 5352 (1592) and until the present day has lived amongst us here in Prague. May God raise up his throne to the loftiest heights!

Most of what we know of the biography of Rabbi Mordecai ben Abraham Jaffe is contained in this description by David Gans. Only a few details are missing: his date of birth, which is uncertain; the date of the publication of the first volume of *Sefer Levush Malkhut* in Lublin (1590), and an exact description (unnecessary for the readers of *Zemah David*) of the powers attached to the post of Supreme Judge of the Three Provinces: Moravia, Bohemia, and Poland. The details of his biography after 1592 are obviously also missing.

We have seen that the Maharal suddenly left Prague for Posen in the month of Iyar 1592, and that was the very date when Mordecai Jaffe settled in Prague. A few weeks later, Mordecai Jaffe was appointed to the position of Chief Rabbi of Prague which had been left vacant by the Maharal, occupying that post until 1598 precisely, when the Maharal took up that position again. And who was it that succeeded the Maharal as Chief Rabbi of Posen? Mordecai Jaffe once more. He remained in Posen until his death in 1612, three years after the death of the Maharal in Prague and one year before the death of David Gans.

This remarkable alternation of positions, which in 1592 Gans could not have foreseen, vividly highlights the ecclesiastical similarity, if one may say so, of the Maharal and Jaffe, and the similar degree of authority which they enjoyed in the rabbinical hierarchy of Central and Eastern Europe.

But this similarity of career, which David Gans was to witness, was complemented by a spiritual affinity which Gans alluded to in the passage we quoted and which became increasingly pronounced as Mordecai Jaffe developed.

Sefer Levush Malkhut comprised ten parts which were published from 1590 to 1604. If the book was conceived as something parallel to Joseph Caro's *Shulhan Arukh* (Gans called it 'a compendium of all the ordinances of the Talmud and the commentators'), it had none of the faults for which the Maharal reproached the *Shulhan Arukh*, so much admired and commented on by Rabbi Moses Isserles. It was not a digest—far from it—but a summation, comparable to Maimonides' *Mishneh Torah*: a summation full of elements which the *Shulhan Arukh* had not incorporated, and which we find at the core of the work of the Maharal.

The spiritual affinity of Jaffe and the Maharal

The entry in *Zemah David* incidentally mentions works connected with three of those elements: a commentary on Maimonides' *Guide to the Perplexed*, a commentary on the ordinances concerning the Sanctification of the New Moon in Maimonides' *Mishneh Torah*, and a commentary on the Recanati.

These three works by Mordecai Jaffe did not appear until 1594, when they were published in Lublin under the general title of *Sefer Levushei Or Yekarot*. How did David Gans know about them in 1952? He had learnt about them from Mordecai Jaffe's general introduction to his *Sefer Levush Malkhut*, published in the first volume which appeared under the title *Sefer Levush ha-Tekhelet* in 1590.

This introduction leaves us in no doubt about Mordecai Jaffe's intentions and ideology, or about the spiritual universe which he inhabited and in which his work was situated—a universe with which David Gans would become increasingly acquainted as it was presented to the public. This universe was the universe of the Maharal, or at any rate of the Maharal in certain of his great works.

Let us examine a passage from Mordecai Jaffe's introduction to the work to which David Gans alludes in a short phrase in his entry. One is immediately struck by the fact that it expresses a profound concern for pedagogy which one also finds in the Maharal, especially in his *Netivot Olam*. Jaffe's general approach, like that of Maharal, is encyclopaedic but methodological. His subject is treated in accordance with an epistemological scheme which, even in its choice of words and metaphors, recalls the terminology of the Maharal:

Every disciple of the Sages who, like the holy angels, seeks to enter the Pardes and to scale the rungs of the ladder [*sulam*] whose foot is on earth but whose top reaches heaven, must raise himself from the base to the summit dominated by the Divine Presence, as it is written: 'Behold, the angels of God ascended and descended on it' (Genesis 28: 12). They first ascended, attaining knowledge by going from the base to the summit, and then descended so as to bestow it abundantly upon the whole universe.

This is the literal order [*seder*] in which students must study.

First the student must study the theoretical and natural sciences which represent the whole of our knowledge of the humble inferior world in which we live: these are all enumerated in the famous treatise known as the *Guide to the Perplexed*.

Then the student will go one rung higher and will study astronomy, embracing the intermediate world: that of the spheres and heavenly bodies with the sun at their head, reigning over them like a sovereign over his army, with the moon as his second-in-command.

Then he will mount progressively higher in order to enter into the Pardes: i.e., the science whose path leads to Bet El, the House of God. I mean the science of the *Kabbalah*.

Only then will he be deemed worthy to attain the knowledge of the First Cause, may it be blessed, which hovers over the three worlds, giving them existence and assuring their permanence.

I have said enough in order to be understood.

But, in case anyone still failed to understand him, Jaffe explained that he felt there was a spiritual correspondence between the triad philosophy–astronomy–*Kabbalah* and three of the spheres of the *Kabbalah*: *bina* (intelligence), *ḥokhmah* (wisdom), and *keter* (crown).

Thus, like the Maharal, Mordecai Jaffe attempts a classification of the different kinds of knowledge. They require a *seder*, a progressive ordering whose hierarchical character is expressed by the metaphor of the ladder. These same terms recur in the Maharal's *Netivot Olam* (Paths of Eternity) which appeared in 1595 and were thus written at the same period as Jaffe's *Levush*. They, too, started with the secular sciences, among which the Maharal, like Jaffe, specifically mentioned the natural sciences and astronomy, and reached their culmination in the *Kabbalah*, whose preeminence the Maharal had vigorously defended in his *Derekh Ḥayyim* of 1589. Finally, the two authors link their methodology to the general concept of the hierarchy of the three worlds, known to Aristotle, but transmuted by the *Kabbalah* into a far more elaborate cosmology, full of theological significance.

The originality of Jaffe: astronomy receives its title of nobility

However, the two rabbis do differ on certain essential points. The requirements of polemics drive the Maharal to make extreme statements which are completely absent in Jaffe. These reveal the basic thinking of the Maharal, for whom no compromise between philosophy and *Kabbalah* is possible even for pedagogical purposes. For Mordecai Jaffe, on the other hand, the Hebrew term *filosofia* has an important place on the educational ladder and is equated with *bina* in the kabbalistic hierarchy of *sefirot*. Here Jaffe obviously takes the side of the Rema, whose pupil he was, and not the side of the Maharal. He too is a conciliator, but he is better able than the Rema to assign philosophy its precise, limited place in a coherent scheme, whereas the Rema posits the identity between philosophy and *Kabbalah* as axiomatic. Could not David Gans have found in

Mordecai Jaffe a compromise solution to the problem which worried him because it tore his two beloved Teachers apart?

In order to deal with this question, we ought to take it a stage further. We see that the Maharal did speak about astronomy, but he simply classed it among the natural sciences (just as he did with those elements of 'philosophy' which he nevertheless deemed to have some validity) in a category which he placed under the heading of *hokhmah*; but Jaffe, on the contrary, took astronomy out of that category, creating an original and remarkable triad:

Philosophy corresponds to *bina*
Astronomy corresponds to *hokhmah*
Kabbalah corresponds to *keter*.

Just as in the cases of philosophy and the *Kabbalah*, he justified the distinguished position of astronomy with verses from the Bible, and he is thus one of the rare Jewish thinkers of the late sixteenth century, if not the only one, to give astronomy scientific and theological titles of nobility. For my part, I have never found this formulation in any other Jewish writer.

It is impossible, therefore, not to ask why David Gans did not use Mordecai Jaffe's ideas to support his own astronomical researches. But the fact is, that after his fulsome praise of Jaffe in his *Zemah David* of 1592 he was completely silent. Neither in *Magen David* of 1612, nor in the manuscripts of *Nehmad ve-Na'im* (nor, obviously, in the printed edition of 1743) did the name of Mordecai Jaffe escape his pen, not even in the place where we would most expect to find it: in the epilogue of *Nehmad ve-Na'im*, where he speaks of the Rema and the Maharal.

When I read this passage in the epilogue, I must admit to a feeling of frustration. Not only did Mordecai Jaffe deserve to be included among the 'contemporary thinkers who had devoted their attention to the methodological problems raised by astronomy within Jewish thought', but Gans could have found in him a model of considered equilibrium which corresponded to his own temperament and to the positions which he himself adopted when face to face with these problems. Could it be the very closeness of that affinity which explains the silence of David Gans?

In 1609 he put the last touches to a work of astronomy which he still called *Magen David* (and which a few weeks before his death in 1613 received the title of *Nehmad ve-Na'im*). That same year saw the publication in Prague of the three last volumes of the *Levush* promised by Mordecai Jaffe in 1590: the volumes devoted to the triad: philosophy, astronomy, *Kabbalah*. The publisher asked Judah ben Natan Halevi Ashkenazi to provide the astronomical section with a few glosses and an introduction, and in that introduction Judah Ashkenazi attempted a 'defence of astronomy' in which he used very similar terms and arguments to those employed by David Gans in his own similar 'defence' at the end of his epilogue— notably the argument that the contradiction of the stellar orbits necessarily implies the existence of a creator (see below III. 2). Moreover, Judah Ashkenazi used expressions which could have suggested to David Gans the new title of his book of astronomy, *Neḥmad ve-Na'im*, which replaced its former title *Magen David*. (See below I. 5 'The Jerusalem Manuscript'.)

If that was so, it would not have been a case of plagiarism but of a kind of blurring of the names used by authors who were too close to David Gans's way of thinking for him not to have adopted their terminology as if it had always been his own. However that may be, among the actors in the spiritual drama in which David Gans was involved, Mordecai Jaffe is something special. Like a phantom which disappears at the very moment when one thinks one has caught sight of it, his thought is present but his name invisible in the work of David Gans, which it is now time to examine.

5

David Gans's works

THE work of David Gans represents an aspect of humanism at its most technical, or at its most Rabelaisian, I might even say. Nearly all the sciences of his day are represented in it, and a classification by subjects will give a fairly accurate idea of the encyclopaedic scope of the mind of David Gans:

1. History: *Zemaḥ David* (Shoot of David), *Sefer al Aseret ha-Shevatim* (Essay on the Ten Tribes).
2. Geography: *Gevulot ha-Arez* (Frontiers of the Land), *Zurat ha-Arez* (Shape of the Earth).
3. Mathematics: *Migdal David* (Tower of David), *Prozdor* (Ante-chamber).
4. Astronomy: *Me'or ha-Katan* (The Lesser Light), *Magen David* (The Shield of David), *Neḥmad ve-Na'im* (Pleasant and Agreeable), translation of the 'Alphonsine Tables' from Hebrew into German.

I say 'fairly' accurate, because in a 'David Gans' bibliographical card index one would have to subdivide mathematics into pure mathematics and geometry, the latter also meaning astronomy; and astronomy would have to be subdivided into astronomy proper, cosmology, cosmography, and geography. Some works cover several areas at the same time, and the line of demarcation which allows us to perceive the limits of David Gans's creative inspiration and his curiosity as a writer seems to me to be the fact that his work embraces all the secular sciences and excludes the rabbinical sciences. No biblical or Talmudic commentary, no attempt at *Responsa*, no sermon has come down to us from David Gans, in whom he have a rather rare example of a sixteenth-century rabbi who occupied himself exclusively with universal erudition, yet without losing touch with religious tradition in which he lived naturally and spontaneously.

David Gans's work can also be approached from another angle

which will give us a better idea of how it came into being, and allow us to examine its sources. Like his Teacher the Maharal, who in his preface to *Gevurot ha-Shem* (1582) drew up a systematic plan of his intended works, parts of which were never carried out, David Gans, in the preface to his first work, *Zemaḥ David* (1592), informed the reader that he intended writing a work of mathematics, *Magen David*, and a work of geometry, *Migdal David*. He also announced his intention of writing a dissertation on the problem of the Ten Tribes and on the discovery of the New World (*Sefer al Aseret ha-Shevatim*) (p. 193a). Thus a plan was taking shape in David Gans's mind, but the way in which it was realized, and its setbacks and failures, lead me to think that there was something tentative and exploratory in David Gans's creative psychology, deriving both from a timidity which we have already noticed in his biography and a progress in his knowledge which caused him to recoil and change his positions.

In the following chapters we shall see how David Gans's astronomical work was bound up with the explosive impact of his meeting with Tycho Brahe in 1599—a meeting which transformed a schoolmaster into a scholar.

I do not feel it unreasonable to claim that this event had an important effect on David Gans's whole make-up. My feeling is (leaving aside the scholarly discussions on the content of certain of his works, examined in a masterly fashion by Freedman[1]) that David Gans's creativity was conditioned by a psychological factor: his strong pedagogical motive. He was above all—as he often said in his prefaces, etc.—a teacher, an initiator, if not on a primary-textbook level, then at least on an exclusively didactic level. But certain challenges which came from the outside—his discovery of Euclid, his frequentation of the Maharal, of Tycho and his circle—raised him, despite himself, on to the far higher level of a researcher and sometimes of an original thinker.

This change is reflected in a number of different ways: in the alteration of the titles of certain works (as we shall see in the case of *Neḥmad ve-Na'im*), in the abandonment of certain projects which no longer seemed feasible on the original didactical level, but whose reshaping in a more scholarly manner would have required a period of maturation which Gans—preoccupied as he was with

---

[1] Freedman. See the ten pages, numbered 1 to 10, entitled I. Bibliography: Manuscripts and Editions of Gans's Works.

rethinking his work of astronomy after his traumatic meeting with Tycho Brahe—probably did not have at his disposal, and in his propensity for writing new works on the same subjects as his previous ones but on a far higher intellectual plane.

Thus, it seems to me that, according to the author's own brief description of these works, *Zurat ha-Arez* was only a very basic geographical textbook, whereas *Gevulot ha-Arez* was an account of the new geographical and cosmographical discoveries and their impact on certain historical problems (the New World, modern cartography, the Lost Ten Tribes.)[2]

And, in the same way, *Migdal David* was an elementary manual of geometry whereas the *Prozdor* included descriptions of complicated instruments such as the quadrant and instructions for their use.[3]

And, finally, *Me'or ha-katan* limits its investigation of astronomy to the purely Jewish preoccupation of fixing the calendar (in fact, it was a kind of pocket almanack), whereas *Magen David* and *Neḥmad ve-Na'im* were the outcome of a real adventure of discovery which we shall later describe in detail.[4]

Be it as it may, out of all this large and ever-fluctuating body of work, only one book was published in David Gans's lifetime—his first, his 'firstfruits', his 'shoot': *Zemaḥ David*—in 1592. The *Magen David* published in 1612 was only a prospectus. As for the two other works published posthumously, one, *Neḥmad ve-Na'im*, only saw the light in 1743 and has never been re-published since, and the other, *Zurat ha-Arez*, is only known to us from a bibliography of the seventeenth century.[5] No copy of the work has come down to

---

[2] Gans himself mentions *Gevulot ha-Arez* in *NN* 27b, referring to its 'second part'. *Zurat ha-Arez*, on the other hand, is known to us only from Plantavitius's bibliography. See n. 5.

[3] Our knowledge of the existence of *Migdal David* is derived only from the mention of the title in the preface to *Zemaḥ David*. On the other hand, *Prozdor* is mentioned by him in *NN* 70a and 75d. In the latter passage, Gans regretted the disappearance of this 'lengthy book'.

[4] All the passages in which Gans mentions *Me'or ha-Katan* (see Freedman) are concerned with the problems of the Jewish calendar.

[5] We refer to the bibliography of the Bishop of Lodève, mentioned in Chapter 3 above. Jean Plantavit de la Pause (1575–1651), under his Latinized name of Plantavitius, published two excellent works: his *Florilège Biblique* and his *Bibliotheca Rabbinica*, in which item no. 591 is *Zurat ha-Arez* by Rabbi David Avsi, published in Constantinople. This item was included by Giulio Bartolocci (1613–85) in his *Kiryat Sefer: Bibliotheca Magna Rabbinica*, ii. 413. He claimed that the book was to be found in the library of Queen Christina of Sweden, but neither Plantavitius's *Bibliotheca* (Lodève 1645) nor Bartolocci's are free from errors and confusions. On the interesting

us. As for his numerous other works, not only did they remain in manuscript, but—worse still—none of these manuscripts has ever been found.

Prozdor went astray during the author's lifetime. The translation of the 'Alphonsine Tables' (really the Tables of Pedro) was never mentioned by Tycho Brahe, although it was for him that Gans undertook this task. The 'Book on the Ten Tribes', which was probably only a chapter of *Gevulot ha-Arez*, was never written. And all the rest lie in the limbo of forgotten manuscripts which we hope that some researcher will one day bring to light as we have had the opportunity of doing for a hitherto unknown manuscript of *Neḥmad ve-Na'im*.

ẒEMAḤ DAVID

We shall not stop here to make an exhaustive examination of *Ẓemaḥ David* (1592), the only work of David Gans to have appeared in his lifetime, and also his 'best-seller', since it went into eight more editions and was translated into Latin. This historical chronicle was mentioned in the scholarly footnotes of all the nineteenth-century Jewish historians who rightly saw David Gans as a precursor in their own field, and in our own day Jirina Sedinova is working on a complete edition of *Ẓemaḥ David*, of which her publications to date provide a fascinating promise.[6]

It will be enough for us simply to draw attention to some of the interesting material contained in the two prefaces to *Ẓemaḥ David*. In the first preface, introducing the Jewish wing of his diptych, David Gans declared enthusiastically that his historical work was only a 'shoot' (*ẓemaḥ*), a pledge or earnest of a whole series of works concerning all subjects of interest to the educated man in the sixteenth century: mathematics, geography, geometry, astronomy. In the second preface, introducing the more audacious non-Jewish wing of the diptych, David Gans twice invoked the authority of Jewish historians who preceded him in their involvement in secular studies, particularly that of a contemporary—his Teacher, the Rema,—adding a touching observation about the persistence of the

personality of the Bishop of Lodève, see F. Secret, *Les Kabbalistes Chrétiens de la Renaissance* (1964), pp. 336–7.

[6] See also Mordecai Breuer's preface to his edition of *Ẓemaḥ David*, (Jerusalem, 1983).

Jewish people which passes through the vicissitudes of the most tortuous periods under the protection of the Divine Wings, giving examples not only from the ancient world in which a succession of mighty empires crumbled while Israel survived, but also, and even more convincingly, from the sixteenth century itself, in which Papists and Lutherans tore one another apart (the Wars of Religion had already claimed hundreds of thousands of victims) while the little Jewish people continued its humble but obstinate existence. This observation of David Gans, expressed in simple and pietistic language, already at the end of the sixteenth century heralded the philosophy of history which at the beginning of the nineteenth century Naḥman Krochmal was to develop in terms of post-Kantian idealism.

Here I shall limit myself to presenting—for the interest and, I hope, the delight of the reader—a few of the entries of *Ẓemaḥ David* devoted to recent events. They have a freshness of flavour and many picturesque features, and at the same time allow us to sense the cultural atmosphere of David Gans's environment. Other entries will be quoted, as the need arises, in later chapters in this book in connection with events experienced or described by Gans.

We shall begin with a subject which is very up-to-date: confrontations in the universities (we translate as 'confrontation' the biblical term *kineah* which we feel that Gans used quite deliberately)—a subject connected with another contemporary manifestation, and one which is dear to me: the courage of Czech students.[7]

EXTRACTS FROM ẒEMAḤ DAVID

1408 In the glorious city of Prague, in the College founded, as we said, by the Emperor Charles IV in 1351[8] which contained more than 30,000 young Christians who are called 'students', great riots and disturbances broke out for the following reason: the Bohemian students objected to the privileges granted to the German students by Charles IV, whereby the dignitaries and heads of this school of higher learning must always be Germans, who enjoyed full jurisdiction in all areas. Finally, the Bohemian students gained the upper hand and forced the Germans to leave their posts. This incident resulted in the departure of twenty thousand students in one week. Most of them left for

[7] Cf. my letter to *Le Monde* of 2–3 January 1969: 'The Czechs and the Jews'.
[8] Gans stated that in 1351 Charles IV founded a School of Higher Learning (*Hochschule* or university) in Prague on the lines of the similar institution in Paris.

Leipzig where a school of higher learning was founded which has existed until the present day.

1440 Printing was invented at Mainz by the Christian Johannes Gutenberg of Strasbourg in the first year of the reign of the Emperor Frederick the Pious (the Jewish year 5200).

Blessed be He who endows man with intelligence and teaches him knowledge.

Blessed be He who in His goodness has granted us such an invention, of universal benefit and unique of its kind. No other invention, no other discovery can be compared to it since God created man upon the earth. It is not only the metaphysical sciences and the seven secular sciences which have profited from this invention, but all the applied sciences—metalworking, architecture, wood-engraving, and lithography— have also benefited. Each day reveals some new aspect, and innumerable books are published which benefit all professions whatever they may be.

1522 Martin Luther, a great scholar of their scriptures, conceived and wrote a large number of works in the spirit of Jan Hus whom I mentioned previously for the year 1414.[9] He set himself against the Pope, and provoked a schism amongst the Christians by proposing a whole series of innovations. He immediately gained the support of many peoples and particularly of a number of Dukes and cities in Germany, namely: the Dukes of Saxony, Silesia, Hesse, Mecklenburg, Brandenburg, Pomerania, Baden, and Switzerland, and the cities of Augsburg, Ulm, Nuremberg, Frankfurt, Basle, and Strasbourg and many others. His doctrine was publicly proclaimed at the Diet of Worms in the year 5280 or 1522 of the Christian era. A number of great wars immediately broke out in most of the countries of Europe. Each year saw a new one, so that since that fatal year until our own days more than a thousand thousand thousands of Christians have been killed and massacred as a terrible consequence of his doctrine.

1554 In the city of Geneva the great scholar Servetus was burned to death because he was accused of denying the divinity of the one whom they considered their Messiah.

1571 In his great love for the Jews, and in order to demonstrate his benevolence towards them, the pious emperor Maximilian (II), together with his wife the Empress Mary, daughter of the Emperor Charles, and the highest dignitaries among his princes and counsellors, passed through the Street of the Jews in the City of Prague.[10]

---

[9] Gans devotes more than two pages of *ZD* to Jan Hus, his martyrdom, and the nearly thirty years of war which followed.

[10] As Gans does not say he was an eyewitness, he was probably not in Prague when this event took place.

1572 The great and remarkable comet was again seen in the year 5332, 1572 of the Christian era. This new star was visible for fourteen months, a longer period than any chronicle, no matter how far back in time it went, had ever recorded for a new star. All the star-gazers in Germany, Italy, France, and Spain gave interpretations of this extraordinary apparition, and many books were written about it, some of them foretelling great catastrophes. But the Lord in His mercy confounds the visions of the foolish. In that year, however, there were earthquakes in Constantinople, Augsburg, and Munich. . .[11]

1572 In that year there was a great massacre in France. The Duke Admiral had been invited to the capital, Paris, to celebrate a marriage. He was struck down with the sword in the Royal Palace, together with many other princes and dignitaries of high rank. The strife and the massacres that have taken place in France since that time have been such that a whole book would be needed to describe them.

1574 The greatest living astrologer, Ptolemy Sultitus of Görlitz, predicted in his annual almanack[12] that from the position of Saturn one could infer great catastrophes of which the Jews would be the victims. His predictions, in fact, came true, for that year was a year of countless massacres and afflictions for the Jews in many regions. In Moravia, our sins caused the martyrdom by burning of many of our co-religionists. The pious Emperor Maximilian, of blessed memory, had to intervene, and after careful enquiry those Jews that remained were snatched from the lions' mouths and placed beneath his protective wings. May God take this into account, as well as all his other good deeds.

1577 Mary, Queen of Scots rebelled against her aunt, the Queen of England, and on 28 November 1577, the latter, through guile, arrested her together with her fifteen-year-old son, and ordered her to be beheaded.

1585 Pope Gregory XIII instituted the new calendar in Rome, replacing that of the Emperor Julius Caesar. . . Instead of calling the day after the fifteenth of October the sixteenth of October, he decided it would be the twenty-fifth of October, so that that year was shortened by ten days. We should note that the new counting of the solar year is very close to the old Jewish computation of Rav Adda bar Ahava. . .

[11] In 1592 Gans did not yet know that seven years later he would meet the most illustrious of the observers of the new star: Tycho Brahe. The essay on it which Brahe wrote that year established his reputation and made him into a kind of 'ambassador' of the kingdom of Denmark to the world of science.

[12] This was Bartholomaus Scultetus, a disciple of Paracelsus, who was burgomaster of Görlitz. His name appears on two documents in connecton with the man who made Görlitz famous: Jacob Böhme. One, dated 24 April 1599, declares that the shoemaker Jakob Böhme has gained citizenship of Görlitz. The other states that in July 1613 he ordered Jakob Böhme to concern himself with his shoemaking and not with abstruse theology.

Emperor Rudolph (II), may his glory be exalted, specially convened an Imperial Diet in his splendid capital the city of Prague so as to solemnly confirm the acceptance of the new calendar.

1588 Henry III of France, who was also King of Poland, as I mentioned above, inclined towards the doctrine of the Calvinists, who scorn the ordinances of the Pope. After long wars and great massacres, the King summoned his opponents on the pretext of wishing to make peace with them: these were the two highest Dukes in the royal line, close relatives of the King—the Duc de Guise and his brother the Cardinal, as well as other dukes and the Bishops of Lyons and Amiens. Just when these delegates were about to enter the royal palace in Paris, assassins in the pay of the King thrust themselves upon them and killed them all, as well as many other princes of high rank. This happened on 23 September 1588.

1589 Henry III, King of France and of Poland, whom we have just mentioned, received his just deserts for his criminal act. The brother of the Duc de Guise who had been assassinated in 1588, plotted against the King in order to avenge his brother. By means of an extraordinary stratagem, he sent the King a priest named Jacob Clemens, aged 23. He, under the pretence of handing the King some letters, had concealed in his hand a little knife half the length of a finger, with a poisoned tip. He plunged it into the King's stomach, in consequence of which the King died twenty-three hours after the fatal blow. Before dying, the King designated as his heir his close relative, Henry, Duke of Navarre.

NEḤMAD VE-NA'IM

A classic work

At first sight, David Gans's *Neḥmad ve-Na'im* appears to be an astronomical treatise in the scholarly sense of the term. It is in the tradition of similar treatises written in Hebrew by Jewish scholars, of which the most recent in date as well as the most important and influential was Isaac Israeli's *Yesod Olam*, written in Toledo in about 1310.

Divided into twelve parts, with three hundred and five chapters of unequal length, *Neḥmad ve-Na'im* begins with a description of the cosmological foundations of the universe which are identified with the Aristotelian and Ptolemaic system of the four elements and the eight spheres. There follow studies of the measurement of time, of the zodiac, of the movements of the sun and moon—all of which are important factors in fixing the Jewish calendar—and, in addition to these items, so indispensable to the Jewish cosmology and liturgy, there is a brief description of the movement of the five other planets.

And yet, within this rigid medieval framework, one sees a few signs of original perceptions revealing a far more modern outlook than that of Israeli. First of all, in the classic table of longitudes, the figures are corrected and updated, the author obviously being conversant with the modifications resulting from the choice of a new zero meridian towards the end of the fifteenth century.[13] There are many mathematical digressions and many geometrical figures drawn awkwardly or with a naïve fantasy in the manuscripts, and carefully reproduced in the printed version. A whole section of the work—the third—is devoted to a vast incursion into geography, and another, the eleventh, describes and demonstrates the use of the quadrant for astronomical and geographical observations and for land surveying. Finally, the twelfth and last chapter, dealing with comets and other strange or inexplicable celestial phenomena, ends with a categorical rejection of astrology, at least where Judaism is concerned.

A nonconformist work

These three chapters—the third, the eleventh, and the twelfth—are enough in themselves to give this book a nonconformist quality. Out of the cocoon of medieval astronomy, one senses the man of the Renaissance emerging. For it is perfectly clear, in this book, that for David Gans, cosmology and geography were inseparable. For him, it was no longer enough to be a Ptolemy of the heavens: one had also to apply the laws of the heavens to the earth, because the earth, for almost a century now, had completely changed its character. The impact of the great maritime discoveries was deeply felt by David Gans, and his description of the face of the earth is one of the most 'up-to-date' to come down to us from the period *circa* 1600. This third section of the book makes it a landmark in the history, not only of Jewish, but of universal geography. There had been a gigantic step forward. The New World had emerged from its baptismal waters, from the mists of mythology, from the realms of fantasy. The map drawn up by David Gans is remarkable in its

---

[13] In chapter 161 of his book Gans draws attention to this problem twice. On the transference of the zero meridian seventeen degrees to the west of the Ptolemaic longitudes and its implications from the Jewish point of view, see B. Cohn's interesting study: *Der Almanach Perpetuum des Abraham Zacuto* (Strasburg, 1918), n. 12.

accuracy, its precision, its truth. The new continents no longer appear to be the inchoate mass which is their image right into the seventeenth century. Here, there was a decisive victory of reason over mythology, and it is to this victory of rational over mystical geography in David Gans that we intend to devote the first part of our study of *Neḥmad ve-Na'im*.

Moreover, the importance given by Gans to the quadrant and to observation and experiment in general is symptomatic of another aspect of the author's great leap forward. For the past thirty years, the quadrant, its improvement, its use for the observation of the heavens but also for measuring altitudes, the height of towers, land-surveying, and many other purposes, had preoccupied the minds of researchers. The gigantic quadrant constructed by Tycho Brahe about 1570 on the hills around Göggingen near Augsburg was one of the first in the impressive series of instruments which the Danish astronomer set up in the course of his brilliant career which was then just beginning. This quadrant aroused the admiration of the great Pierre de la Ramée, who saw it at Göggingen a few months before returning to Paris where he fell victim to the St Bartholomew massacre. An anonymous German almanack published at Frankfurt-on-Main in 1571[14] describes this quadrant and its uses at length. It is not impossible that Tycho Brahe himself was the inspirer of this almanack, as he stayed in Frankfurt in 1568.

Be that as it may, the eleventh chapter of David Gans's *Neḥmad ve-Na'im* reproduces literally whole pages of that almanack, with its picturesque illustrations, but, since David Gans is Jewish and is writing in Hebrew, he is bold enough, in order to describe this simple and useful instrument, to substitute for the Latin 'quadrant' the Hebrew term *anak*. This term appears in the Bible (Amos 7: 7–8), and is usually translated as 'plumb-line'. We can already recognize Tycho Brahe's hand in the creation of that first instrument whose later forms would be perfected by him.

---

[14] This was one of the many different editions of *Astronomia Teutsch* contemporary with the rise of Protestantism in Germany. The almanack which David Gans must have seen and which we assume was produced on the initiative of Tycho Brahe was mentioned by E. Zinner in *Geschichte und Bibliographie der astronomischen Literatur in Deutschland zur Zeit der Renaissance* (Stuttgart, 1964²), where it is listed as item no. 2806. It was published by the successors of Christian Egelnoff who in 1530 had moved his press from Strasbourg to Frankfurt.

A modern work

But, over and above the value of the description of the quadrant as such and what one might describe as its linguistic conversion to Judaism, the importance which David Gans confers on it confirms the modern character of his book of astronomy. As we shall soon see, anyone, around the year 1600, who no longer confined himself to pure mathematics but took an interest in instruments, belonged to that small group of 'revolutionaries' in astronomy who had turned their backs on Ptolemy (even when not aware of it) and looked towards the future.

Finally, Gans's distinction between astronomy and astrology, and his recognition of the first as an exact science and the second as an illusion, is still more striking in that turn of the century when the foremost astronomical geniuses, Tycho Brahe and Kepler, cast horoscopes in which they believed as firmly as in their mathematical or physical discoveries.[15] Here, Gans took up a specifically Jewish point of view or, rather (since a confusion between astronomy and astrology was, and remained, common in Judaism), he made a specifically Jewish option.

I cannot insist too strongly on this point. David Gans's *Neḥmad ve-Na'im* is a work of astronomy. Astrology has absolutely no place in it. And when it *is* referred to in a series of chapters at the end of the book, it is only in order to rule it out. How many times, when speaking with my colleagues about my research on a book of astronomy by a pupil of the Maharal of Prague, have I not met with the quasi-automatic reaction: 'But you mean a book of astrology'? The myth of the 'Maharal the astrologer' being as persistent as it is, how could it be otherwise with one of his pupils?[16]

Neither the Maharal nor his disciple David Gans were astrologers or believed in the scientific value of astrology. That, of course, did not prevent them from including in their writings

[15] On the controversial place of astrology in astronomical literature in Germany in the Renaissance, cf Zinner, pp. 23 ff. Tycho Brahe was quite cautious where astrology was concerned, Kepler somewhat less so. Kepler was obliged to practise astrology in order to earn his keep. In his defence of astronomy, *Tertius interveniens*, he voiced some reservations about astrology tinged with humour. In that same essay, he also expressed reservations about the crude anti-Semitism of the period.

[16] Cf. article on astronomy, *Encyclopaedia Judaica* (1972): 'In the 16th century Judah Loew ben Bezalel had a high reputation as an astronomer. However, apart from his few astrological discussions, nothing can be found in his few writings to support this.' Fortunately, this was corrected in the article in the *Encyclopaedia* on the Maharal (Judah Loew) himself.

(particularly David Gans, in one of the last entries of *Zemaḥ David*, previous to his discovery of Tycho Brahe's astronomy) comments on the providential character of certain celestial phenomena such as comets, storms, etc., but this purely religious faith in an all-embracing Providence obviously had nothing in common with the sixteenth-century belief in the scientific value of horoscopes and astrology as such.

Although, as a concession to the fashions of the day, David Gans included in *Neḥmad ve-Na'im* a table demonstrating the influence of the signs of the zodiac on different regions of the earth (chapter 303), this chapter is only a diversion. It is preceded and followed by a series of chapters (296 to 302) in which the question of astrology and horoscopes (called 'nativitäten' by David Gans) is examined in full.

Gans against astrology

In chapter 297, David Gans raises himself to the level of the philosophers. Although forced to admit that there often appears to be some interrelationship between eclipses and certain physical or historical catastrophes, he refuses to consider eclipses as accidental phenomena, brought on by some caprice of God. Everyone knows and has to acknowledge that the occurence of eclipses depends on mathematical laws of unchanging regularity and that their appearance is predictable from the Creation until the end of time. This being the case, in considering the relationship between eclipses and catastrophes, does one have to accept a rigid determinism which would imprison the course of history in a mathematical sequence of disasters? That would mean denying the great fundamental principle of free will, which Gans adheres to as much as Maimonides. Gans therefore suggests an explanation which has elements both of the pessimism of Abravanel and of biblical optimism. Humanity having an unalterable tendency towards evil (as claimed by Abravanel), God placed within nature the mathe-matically predictable occurrence of eclipses. It serves as a warning, and the eclipses announce catastrophes only in the manner of the biblical prophecies of disaster which are made not in order that the disasters should take place, but in order that men should alter their conduct in such a way that the disasters will be averted. Eclipses are thus not accidents strewn upon the path of mankind but protective railings set along this route from the moment of the Creation until the End of Days.

In chapter 298, Gans carries his polemic against astrology a stage further. This chapter is entitled 'On the real or imaginary value of horoscopes', and it could have as its motto Tycho Brahe's slogan *'Contra Astrologos pro Astrologia'* (for astrology against the astrologers), but with the difference that Gans understated the 'pro' and put all his stress on the 'contra'.

'Against the astrologers. . .' One finds in this chapter written by a sixteenth-century rabbi the passionate tone of the biblical prophets whom Gans does not fail to quote, citing chapter and verse. Astrologers, he claims, are charlatans, impostors, smooth talkers who sell their wares to gullible fools in the fairground.

Gans, of course, was not unaware that among contemporary astrologers there were some genuine scholars, astronomers whose horoscopes had often been surprising in their accuracy. But the more serious the astrologers were, the more they queried their own predictions. All were agreed that an infinite number of factors could counteract the horoscope or render it ineffective.

'Our sages', wrote Gans,

were right to give first place among these factors to men's moral attitudes, their virtues and shortcomings. Basing myself on the opinion of Abraham Ibn Ezra, Joseph Albo, and the Masters of the Talmud, I conclude as follows: the phenomena of the lower world are all indeed dependent on the phenomena of the upper world, to such a degree that there is no blade of grass below which does not have its star above which says to it: the time has come to grow! But the phenomena of the upper world—the stars, the planets, the forces that move them—are all, without exception, dependent on the divine Will. To Him alone who said: 'Let the world be!', and the world was, to Him alone belongs the power of increasing and sustaining the influence of the constellations and also the power of destroying them completely.

Gans, however, did not limit himself to these ethical observations. Like his Teacher the Maharal whose remarkable criteriology mentioned in our *Puits de L'Exil* (p. 109) clearly distinguishes between the exact science of astronomy which has a place in Judaism and the pseudo-science of astrology, a plaything for childish minds which is inconsistent with authentic Jewish doctrine, David Gans expounds a systematic criteriology opposing astrology (*ḥizayon*) to astronomy (*tekunah*). 'For divination [*ḥizayon*],' he says, 'the prediction of the future, cannot be counted among the seven basic sciences to which astronomy [*tekunah*], on the contrary, belongs. Divination does not have philosophical foundations; it is not concerned with argument by proof. Its aim is experience, and for that reason it is not considered a science.'

Gans reminds us that in the preface to his book *Zurat ha-Arez*, the medieval writer Abraham bar Ḥiyya had already stated: 'We do not count astrology among the natural sciences. I would call it an experimental craft (*melekhet nisayon*], for it is only a by-product of the science of astronomy [*ḥokhmat ha-Tekunah*].'

There is something contemptuous in Abraham bar Ḥiyya's terminology which is perfectly in keeping with David Gans's attitude, and which implies: the astronomers are disinterested scholars, while the astrologers are careerists whose aim, like the false prophets of old, is not to discover the truth but only to make money.

And finally, after launching a sarcastic attack on the prophets of millenary doom (How many times have not the dates of the millennia had the absurd privilege of being chosen by the astrologers to coincide with the direct catastrophes? And yet never has mankind enjoyed a more perfect happiness, and a greater abundance of wealth and goods!), Gans ends his chapter with a quotation from Maimonides' famous letter to the Yemenites in which the medieval philosopher, a determined advocate of free will and a relentless opponent of all forms of fatalism, nobly declared that no astrological prediction or horoscope, no deterministic influence can stand in the way of the divine Will or of human freedom of choice.

And, in case the reader is still not convinced, as a parting shot David Gans claims that the influence of the stars is to be discounted, at least where the Jewish people is concerned. Let the other peoples go in for that kind of determinism! Who knows if, in the end, the difference between Israel and the Gentiles is not precisely that the Gentiles are subject to a cosmic fatalism, whereas the Jewish people acts freely throughout history? David Gans puts this question in the last chapter but one of *Nehmad ve-Na'im* (304) entitled: 'Is the Jewish people subject to the influence of the stars?' He recalls the famous Talmudic controversy in which the Jewish sages were divided on this point (Tractate *Shabbat*, 156 a,b), and he insists on the fact that the overwhelming majority of the sages, including Mar Samuel, the leading Talmudic astronomer, gave a negative answer to the question: (i.e., '*Ein mazal le-Yisrael*', Israel is not subject to the influence of the stars). Now, this, undoubtedly, was also the belief of David Gans. If he sought to support his views by the authority of Isaac Abravanel, we think it is because this, better than his reference to Maimonides, demonstrates the modern character of his book of astronomy, since Abravanel lived at the beginning of the sixteenth century of which *Neḥmad ve-Na'im* was the organic product.

An existential work

But, above all, *Neḥmad ve-Na'im* bears living witness to an experience which, quite apart from the factors we have just mentioned, gives David Gans's astronomical work a most unusual character: that of a genuine autobiography, or rather, of a spiritual diary whose progress may be followed from one end of the book to the other.

The fact that he belonged to a group of 'astronomical revolutionaries' was not a vague unconscious understanding with David Gans, nor was it a *Bildungserlebnis*, to use Gundolf's terminology: an experience inherent in the spiritual climate of the period. *Neḥmad ve-Na'im*, as we shall try and show in this study, was essentially an *Urerlebnis*: the conscious, living, breathing encounter of the knowledge of David Gans with the knowledge and above all the experience of Tycho Brahe and Johannes Kepler, whose intellectual and life-experience he shared. It was a continuous dialogue between a Jewish way of thinking and the leading figures in contemporary astronomy whom he frequented, stimulated with his questions, and supported with his work.

From the manuscripts, we become acquainted with two important aspects of this dialogue. One, running like a thread through the whole book, is David Gans's account of the story of his personal contacts with his great non-Jewish contemporaries.

Later we shall examine this first aspect—the most interesting and alive—of *Neḥmad ve-Na'im* in some detail. One finds in it the doubts, perplexities, searchings, as well as, sometimes, the convictions of the Jewish scholar which he submits for elucidation, solution, confirmation, or criticism to the astronomers with whom he worked in the castle of Benatek near Prague. Tycho Brahe, Johannes Kepler, and Johannes Muller are referred to specifically a dozen times, and also, on one occasion, in one particularly memorable chapter (161), in a collective manner as 'the whole group of scholars making up the team gathered together by the Emperor Rudolph in Prague'. We thus enter into an experimental arena where one school of thought brushes against another and where there are flashes of illumination, but also often a recognition of the existence of problems rather than their solution.

The other aspect of this encounter emerges in what, like Alter, we shall call the 'epilogue' of *Nehmad ve-Na'im*. This 'epilogue' is a theoretical exposition in which David Gans rediscovers his original vocation of historian. We find there a brief history of astronomy divided, like *Zemah David*, into two parts: the history of Jewish astronomy and the history of non-Jewish astronomy, both of which are followed by a demonstration of the *Jewish* origins of general astronomy and by a defence of astronomy as a science deserving to be treated with respect by Jews observant of the Torah.

If this 'apology' is addressed solely to the Jewish community, the rest of the epilogue concerns humanity as a whole, and it is studded with continual references to the team of astronomers in Prague, thus transforming the historical exposition into a living description of David Gans's researches on the spot. This ties up with the thread which, as we said, runs through the astronomical treatise itself, giving it its exceptional documentary interest. Later, we shall provide a detailed account of this also.

In the two complete manuscripts of *Nehmad ve-Na'im*, these pages appear at the end, forming an epilogue, but the editor of the published version of 1743 decided to transform the epilogue into a preface, at the same time taking out the final page of this pseudo-preface in order to form—in accordance with David Gans's intentions as we see from the manuscripts—the *hatimat ha-hatimah*, 'the conclusion of the conclusion', the super-epilogue, the high point of David Gans's researches: what I would call his 'astronomical testament'. No doubt the editor, a contemporary of Newton, felt that in these very last lines of his manuscript David Gans revealed himself as an important link in the chain which, passing from Ptolemy to Copernicus and from Copernicus to Newton, had known so many strange vicissitudes.

David Gans's 'astronomical testament' reaches its culmination in the moving description, full of feeling, of Tycho Brahe's observatory at Benatek which we quoted earlier, and in a brief but heartfelt and admiring exposition of Tycho Brahe's astronomical system.

This coronation of Tycho Brahe which at the same time is a crowning of *Neḥmad ve-Na'im* is undoubtedly in contradiction with the main thrust of the book, faithful to the Ptolemaic system. But is not this contradiction one sign among others that David Gans belonged body and soul to his period, the second half of the sixteenth century—a period so steeped in contradictions that two of its most illustrious representatives, of whom David Gans was the disciple, made contradiction into the corner-stone of their doctrine and philosophy? I am referring to Tycho Brahe himself and to the Maharal of Prague. And the conclusion of our own research links up with the conclusion of *Neḥmad ve-Na'im*: in David Gans's thinking, Tycho Brahe's astronomical system is ultimately associated with the Maharal's astronomical ideas. These two systems which dare to raise the challenge of the contradiction between Ptolemy and Copernicus form the substructure of the treatise, or—dare I say?—of the astronomical system of David Gans.

POINTERS TOWARDS A CRITICAL EDITION

A book published one hundred and thirty years after its author's death raises a host of problems which are easy enough to state, but to which it is more difficult to find an answer. Moreover, if this book has only one edition which is now two hundred and forty years old, it becomes almost impossible to re-edit it if one does not apply the strictest rules of textual criticism to the comparison of the published text and the manuscripts from which it is taken.

Neḥmad ve-Na'im was published by Israel bar Abraham at Jessnitz in 1743 under the auspices of Rabbi Joel ben Yekutiel Sachs, Rabbi of Austerlitz. The book is a quarto consisting of eighty-two pages in Hebrew (really 164 pages since, in accordance with Hebrew usage, the numbering includes both the recto and the verso), and twenty pages in Latin. The printing is careful, and the title-page is simply decorated in a taste reflecting the transition from the classical to the Baroque in the mid-eighteenth century.

The first two pages contain the editor's preface. In the traditional style of *melizah*, but with much simplicity, the Rabbi of Austerlitz explained how in Breslau the manuscript of *Sefer Neḥmad ve-Na'im* came into his hands by chance. The book seemed to him so clear and so consistent with Jewish astronomical tradition that he immediately thought of taking it out of its more than hundred-years-long hibernation.

With the same simplicity, he explained the difficulties which this task presented: the manuscript was full of over-writings, repetitions, gaps, contradictions. One had to proceed carefully. In order to remain faithful to the author, the editor touched the text of the manuscript as little as possible, even if that meant presenting the public with a work which, on many points, left much to be desired. The publisher, he said, helped the editor to reproduce as faithfully as possible the many figures which elucidate the text when the text is unclear.

Only one major change was made in the book. The Rabbi of Austerlitz felt justified in placing at the beginning of the book as a kind of introduction a lengthy exposition which, in the manuscript, is not only placed at the end, but begins literally with the words 'As a conclusion. . .'.

Here the rabbi's apologetic intention prevailed over his desire for fidelity. What impressed the Rabbi of Austerlitz in these concluding pages was (1) the proofs provided by Gans of the Jewish origins of universal astronomy, and (2) Gans's bold controversy with those among the Jews who denigrated astronomy and accused those who studied it of wasting their time.

It was likewise with an apologetic intention that the publisher or the editor, or both of them together, asked Professor Christian Hebenstreit (1686–1756) to provide the book with an introduction in Latin. This Protestant professor in charge of Hebrew studies at the Leipzig Academy acquitted himself of this task with tact and intelligence. He was not content, using Wolf's *Bibliotheca Hebraica* as his source, simply to give David Gans's biography and to describe the circumstances in which he lived. He also gave a summary of the book's contents, stressing the importance of the 'Preface' which interested him less for its apologetics than because of David Gans's historical survey of astronomy from its origins until 1613, the year the manuscript was finished. Hebenstreit also furnished us with some important etymological and historical clues through his transposition of Hebrew proper names into Latin. Although often hypothetical, these transpositions allow us to follow certain leads which the Hebrew text in its unpolished state without a Latin introduction would not have permitted us to find.[17]

---

[17] The deciphering process begun by Hebenstreit was successfully continued by Bruell and Alter.

Finally, Hebenstreit drew attention to a number of important points which the Rabbi of Austerlitz had completely overlooked, such as the reference in David Gans's 'Preface' to Copernicus and the revolutionary importance of his book, and the general conclusion of the work which is an exposition by David Gans of the theories of Tycho Brahe.

We should point out in passing that the rabbi and the Christian professor both lived after Isaac Newton, but they did not pass any value-judgement on David Gans's obviously antiquated astronomical conceptions. No doubt they themselves were influenced by the general atmosphere of the first half of the eighteenth century when only a few specialists had definitely broken with Ptolemy. What particularly interested them about the book was thát David Gans, who had hitherto been known only as a historian, was now shown to have been also a remarkable astronomer.

They did not say anything about textual criticism. The textual problems raised by the manuscript found at Breslau by the Rabbi of Austerlitz, its authenticity, its related material, were mentioned neither by the rabbi nor by the professor. This, too, tells us something about their period. In the eighteenth century, textual criticism was still unborn. We have to await the nineteenth century for these problems to be considered, and even then only in the form of a few scattered and generally unrelated notes, without any attempt to make a total assessment of the situation.

The editor of the book of 1743: Rabbi Joel Sachs

Before attempting to make such an assessment ourselves with a view to a second edition of *Neḥmad ve-Na'im*, we should say a little more about the editor of the first edition, Rabbi Joel ben Yekutiel Sachs, who gave the date of his preface as Purim 1743. The year 1743 marked a turning-point in the rabbinical career of Joel Sachs. Born at Glogau at the beginning of the eighteenth century, he left his rabbinical position at Austerlitz a few weeks after Purim 1743 to take up the important post of *dayyan* (judicial deputy) to a new Rabbi of Berlin, and it was in Berlin that he died in 1764 after having written a number of works in which the *Kabbalah* played an important role.

This new Rabbi of Berlin who had called the Rabbi of Austerlitz to his assistance was by no means an unknown figure. He was David Fränkel, Rabbi of Dessau, who had brought with him to Berlin his favourite pupil, a boy prodigy of 14 years of age called Moshe ben

Mendel who was soon to become famous in Berlin under the Germanized name of Moses Mendelssohn.[18]

Thus, the very year when *Neḥmad ve-Na'im* was published was the one when Moses Mendelssohn began his path to celebrity. This is not the only 'coincidence' to which we shall have occasion to draw attention in this book. The coincidence, moreover, becomes even more fascinating when one realizes that there was another connection besides the mere date 1743 between Rabbi Joel Sachs, editor of *Neḥmad ve-Na'im*, and Moses Mendelssohn.

Joel Sachs was the son-in-law of Jehiel Michel, better known as Michel Ḥasid (1680–1728), who was Rabbi of Berlin (in 1718 he received King Frederick William I and his Queen in the Berlin Synagogue—a gesture of royal sympathy towards the Prussian Jews which recalls that of Louis XIV towards the Jews of Metz[19] and that of the Emperor Maximilian II towards the Jews of Prague).[20]

One of the sons of Rabbi Michel Ḥasid (and hence a brother-in-law of Rabbi Joel Sachs) converted to Christianity in 1735 and entered into history under the name of Aloys von Sonnenfels, after having adopted as his first Christian names the names Lipman Perlin and Aloys Wiener. These names reveal the itinerary which took him from Berlin to Vienna, where he was ennobled. His wife remained Jewish, and he himself, a converted Jew, was an ardent defender of the Jews and Judaism. He particularly insisted in participating in a commission set up by Pope Clement XIII which decided that the ritual murder legend was completely unfounded, and he published a vigorous pamphlet disproving that legend, which was again being disseminated by the followers of the Jewish false Messiah Jacob Frank, who had been converted to Christianity in the same way as his predecessor Shabbetai Zevi had been converted to Islam.

Aloys's son, Joseph von Sonnenfels (1732–1817), converted to Catholicism by his father at the age of three, was one of the greatest jurists of the Austria of Maria Theresa and Joseph II. A statue at the Vienna City Hall perpetuates his memory. Taken down by the Nazis during the Anschluss of 1938, it was replaced in 1945. It was

---

[18] David Fränkel had just re-edited Maimonides' *Guide to the Perplexed* which he published in Jessnitz in 1742, just one year before Joel Sachs's publication of *Neḥmad ve-Na'im* in the same printing-press.

[19] See J. Meisl (ed.) *Pinkas Kehillat Berlin* (1962), index, and see. p.254.

[20] See the extracts from *Zemaḥ David* above (under the year 1571).

not only his racial origins which the Nazis could not forgive him. Joseph von Sonnenfels worked as much as his father and even more for the emancipation of the Jews. He laid down the general principles of the Edict of Tolerance proclaimed by Joseph II in 1781.

Joseph von Sonnenfels like his father, however, regarded the emancipation of the Jews as complete only when they had submitted to the same process as they themselves had done: conversion to Christianity. And it is just here that Moses Mendelssohn—the 'refractory' Jew who fought for Jewish emancipation together with absolute fidelity to the Jewish religion—reappears.

People have long wondered who the anonymous interlocutor was to whom Mendelssohn addressed his *magnum opus*, *Jerusalem*, published in 1783, three years before his death. Only in the last ten years have we known the answer, thanks to the researches of Professor Jacob Katz.[21] It was none other than Joseph von Sonnenfels who in 1782 had published a booklet *Das Forschen nach Licht und Recht* in which he called upon Mendelssohn to convert, just as Lavater had done a few years previously. Mendelssohn had replied to Lavater with a long and exhausting polemical correspondence. To Sonnenfels he replied with the little masterpiece of political theology which is his *Jerusalem*.

Thus, Mendelssohn's *Jerusalem* constitutes a rejection of the arguments of the nephew of Rabbi Joel Sachs, with whom he had come to Berlin together with his teacher David Fränkel forty years earlier in 1743, the year of the publication of David Gans's *Nehmad ve-Na'im* under the auspices of this same Rabbi Joel Sachs.

I feel that these interrelationships have to be pointed out to enable us to sense the intellectual atmosphere in which *Nehmad ve-Na'im* was published one hundred and thirty years after the death of its author and forty years before the appearance of Mendelssohn's *Jerusalem*; in the very year when Mendelssohn, a provincial Jewish adolescent, began his transformation into a German Plato of the eighteenth century while remaining to the end, like David Gans, despite all the shocks and assaults of the gigantic philosophical and scientific revolutions they witnessed, faithful to their Jewish convictions. We shall return to this in our appendix.[22]

[21] Jacob Katz, 'Le-mi ana Mendelssohn bi-yerushalayim shelo?', *Zion*, xxix (1964), pp. 112–32. [22] See Appendix: Copernicus in Hebrew Literature.

Assessment of the situation

Chronologically, the references to the manuscripts (or pseudo-manuscripts) of David Gans's *Neḥmad ve-Na'im* in the nineteenth century all appear between the years 1848 and 1878. They are listed in the following pages and in our bibliography. The following facts come to light:

1. There is an incomplete manuscript of *Neḥmad ve-Na'im* in the Municipal Library in Hamburg. It bears the old title *Magen David* and is dated 1596. We shall call this the Hamburg manuscript.[23]

2. This manuscript was published, again under the title of *Magen David*, in Prague in 1612, one year before David Gans's death. Only one copy of this book has so far been traced, in the Bodleian Library in Oxford.[24]

3. There is another manuscript, this time complete, bearing the title *Neḥmad ve-Na'im* in the Museum in Brünn (today Brno) in Czechoslovakia. We shall call it the Brno manuscript.

From 1878 to 1958 historians, bibliographers, and epigraphists let matters rest there, convinced that the manuscript which the Rabbi of Austerlitz used for the publication of the book in 1743 was the Brno manuscript.[25]

In 1958, however, there appeared the first serious critical study placing the problem in its true perspective. The author of this study, Dr George Alter, carried out this task with remarkable conscientiousness. In a paper addressed to the Czech Academy of Sciences on 18 June 1957 he paid tribute to both David Gans and Joseph Delmedigo, and his paper was published in English in the review *Rozpravy Ceskoslavenske Akademie Ved* (68, 11, 1958) under the title 'Two Renaissance Astronomers.[26]

Alter devoted thirty pages to David Gans, and thirty to Delmedigo. It is obvious from the modest scope of his study that Dr Alter left the task of elaboration to others, but it is not only the brevity of his work which made Alter a precursor. His field of

[23] Ḥayyim Michael, *Or ha-Ḥayyim*, ed. Berliner (Frankfurt-on-Main, 1881), no. 782. Moritz Steinschneider, *Catalog der hebraischen Handscriften in der Stadtbibliothek Hamburg* (Hamburg, 1878), no. 299, photostatic reproduction (Hamburg, 1969).

[24] Moritz Steinschneider, *Catalogus Librorum Hebraeorum in Bibliotheca Bodleiana* (Berlin, 1852, 1860), no. 861. Ch. B. Friedberg, *Bet eked Sefarim* (Jerusalem, 2, 1954), ii, no. 602.

[25] M. Stoeszel: 'Aus dem Museum in Brunn', *Ben Chananja* (Szegedin, 8, 1865), pp. 601 and 910. N. Bruell, *David Gans als Astronom*, p. 718.

[26] Alter was not acquainted with Ch. S. Freedman's stencilled dissertation.

competence being chiefly astronomy, Gans's concern with the specifically Jewish problems raised by the study of astronomy are hardly touched on at all. Our own work thus complements that of Dr Alter, whose learning was equalled only by his courtesy, and whom I subsequently had the pleasure of meeting in Israel, where he later lived.[27]

George Alter based his study on a comparison between the printed book and the Brno manuscript. He insisted on the fact that the differences between the Brno manuscript and the printed book were so great that the Rabbi of Austerlitz must have used another manuscript for his 1743 edition. Alter adds: 'But we do not know its whereabouts' (p. 34).

Thanks to certain 'strokes of luck' which lead to unexpected discoveries, we have been fortunate enough to find the missing manuscript on microfilm (no. 10408) in the National and University Library in Jerusalem. The original is in the Library of the Jewish Community in Geneva. We shall call it the Geneva manuscript.[28] In the National and University Library in Jerusalem there has also been found a third, incomplete manuscript, no. HEB 8° 2747. We are the first to have identified it, and shall refer to it as the Jerusalem manuscript.[29]

We now have the essential material for a critical edition of David Gans's *Neḥmad ve-Na'im*. We are now going to place it in its proper perspective by a brief examination of the manuscripts and texts we have just mentioned, limiting our efforts to the correction of certain errors of interpretation which have arisen from the manuscripts and attempting to gain a better understanding of David Gans's personality and thinking. We postpone to a later stage the purely technical considerations of a critical edition about which we need say only that it has now become a practical possibility.[30]

[27] Dr George Alter was a well-known astronomer and musicologist in Czechoslovakia. He settled in Israel in 1962 and died at Beit Yitzhak in 1972. He left the Hebrew University his 'Arnold Schoenberg Collection', and his 'David Gans–Delmedigo collection' he was kind enough to leave to me. May he rest in peace.

[28] It was one of the series of manuscripts in the Library of the Jewish Community in Geneva microfilmed by Dr Allony for the National and University Library in Jerusalem. *Neḥmad ve-Na'im* was no. 2.

[29] We wish to express our gratitude to Mrs Margot Cohn and Dr Moshe Catane of the National and University Library in Jerusalem, to whom we owe our discovery of this manuscript.

[30] Together with Mordechai Breuer's edition of *Zemaḥ David* (1981), the projected edition of *Neḥmad ve-Na'im* would greatly increase the scope of our knowledge of the work of David Gans.

Nothing illustrates the lack of seriousness with which the most conscentious scholars have approached the work of David Gans better than the story of what they call the 'Hamburg manuscript'. Only one man saw it: Ḥayyim Michael, who described it briefly in his catalogue *Or ha-Ḥayyim*.[31]

Relying on his testimony, Steinschneider, Freedman, Alter, and Huminer considered the Hamburg manuscript to be the manuscript of the *Magen David* which Gans published in 1612, and which these scholars unanimously believed to be part of the first draft of *Neḥmad ve-Na'im*. If this last point, as we shall shortly see, requires some modification, the first one—linking the Hamburg document dated 1596 by the scribe to the *Magen David* of 1612 as the manuscript of the printed text—is completely erroneous.[32]

At first, I was inclined to trust the interpretation of our illustrious and most competent predecessors, especially as I was uncertain whether, after the bombardment of Hamburg in the Second World War, the manuscript was still in that city. However, I learnt from Hellmut Braun's preface to a 1969 photostatic reproduction of Steinschneider's catalogue that the Hebraica mentioned by Steinschneider 'had survived all the hazards of the Second World War and were again available for research'. In that case, why not return to the source? Through a brief exchange of letters, I had the pleasant surprise of learning that David Gans's manuscript was still

---

[31] The catalogue *Or ha-Ḥayyim* of Ḥayyim (Heimann Joseph) Michael (1792–1846) was published only in 1891. Zunz, however, mentioned it in 1848 in *Ozrot Chajim: Katalog der Michaelschen Bibliothek* (Hamburg).

[32] Previous to Michael's reference, Gans's manuscript was mentioned by J. Chr. Wolf in *Bibliotheca Hebraea* (Hamburg, 1733), iv, 803, but in a very imprecise manner (i.e., *Liber quidam ejus Astronomicus Ms in codice chartacco foliorum 48*). Michael's opinion, on the other hand, is quite definite ('the book of astronomy *Magen David* is here in the Library of Hamburg in a 48 folio manuscript ... and this book *Magen David* was published in Prague in 1612 ...').

Steinschneider, basing himself on Zunz and Michael, voices a similar opinion in his *Cat. Bodl.* (Berlin, 1852–60). In his Hamburg catalogue (1878), however, Steinschneider is content simply to mention the Hamburg manuscript of *Neḥmad ve-Na'im* without indicating any connection between the printed *Magen David* and the 1596 manuscript of the same name. Perhaps a reading of the manuscript had made him doubt whether the two were related. However that may be, later scholars followed Michael's opinion which Steinschneider himself had seemed to support in his Oxford catalogue.

in the Hamburg City Library which meanwhile had become the State and University Library, and I soon had a microfilm of the precious manuscript in my possession.

Michael's error is very easily explained: the scribe stated that these hundred and nineteen chapters were a large section of an astronomical work for which its author David Avuz had already chosen a title which he would elucidate in the part which had not been copied out. That title was *Magen David*.

An astronomical work of ten printed pages by this same Avuz-Gans was in fact published under the name of *Magen David* in Prague in 1612. But, at the time when the scribe copied out (in three days, he said) the large section of the work which the author would one day call *Magen David*, it was still Kislev 5357—that is, 1596.[33]

Now, between these two dates—1596 and 1612—a traumatic event took place in the life of David Gans: his meeting with Tycho Brahe who, we should remember, arrived in Prague only in 1599. The revolutionary effect of this meeting on David Gans's concept of the astronomical universe is strikingly illustrated by a comparison of the *Magen David* manuscript of 1596 and the *Magen David* published in 1612. One has only to scan the two texts, and the organic connection which the experts have claimed exists between them will completely disappear. The only similarity which remains is the fact that both texts have the same title and both deal with astronomy.

But the astronomy of the *Magen David* published in 1612 betrays the revolution which had taken place in the author's outlook since his meeting with Tycho Brahe, whereas the manuscript of 1596 in relation to what is called the 'sixteenth-century astronomical revolution' is an archaic and prehistoric document.

A comparison of the two texts, far from demonstrating the continuity of the work of David Gans, shows the break that was caused in it by Tycho Brahe's arrival in Prague. In the methodology of heuristics, this comparison can teach us a lesson of general significance: it can teach us to beware of superficial identifications by forcing us to realize that a living experience, insignificant though it may sometimes appear, can completely transform a man and his work. The two texts show that David Gans was changed by Tycho

---

[33] Kislev 5357 is 1596, not 1597 or 1598 as Steinschneider erroneously stated in his *Cat. Bodl.* This error was awkwardly corrected in his *Hamburg Cat.*

Brahe in much the same way as Isaac Newton was changed by the celebrated apple. With the difference, of course, that Newton's apple is probably a legend while Tycho Brahe came into Gans's life through the front door of history.

If we wish to assess David Gans's importance as an astronomer, there is little point in our wasting our time in a detailed study of the Hamburg manuscript. It is one of those didactic works of which Gans wrote quite a number in the areas of mathematics and geography, a simple introduction to the subject in a monotonous style, with almost every chapter beginning with a pedantic admonition to the pupil-reader: 'Know that . . .'. Everything, of course, is based on the Ptolemaic system, and nowhere is there any evidence of problems or difficulties, nowhere is there any sense of that effort of adjustment to a new universe which lends such charm and interest to the printed *Magen David* and, later, *Neḥmad ve-Na'im*.

In the manuscript of 1596, David Gans was not yet an astronomer, but merely a teacher of astronomy. He had not yet entered the observatory at Benatek; he had not yet scanned the heavens himself. He had not yet held discussions with Tycho Brahe and Kepler. Everything is still dry and academic.

There is just one slight exception at the beginning, in the dry preface which outlines the problem that the epilogue promised in the *Magen David* of 1612, and which exists in the manuscripts of *Neḥmad ve-Na'im*, expounds with such vibrant intensity: the frequent contradictions between the Ptolemaic system and certain astronomical observations in the Talmud. Maimonides, Isaac Israeli, Azariah dei Rossi, and the Rema are all quoted, ending up with the latter's reassuring conciliatory conclusions.

In 1596, of course, things could hardly have been otherwise. The Maharal's astronomical reflections only appeared in *Be'er ha-Golah*, which was published in 1600. Gans was therefore not yet able to correct the Rema's conciliatory positions with the mysticism of the Maharal, and still less was he able to perceive a connecton of some kind between the Maharal's mystical insights and the revolutionary astronomy of Tycho and Kepler. He was still obviously unacquainted, moreover, with the name and work of Nicholas Copernicus. The geocentric (earth-centred) Ptolemaic figure in the Hamburg manuscript is like a negative replica of the heliocentric (sun-centred) diagram in the book of Copernicus (p. 9 verso).

The eulogistic reference to Copernicus in the printed *Magen David* and *Neḥmad ve-Na'im* is the clearest proof of David Gans's gigantic step forward between the manual of astronomy of 1596 and his great work of 1612.

MAGEN DAVID: BODLEIAN LIBRARY, OXFORD.
HEBRAICA OPP. 4 417

A hostage to fortune

Magen David was a hostage offered to fortune by its author one year before his death, but no one, alas, took any notice of it. These few pages of proof given to the publisher in 1612 awaited a response which would have encouraged David Gans to publish the whole of the work of which these pages were an extract. Gans, however, died before he was able to do so, carrying with him into the grave several unsolved problems concerning this preliminary booklet compared with the manuscripts and, obviously, even more with the printed book which appeared a hundred and thirty years later.

Yet, *Magen David* possessed all the qualities which could have made it a success. Even the very title-page offers attractions which it would be hard to resist. It promises a treatise of astronomy, but an astronomy replete with new marvels; a treatise of cosmography, but a cosmography in which the New World has the place of honour. It promises a straightforward explanation, finally, putting these sciences within the reach even of the layman. Three figures decorate the bottom of the page, as though to insist on the plastic, visual character of the book.

There follow three pages of eulogies by four Jewish Sages of Prague who belonged to the circle of the Maharal of which David Gans himself was a member: Yom Tov Lipmann Heller of Wallerstein (the author of the famous *Tosafot Yom Tov*); Solomon Ephraim Luntschitz the popular preacher; Isaac Cohen, the Maharal's favourite son-in-law; and the *dayyan* Mordecai Lipschitz.

Then there are four pages by the author addressed to his sons, but also intended for the public at large. It is in this preface that, for the first time in history, we find Copernicus mentioned (and praised) in a Hebrew work; we have used the passage in question as an introductory quotation for this book. After speaking of Ptolemy and the great Jewish astronomers Maimonides, Abraham bar

Ḥiyya, and Isaac Israeli, Gans also mentions the 'contemporary non-Jewish astronomers' (i.e. Tycho Brahe, Johannes Kepler, and Johannes Muller) who, he says, inspired him as much 'by their books as by what he heard from their own mouths'.

The preface, like that of *Ẓemaḥ David*, dwells on the reasons why Gans gave his book the title of *Magen David*. We shall return to this shortly. Finally, there are nine pages giving the table of contents of the work which was to appear a hundred and thirty years later under the title *Neḥmad ve-Na'im*.

This change of title is a puzzle which we shall deal with at the end of this chapter. But even more puzzling is the miserable reception which *Magen David* must have encountered. We know that the author died a year after the publication of this booklet, but ought not his death to have caused the lax subscribers to have encouraged the publisher, who asked no better than to publish the entire work, provided only that he was granted the wherewithal to do so? And yet (we have to say again) the promised work was published only a hundred and thirty years later, in a quite different social and cultural context from that of Prague in 1612. And even *Magen David* itself, which was probably treated merely as a publisher's prospectus and of which very few copies must have been printed, completely disappeared from circulation. The copy preserved in the Bodleian Library is unique: to this very day it is the only copy of David Gans's *Magen David* of which we know.

Yet however that may be, *Magen David* remains, for our purposes, an invaluable document. It furnishes the proof that, despite all we have said, David Gans, modest worker though he was, had his moment of glory. More than the sober tombstone erected in the Prague cemetery in 1613 with its goose and its 'Magen David', the four 'testimonials' of *Magen David*, appearing in the lifetime of the author in 1612, constitute a homage to David Gans. It is the only one to have come down to us, but it compensates, to some degree, for the deep silence with which he is otherwise surrounded.

We can easily pass over the testimonial of Rabbi Israel Mordecai ben Elijah Lipschitz, whose name has not entered into history. But the other three testimonials must be appreciated at their true value, for they are from people who have an important place in the history of sixteenth-century Jewish culture, and particularly in what we call the 'School of Prague'.

The 'imprimatur' of Rabbi Luntschitz

The seven lines written by Rabbi Solomon Ephraim Luntschitz are defective, but what remains only draws all the more attention to their importance. Rabbi Luntschitz wrote that on the evidence of the specimen he had seen and the testimony of reliable men who had read the whole manuscript, he had given David Gans authorization to publish this major work of astronomy which was a worthy complement to the previous works on the same subject.

This amounted to a real 'imprimatur' for a book considered modern and, one might even say, 'progressive'. It came from a person of authority close to the School of the Maharal, as Rabbi Luntschitz had succeeded the Maharal as Rabbi of Prague in 1604. The Maharal would have preferred his own son Bezalel to have been nominated to the position which he left on account of his advanced age, but in Luntschitz he found a worthy successor: the author of *Kli Yakar*, a commentary on the Torah steeped in the ideas of the Maharal, an inspired orator as the Maharal had been and, above all, like the Maharal, a fierce adversary of *pilpul* and the teaching methods used in the *yeshivot* and Jewish communities of Bohemia and Poland. Thus, in 1612 Luntschitz took up the work of reform which had been initiated by the Maharal and pursued it till his death in Prague in 1619. In his *Ammudei Shesh*, published in Prague in 1611, he placed himself explicitly under the authority of 'the Gaon Rabbi Loew', as he called him (p. 38c). This gives his 'imprimatur' of the *Magen David* all the more significance: a faithful disciple of the Maharal and his successor in the rabbinical hierarchy had bestowed it upon another disciple of the Maharal.

The enthusiastic approval of Tosafot Yom Tov

Yom Tov Lipmann ben Nathan Heller Halevi (1579–1654) is one of the great figures of Jewish history, which he has entered under the name of Tosafot Yom Tov, the title of his commentary on the Mishnah, which accompanies that of Rabbi Ovadia Bertinoro (Bartenura) in nearly all editions.

A strong personality, who played a positive and effective role among the persecuted Jewish communities in Bohemia during the Thirty Years War and then in Poland from 1648 (the year of Chmielnicki's massacres, a turning-point in the history of the Polish Jewry), Tosafot Yom Tov, through the popularity of his work, universally known, and through his activities as a rabbi, sometimes seemed to be the prototype of Talmudic Judaism. Heinrich Heine took him into general culture with a famous verse in his satirical poem 'The Disputation':

Gilt nichts mehr der Tausves-Jontof
was soll gelten? Zeter! Zeter![34]

In 1612, Yom Tov was still young. He was working on his commentary, whose first edition only appeared between 1614 and 1617 (the second edition appeared in 1643). But he was already known for some minor works, and, above all, from 1597 (when he was 18 years old) he had been a *dayyan* in Prague, where he was one of the closest disciples of the Maharal. He left Prague for Poland only in 1631.

From the Maharal he had inherited a desire for a methodical and rational approach to pedagogy, a passion for the rehabilitation of the Mishnah at the expense of *pilpul* (the *Tosafot Yom Tov* demonstrate the method of teaching the Mishnah which he practised with his pupils), and also a taste for the sciences, including astronomy.

In the Maharal's best style, Yom Tov Heller wrote a real 'praise of astronomy' in the form of a testimonial to Gans's *Magen David*. At the time when he wrote, it was summer, on the eve of *Shabbat Ekev* when they read the verse: 'Behold, the heaven and the heaven of heavens is the Lord's. . .' (Deuteronomy 10: 14). This, he said, was a call addressed to the human being, the only creature not naturally inclined to look downwards to the earth, but who raises his eyes 'to the lofty heights, seat of the glistening stars and planets'. For a long time, young Heller had been convinced that, as the sages of the Talmud had taught, the 'wisdom of Israel' spoken of in Deuteronomy 4: 6 was possession of the 'secrets' of astronomy, the basis of the Jewish calendar. These 'secrets' had been lost during the various exiles of the Jewish people, and it was now the Gentiles who boasted of their pre-eminence in a science which they claimed had originated in Athens, since it was founded entirely on the principles of Euclid the Athenian.

What a tragedy this was for Judaism, and how great a joy it

---

[34] 'If Tausves Jontof is not worth anything, what can be worth anything? Blasphemy, O blasphemy!' Here Heine has made a major error. His 'Disputation' was supposed to have taken place in Spain previous to the expulsion of the Jews in 1492 and so a good century and a half before the appearance of *Tosafot Yom Tov*. This was not Heine's only error in Jewish matters.

consequently was (even if it meant drawing on one's own funds) to be able to welcome and help in the publication and dissemination of this *Magen David* which Rabbi David Avuz (Gans) had now submitted to him!

From the language used by Yom Tov Heller, it is not difficult to imagine why he was so enthusiastic about *Magen David*—he, who was well acquainted with the other astronomical treatises: the medieval ones, but also the more recent ones such as that of Moses Isserles (the Rema) or that of Mordecai Jaffe, on which he himself had written a commentary.

The reason was that in *Magen David*, unlike in previous works, for the first time the main question involved is not that of the Jewish calendar. In this book, science is not the servant of *halakhah* (Jewish law). It is studied for its own sake, and is based, precisely, on the principles of the celebrated Euclid.[35] But this autonomous science, entirely in conformity with that of the Greeks, is shown to be Jewish, both in its origins and nature, its form and content.

I feel that chapter 25 of *Magen David* must have particularly captivated Yom Tov Heller: that chapter in which David Gans, on the strength of the testimony of Tycho Brahe and Johannes Kepler, snatched astronomy away from Athens and brought it back to its true home in Jerusalem. David Gans was talking, here, about 'new' secrets of astronomy, and perhaps there is a discreet reference to Copernicus (mentioned by name, as we said, in *Magen David*, while Tycho Brahe and Kepler are referred to by the anonymous title of 'contemporary astronomers') in the fact that Yom Tov Heller, describing David Gans's entry into his study, states that he carried *Kaduro al shikmo*, 'his globe on his shoulder': an expression which juxtaposes strangely with the biblical expression which follows it: *u-be-yado megillat sefer*, 'carrying a written scroll in his hand'. In astronomical terminology, *Kadur* is the terrestrial globe. In Yom Tov Heller's metaphor it is mobile and could naturally refer to David Gans's instrument, or it could refer to the new concept which Gans mentions in his preface of a terrestrial globe which is not motionless as in Ptolemy, but has continuous and perpetual motion as visualized by Copernicus (*'Kadur ha-arez yesovev sibub tediri'*).

---

[35] In his commentary on the tractate *Kilaim* III, Tosafot Yom Tov claimed that the mathematical problems raised by the Mishnah cannot be understood without reference to Euclid.

David Gans receives the blessing of the Maharal's son-in-law

Isaac Cohen was a sufficiently picturesque figure for his name to make an impression on the readers of *Magen David* even if he had not been the Maharal's son-in-law. He was the great-grandson of Akiba Cohen who died in Prague in 1496, and who was famous for the fact that, together with his sons and grandsons, he formed a group of twenty-five *cohanim* (priests), a sufficiently large number to be able to perform the priestly blessing (*birkat cohanim*) according to the specifications of the Bible: '*Ko tevarkhu et bnei Yisrael*': 'Thus will you bless the children of Israel' (Numbers 6: 23)—the Hebrew word *ko* [thus] having the numerical value twenty-five. Chroniclers give touching accounts of these blessings made from the *duchan* (platform) of the Prague synagogues by the members of a single family of which Isaac was a descendant.[36]

In his first marriage, Isaac had married Leah, the Maharal's eldest daughter, who died young, without leaving any children. Then he married Leah's sister, Vogele, by whom he had a daughter, Eva, who has entered into the Maharal legend. She is said to have been his favourite granddaughter, and, like many other Jewish women, she was learned in every aspect of the written and oral Law.[37] Eva followed her husband Samuel Bachrach to Worms but, widowed very early, she returned to Prague in 1615, where Isaiah Horowitz, the famous 'Shelah' (author of the *Shnei Luhot HaBrit*), asked to marry her. Was it because she refused him that in 1621 the 'Shelah' decided to leave Europe and make his *aliyah* to the Holy Land, where he lived surrounded by a halo of glory as the

[36] See Frederic Thieberger, *The Great Rabbi Loew of Prague* (London, 1955), pp. 16 ff.

[37] Eva was by no means unique. We know that Rashi's daughters (whose sons-in-law were the first Tosafists) took part in the Talmudic debates in their father's school at Troyes. The popular image of the ignorant and unlettered Jewish woman is completely false, at least in the Middle Ages and Renaissance. See the statement of one of the pupils of Abelard in the twelfth century (quoted in Jean Servier's *Historie de l'Utopie* (Paris, 1967, p. 101): 'The Christians who educate their sons do not do so for the sake of heaven but for the love of riches. . . . It is not so with the Jews. It is out of the love of God and His Law that they send their sons to learn the Torah in order to understand it. The poorest Jew, even if he has ten sons, will give them all a thorough religious education, not in order to acquire a profession as the Christians do, but so as the better to be able to understand the law of God; and not only their sons, but also their daughters.' If we restrict ourselves to Prague in David Gans's period, we can also mention the remarkable case of Rivka, daughter of Rabbi Meir Tiktin, who wrote a number of poems and a book on the education of children, *Meneket Rivka*, published in Prague in 1609 and, in a second edition, in Cracow in 1618 (O. Muneles, *Prague Ghetto*, pp. 98–9).

Kabbalist who had succeeded in synthesizing the various mystical movements which had illuminated the sixteenth century? Was it because Eva had tardy regrets that she too began to travel to the Holy Land? But Providence works in mysterious ways. When Eva left Europe, the 'Shelah' had already died in 1630 in Jerusalem, and Eva never reached the Holy Land. She died on the way, in Sofia, in 1650. Here was a mysterious interlacing of false encounters and unsatisfied longings in which one already catches a whiff of the universe of Shabbetai Zevi in the second half of the seventeenth century, of the great masters of Hasidism in the eighteenth century, and, finally, of Franz Kafka who breathed its aroma in Prague in the twentieth century.

So it was Eva's father Isaac Cohen, who missed being the 'Shelah's' father-in-law, who had a possible son-in-law who reached Jerusalem and a daughter who never did, who provided *Magen David* with his warm recommendation. Modest and warm-hearted, Cohen said that he was no longer sufficiently up-to-date in his knowledge of astronomy to be able to judge the work, but he at least knew the author and deferred to his superior knowledge.

Where, in that case, had Isaac Cohen learnt astronomy in his youth if not at the feet of his father-in-law the Maharal, whose disciple he had been?

He was both his disciple, his son-in-law, and his close companion, for it was probably he who served as his secretary, copying out from his dictation the Maharal's glosses on the Talmudic *Aggadah*,[38] and, in particular, he had had the exceptional privilege of being one of the three Jewish witnesses at the historic meeting between the Maharal and the Emperor Rudolph at the Hradschin Palace in 1592.

We have previously quoted, among the news-items and minia-tures, David Gans's reference to this meeting in his *Zemah David*. For a long time, this entry was the only source of information about the meeting that we had, and in its deliberate spareness it hardly permitted us to reconstruct the atmosphere.

Since then, however, a far more detailed account of the meeting has been discovered, written, precisely, by Isaac Cohen. It was a very common Jewish practice, if one did not keep a diary, to note

---

[38] These glosses, which were believed lost, were found and revised by Steinschneider at the Bodleian in Oxford and published simultaneously by Kasher–Blacherovitz in Jerusalem and Honig in London in 1960.

important events in the fly-leaves of a Bible or a Talmud. Isaac Cohen's account was written in the fly-leaves of a Venice Bible which was probably his copy for daily use. We learn from this source that the invitation to the meeting had been transmitted to the Maharal by Prince Bertier through Mordecai Meisel and that during the audience the Emperor first sat behind a large curtain listening to the conversation between Prince Bertier and the Maharal, and afterwards revealed himself in all his majesty and exchanged a few words with the Maharal directly. Concerning the subject of the interview, Isaac Cohen was as discreet as David Gans: 'The conversation having dealt with questions which affect the person of our Sovereign, discretion requires us to pass over it in silence. But if God grants us life, we shall reveal it when the moment is ripe.'[39]

At this meeting, the Maharal was accompanied by three of his co-religionists: the Gaon Rabbi Sinai, his brother,[40] the layman Isaac Weisl, a leader of the Jewish community in Prague,[41] and Isaac Cohen, the Maharal's son-in-law. Isaac Cohen tells us that the four men were all treated with great courtesy by Prince Bertier and the Emperor himself, who next day informed the Maharal that the meeting had been entirely to his satisfaction.

In his account, Isaac Cohen gave the date of the audience as Sunday, the tenth of Adar 5352 (23 February 1592). David Gans made it one week earlier,[42] but we can rely on Isaac Cohen, firstly because chronological errors are frequent in *Zemah David*, even for the most recent events, and then because Isaac Cohen was a witness, whereas David Gans knew about the audience only from hearsay. Thus, it is in no way surprising if we find that in two places, at the beginning and end of his testimonial, Isaac Cohen declares that he is the son-in-law of the famous Gaon Rabbi Loew, the Maharal.

The Maharal himself had died three years earlier. It was as though David Gans had finally received the explicit approval and blessing of his Teacher, of whom his son-in-law was the posthumous representative.

[39] See F. Thieberger, pp. 38–40.
[40] See Chap. 4 above.
[41] As Rabbi Sinai's wife was Anna Weisl, Isaac Weisl was probably the brother-in-law of Rabbi Sinai. The delegation would therefore have had a strong family character (O. Muneles, *Die Rabbiner der Altneuschul*, *JB* (1969), 105).
[42] See Chap. 4 above.

The rationalization of the symbol of the Star of David

We should say something about the title of this work of astronomy: *Magen David*. This title, which incorporates the first name of the author, has three different levels of significance. The first is a very general one. Is not the term *Magen David*, star (shield) of David, generally taken to mean a hexagram composed of two superimposed triangles, on the supposition that that was the emblem of King David? And is not the triangle the basic figure of geometry, which is essential to astronomy?

The second level has a more direct bearing on astronomy. In his book, the author humbly admits that he has done no more than to pass on what he has gleaned from other books and other writers. Astronomy is not only an abstract, geometrical science, but it is also (in the author's own day, at least) a science of observation. Certain celestial phenomena recur only after long periods: centuries or millennia. We must therefore rely on the observers and be content to be a modest organ of transmission. In this sense, *magen* no longer has the meaning of 'shield' but derives from the root *mgn*, meaning 'to pass on'.

On the third level, *magen* regains its warlike character. It is a 'shield' which permits the author, from the title onwards, to put forward his own *apologia* for astronomy in opposition to the obscurantists who consider it a worthless occupation.

The first two levels of significance are interesting in that they are related to the history of the symbol of Judaism which the *Magen David* (incorrectly translated as the 'star of David') has become.

This symbol, which in David Gans's time had not yet gained this *national* significance, would appear to have originated in Prague. In 1354 the Jewish community of Prague received from Charles IV the privilege of carrying a banner, and on this banner figured the star of David. At that time, it possessed only a local significance, and did not concern the Jewish people as a whole, who adopted it only from the end of the eighteenth century, and even then it was only Zionism, at the end of the nineteenth century, which made it into the definitive symbol of the Jewish people.[43]

One other detail connecting the star of David to Prague: the first Hebrew book published in Prague in 1512 (a prayerbook) carried

[43] See article on Magen David, *Encyclopaedia Judaica* (Jerusalem, 1972). As with the legend of the golem, Scholem was one of the first to demystify the legend of the Star of David.

this emblem as a frontispiece, but with a ritualistic, possibly magical purpose with which it had been associated since its origins. This emblem, which the Arabs called the 'seal of Solomon' from the Middle Ages onwards, the Jews called the 'shield of David'. From the twelfth to the eighteenth centuries it appeared in hundreds of Jewish and non-Jewish documents all dealing with practical *Kabbalah*, spells, and magic.[44] There were no exceptions except, precisely, David Gans's 'Shield of David'. In giving his book of astronomy the title *Magen David*, he was playing on the meaning of his first name David, but at the same time he was demystifying the nature of the symbol expressed by the hexagram. As far as we know, he was the first to have done so, and here we encounter something characteristic of his general attitude to the sciences. David Gans rationalized a symbol which until then had possessed purely mystical associations. The 'star of David' was not for him a magical, but a geometrical formula: the *Magen David* was not an incantatory symbol but the emblem of an exact science: astronomy.

This was undoubtedly the significance which, one year after the publication of *Magen David*, when David Gans was buried in the Prague cemetery near the tomb of his Teacher the Maharal, the carvers intended to give the star of David which adorns Gans's tombstone. Above the symbol of the goose (in German, *Gans*) expressing his surname, appears the star of David, recalling both his first name and the science for which he had recently made himself known with the publication of an extract of his *Magen David*: astronomy. Thus, in this modest tombstone are combined the two sciences in which David Gans excelled: history, since the fact that Rabbi David Gans was the author of *Zemaḥ David* is specifically mentioned in the inscription, and astronomy, symbolized by the star of David.

We should also point out that David Gans's tombstone in Prague was the first Jewish tombstone to carry the symbol of the star of David. The next to do so appeared more than a century later, in 1726 in Bordeaux and in Prague in 1736.[45] The symbol began to be used frequently only towards the end of the eighteenth century. It was above all in the twentieth century, however, when two World

---

[44] See Abraham Yaari, *Hebrew Printers' Marks* (Jerusalem, 1943).

[45] On the tomb of Rabbi David Oppenheimer (1664–1736) in Prague; see plate 9. The copy of David Gans's *Magen David* now in Oxford was in David Oppenheimer's library.

Wars had reaped their grim harvest of millions of human beings, that the military cemeteries made the star of David into a normal sight, indicating that here, side by side with the remains of a Christian comrade with his cross or of a Muslim comrade with his crescent, lay those of a Jewish soldier who had died for his country. Who, seeing these graves, could imagine that the first time the star of David appeared on a Jewish grave it was not a sign of membership of the Jewish people but of an early seventeenth-century rabbi's enthusiasm for astronomy and the Copernican revolution?

THE BRNO MANUSCRIPT: STATE ARCHIVES, BRNO, MS 515

The Brno manuscript has been well described and commented on by Alter.[46] This cannot be, as Stoeszel suggests, the original manuscript of *Nehmad ve-Na'im*, contemporary with Gans, written in his own hand or under his supervision. Although the manuscript is not dated, everything suggests that it is from the eighteenth century: the elegant, careful, sometimes even refined script, the two title-pages in a very modern German language and lettering;[47] the beauty of the frontispieces to the twelve chapters; the clarity of the figures, and, finally, the amusing allusion to Gans's name in the form of a goose emerging now and again from the Hebrew letter *qof*.

It is a fine example of a Hebrew manuscript in the style of the second half of the eighteenth century such as wealthy patrons in Central Europe commissioned expert scribes to execute for their libraries.[48]

The name of the owner of the manuscript, Marcus Turnauer (alias Mayer J. Turnau), which appears twice in the title-pages, is also to be found in a register of Moravian Jews of 1787,[49] and it is

[46] Pp. 16–19.

[47] 'Manuscript des Buches Nehmad Wenaïm—Sepher Nehmad Wenaïm enhält vermischte Abhandlungen über das Weltgebäude nebst einer ausführlichen mathematischen Geographie nach dem Tychinischen Systeme verfasst von Rabby David Gans, Verfasser des chronologischen Buches Zemach David, lebte im Jahre 1590.'

[48] Cf. E. Namenyi, 'La miniature juive au XVIIe et au XVIIIe siècles, *REJ*, xvi (cxvi) (Jan.–Dec. 1957), pp. 27–71.

[49] It is a register of the Jews of Triesch in Moravia. Alter suggests the manuscript may have belonged to two different members of the Turnau family. In that case, either the elder would have acquired it about 1740 or the younger would have lived about 1830.

not inconceivable that he was not only the owner but also the person who commissioned the manuscript.

This magnificent folio of 166 pages was certainly not the manuscript used for the book printed at Jessnitz in 1743, firstly because its luxurious presentation and legible script in no way correspond to Rabbi Joel ben Yekutiel Sachs's description of the disordered, jumbled, and sometimes indecipherable manuscript from which he had worked, and secondly because a number of important variations in the text invalidate it as the model for the book published at Jessnitz. Alter has pointed out the main ones, and I have been able to make a few slight additions to the list; but, as I have already made it clear, I reserve the detailed critical study of these variants for a later publication.

For the present, we conclude, like Alter, that the Brno manuscript, interesting though it is, has no direct connection with the manuscript used by the editor of the book published in Jessnitz. As Alter says, this manuscript must be somewhere else, and, happily, we have succeeded in identifying it on a microfilm in Jerusalem. It is the Geneva manuscript.

THE GENEVA MANUSCRIPT: NATIONAL AND UNIVERSITY LIBRARY, JERUSALEM, MICROFILM 10408

A quarto manuscript of a hundred and seventy recto-verso pages entitled *Nehmad ve-Na'im*, preceded by an unpaginated table of contents (eight recto-verso pages), written haphazardly, without any concern for elegance or clarity, with superscriptions, blots, whole lines of writing almost effaced: this is indeed the manuscript described in his preface by Rabbi Joel ben Yekutiel of Austerlitz in the edition of *Nehmad ve-Na'im* published at Jessnitz in 1743.

There are no decorative motifs, no care in the execution of the figures, no pen-strokes crowning the Hebrew letter *qof* with the form of a goose in reference to the name of the author:[50] in fact, none of those features which make the Brno manuscript so singular and charming.

Should any doubts remain concerning the connection between the Geneva manuscript and the printed book, they should be

[50] This is the answer to Alter's question, p. 18: 'One might wonder whether the original manuscript, too, contained these initials, or whether they were the copyist's invention and intention.'

dispelled by the following observation: the Brno manuscript is not dated, while the Geneva manuscript is. At the end of page 170 one learns the date of the completion of the manuscript: Friday the eighth of Ab 5373, or 26 July 1613. And that is precisely the date given at the end of the printed book (folio 82d).

It is also, as we pointed out, a date relevant to David Gans's biography, as he died three weeks later, on 22 August 1613.[51] Accordingly, there are several possible explanations of the origins of the manuscript: it could have been written by Gans himself,[52] or dictated by him, or, following the publication of *Magen David* the previous year, it may have been a revision for publication of a previous manuscript on which Gans had worked uninterruptedly since his meeting with Tycho Brahe.[53] At any rate, the occurrence of Gans's death only three weeks after the completion of the manuscript makes it seem probable that at the time when the manuscript was being prepared for publication Gans was already ill, which would explain the hasty script, the obviously improvised 'final touches', the clumsy alterations: in fact, all the things which Rabbi Sachs complained about one hundred and thirty years later, and which he admitted having succeeded in correcting only very partially.

As for the contents, there are indeed differences between the printed book and the Geneva manuscript, less numerous than in the case of the Brno manuscript, but real nevertheless.[54] We are convinced, however, that a careful critical comparison of the documents will reveal that these variations are all to be attributed to Rabbi Sachs. The Rabbi, moreover, gave a very honest account of his actions in his preface, which at the same time is an apology (*hitnazlut*) and an admission of the occasional need for retouching the precious manuscript.[55] This being the case, these variations do not seem to me to cast any doubt on the identification of the Geneva manuscript as the original manuscript of the book published a hundred and thirty years after its completion and the death of its author.

[51] See Chap. 3 above.

[52] See Part II, Chap. 5, n. 5 for the reasons why this is unlikely.

[53] The main reasons why this could be the case: Tycho Brahe (died 1600) and the Maharal (died 1609) are described as still living; the date 1610 is given in the epilogue in connection with Ptolemy. [54] See above I. 3 n. 21 and below II. 5, n. 5.

[55] The most daring alteration was to make the conclusion of the work (with the exception of the very last lines) into an introduction.

Alter's interesting observation about the omission of the term *Kaduri*, which appears in the printed book,[56] from Gans's account of Copernicus in the Brno manuscript, only serves to bear out our contention: the term *Kaduri* appears quite legibly in folio 167b of the Geneva manuscript.

THE JERUSALEM MANUSCRIPT: NATIONAL AND UNIVERSITY LIBRARY, JERUSALEM, MS HEB 8° 2747

The table of contents in this manuscript of *Sefer Neḥmad ve-Na'im* is complete, but the manuscript itself is unfortunately defective. It lacks an introduction, and ends abruptly at the beginning of chapter 287, of which only the title is mentioned, on p. 123. Chapter 287 (the last chapter of the eleventh section) is consequently missing, and so is the interesting epilogue. The epilogue, however, and what we have called the 'methodological parenthesis' in the epilogue are referred to in many passages previous to chapter 287.

Thus, we have here an uncompleted manuscript which it is impossible to date. One can only say that the script is clear, legible, and not particularly decorative. We have not found any geese, and the figures (particularly the towers in chapters 281 and 283 with their little flags) are unskilfully drawn, and often the opposite way round from the one in which they appear either in the printed book or in any of the other manuscripts which we have studied.

This version is probably intermediate between the Geneva and Brno manuscripts. It is perhaps an attempted restitution of the Geneva manuscript made at the time when the publisher was preparing to print it at Jessnitz in 1743. Whatever the case, the discovery of this manuscript bears out Alter's observation that Gans's astronomical work did have its devotees and the manuscripts produced before and after its publication were numerous,[57] and some agreeable surprises may still be in store for us. Among those which have been provided by an examination of the Jerusalem manuscript, I will describe one in this book,[58] reserving others for the definitive edition which now seems to me within the bounds of possibility.

I postpone until the appearance of this critical edition the detailed consideration of a problem to which I will devote only a

[56] Pp. 29 and 34.   [57] P. 34.   [58] See below II. 5, n. 4.

few lines here which can serve as a conclusion to this part of the book: namely, the reasons for the change of title of David Gans's astronomical work from *Magen David* to *Neḥmad ve-Na'im*.

I must confess that I was tempted, before making a careful reading of the manuscripts, to see in the title *Neḥmad ve-Na'im* a rather complicated allusion to the 'astronomical revolution'. According to this idea, *naḥ* and *na'*, the two first syllables of the two Hebrew words, refer to the conflict between the 'movement' and the 'stability' of the earth, exemplified by the opposition of Ptolemy and Copernicus, whereas the two last syllables, *mad* and *im* would be a reference to *mad'im*, the planet Mars on which Kepler was working at Benatek under Tycho Brahe.

I have abandoned this conjecture for the following reasons:

(1) the adjectives *neḥmad* and *na'im* are employed by David Gans himself in connection with the astronomical works of Judah Halevi (*ZD*, 68a, *Sefer neḥmad ve-yakar*) and the Rema (*NN* 8a: *ma tov u-ma na'im*). They also appear in the 1609 edition of Mordecai Jaffe's *Levush* (see p. 49), in the publisher's note on Recanati (*biur neḥmad ve-na'eh*), and in a note on the *Levush* by the commentator Nathan Halevi Ashkenazi (*amadti al devarav ha-ne'imim*). These are standard formulas used about astronomy whatever the period or whatever the writer's approach.

(2) We have seen that David Gans had a reason for choosing the title *Magen David*. It echoes the title of his first book, *Ẓemaḥ David*. It appears on the prospectus published in 1612, and provides the symbol for his tombstone a year later. On the other hand, the manuscripts provide no explanation for calling the book *Neḥmad ve-Na'im*. In the oldest manuscript (the Geneva manuscript, completed three weeks before Gans's death), this title suddenly replaces that of *Magen David*, without any reason being given for this last-minute alteration.

I am therefore inclined to think that Gans intended the book to be called *Magen David*. The stereotyped, impersonal title *Neḥmad ve-Na'im* must have been added to the Geneva manuscript after Gans's death by a copyist or even by a binder, using the terms current at that period to describe works of astronomy.

PART TWO

DAVID GANS, COSMOGRAPHER

I

The reality and myth of the New World in the Sixteenth century: the Exodus towards Infinity

A FLUID AND COMPLEX MUTATION

THE discovery of America in the sixteenth century was one of the fluid and variegated elements in the mutation which was taking place at that critical juncture of history in the human spirit.

It was a fluid element, for if the sheer process of discovery—the blind but obstinate thrusting forward from Christopher Columbus's first voyage in 1492 to the second voyage round the world by Sir Francis Drake in 1576—had something progressive about it, the knowledge which scholars had of that process in the second half of the sixteenth century was still very incomplete. A new world had been revealed: that was an indisputable fact which no one doubted. But there were so many different accounts of the nature of that revelation, so many famous names were associated with it (Columbus, Amerigo Vespucci, Vasco da Gama, Magellan, Fernando Cortès, Jacques Cartier, Guillaume le Testu, de Noligny), so many nations were in rivalry because of it (Spain, Portugal, France, England, Holland), so many countries, oceans, straits, and isthmuses had appeared in rapid succession, with each phase overtaking the previous one or superimposing itself, creating new names and changes of contours, that the New World, a century after Christopher Columbus, was like a puzzle which no one was able to put together. Neither dates nor names nor latitudes nor contours were definitely fixed yet, and a writer on the subject could pile up contradictions without fear of getting entangled, for if the New World had for a century been a terra firma for those who had been bold enough to set foot there, for those who saw it from afar it was a kind of mirage, something nearer to dreams than to reality.

How could it be otherwise when the discovery of America was not felt to be a scientific fact but a leap into the unknown, or rather, a symptom of the crisis of knowledge? Even if the means of communication and transmission had permitted sixteenth-century man to gain rapid and reliable information about the adventure which he witnessed, and even if the scientific instruments had been sufficiently developed to provide him with an exact knowledge of what was taking place, what would he have done with that knowledge whose acquisition was neither his aim nor his ideal?

In the sixteenth century, knowledge was passing through a crisis whereby it was nourished by its own disintegration. One's enrichment did not take the form of the daily acquisition of new knowledge but of the daily pulverization, at an ever-increasing rate, of the concepts of the Middle Ages. Traumatized by a phenomenon like the discovery of the New World, which would normally have required a patient redrawing of maps and a rethinking of geographical conceptions, the man of the sixteenth century saw it instead as an invitation to hurl himself into the breach opened in the cosmos. The humblest doctor, rabbi, monk felt like a conqueror. He, too, in his own way, equipped armadas, touched land with Christopher Columbus, explored it with Amerigo Vespucci, sailed around it with Magellan, died with him in battle, and rose again with El Cana with the wonderful feeling that he, too, even if he did not make the voyage, could, in producing a book, a map, a chronicle, claim for himself the glorious inscription: *Primus circumdedisti me*: 'You are the first to have circled the globe!'

REASON IS RIGHT IN BEING WRONG

But if, unlike the *conquistadores*, the sixteenth-century scholar did not make this round-the-world voyage out of the love of gold and honours, it would be wrong to imagine that he made it out of the love of scientific knowledge. In his case, reason had reasons that reason might have preferred not to be aware of, but which it sought out all the more earnestly and with which it had always been associated. It only needed an event like the discovery of the New World to bring this association out into the open.

The association in question was the alliance of reason and mysticism, of nature and the supernatural, of physical fact and the fantasies of the occult. And here, together with the fluid character of this event, we may perceive its hybrid character: for the man of the sixteenth century, the discovery of America was both a reality and a myth. In it, his reason sought desperately, or rather with a magnificant persistence in a hope which had now grown infinite, the key to its incomprehensible mystery, a sign to justify this new-found certainty, after a millennium of narrow dogmatism, that reason is right to doubt its own values, that reason is right in being wrong.

Today, at the end of the twentieth century, when men plan and carry out the conquest of the moon, there are few who see in the prodigious escapade of the Apollos anything but a natural consequence of scientific developments resulting from the splitting of the atom. The adventure is tied to the logic of physical laws which we believe must necessarily lead us ever further and higher, and no rocket, however perfected it may be, will ever go through the roof of a cosmos whose dimensions human reason knows itself capable of measuring, and in which it feels itself to be entirely at home.

If these cosmonauts happen to be Marxists, they bring back from their voyage to the farthest stars proof that everything is physical and that the prefix 'meta' is only the fantasy of sick or childish minds. When they happen to be Christians, the biblical verses with which they accompany their first steps on the moon only go to show that American society has its catechisms as the Soviets have theirs, without this purely sociological throwback having any effect on the purely scientific character of the spacial adventure, inspired entirely by pure and simple rationalism.

There are few, I say, who see some philosophical connection between the lunar expeditions and the end of the twentieth century: something like the sign of an approaching apocalypse or the exodus of man towards a new Promised Land. And even these would be a handful of visionaries who would be quite incapable, if the American space agencies made use of them, of doing anything to advance the space programme in a practical manner.

But, in contrast to this, the great navigators, the conquerors, and those who fitted out great naval expeditions and who organized the discovery of the New World at the end of the fifteenth and in the first half of the sixteenth centuries and brought it to a spectacular conclusion were, all of them, visionaries.

Their programme did not aim at drawing a map of the earth or at finding the true dimensions of the natural universe, but at discovering the image of man and his supernatural dimensions. In a deeper sense, their programme did not aim at anything, in so far as it had no objective outside itself: an advance towards a new horizon, an opening-out of a landscape of which the human race had long wearied. The discovery of the New World did not aim at anything. It was a vision in itself: a complex vision, as difficult for these men of the Renaissance to grasp and to express in concrete form as was their amazed penetration into the world of the ancients, their sublime artistic creativity, their eager observation of the heavenly vault, their astounding intuition of the great scientific laws which would be formulated only one or two centuries later. Man discovering the New World was, as Jean Babelon has well said, Oedipus before the sphinx, the human traveller before the mystery of his own being.[1] Leonardo da Vinci, Pico della Mirandola, and Michelangelo were not alone in having the aura of seers and prophets. Christopher Columbus was also a visionary. His third voyage was a feverish adventure, something fashioned out of the dreams he described in his *Book of Prophecies*. The letters of Amerigo Vespucci to René de Lorraine who still proudly bore the title of King of Jerusalem (a relic of the distant Crusades) were responsible for the first appearance of the New World in a cosmography (that of Martin Waldseemuller at St Dié in 1507), but they also—as Jean Servier has convincingly demonstrated[2]— inspired Sir Thomas More's *Utopia* and so embodied both geographical science and philosophical illusion. Magellan and the *conquistadores*, finally, those fiery sea-captains, carried on until death quixotic battles against the windmills of the Apocalypse.

THE NOSTALGIA FOR THE LOST PARADISE

The motivations of that great mutation of human nature which was the search for and discovery of America are known to us. Even stated in their simplest form, they electrify a reading of the Bible. The spices, the gold, the exotic animals which Solomon brought back from Tarshish and Ophir: it was thought that they must still be somewhere, and since navigation towards the East proved to be unavailing, perhaps, by changing course towards the West one could bring before the sovereigns of Spain, Portugal or France the treasures which the fearless sailors once brought to Jerusalem.

But since there is so much in the Bible and all parts are so much interconnected, Solomon's Ophir takes us back to the Ophir in

[1] Jean Babelon, *L'Amérique des Conquistadores* (Paris, 1947), p. 16.
[2] Jean Servier, *Histoire de l'Utopie* (Paris, 1967), pp. 121–41.

Genesis. Thus, through a purely linguistic association, the Bible suggested to Christopher Columbus's seething imagination not only the spice-route but also the way to Paradise, and—let us make it clear from the start—the way to the Lost Paradise.

So this was the first mutation in the soul of the sixteenth-century Bible-reader: it no longer looked forward to the consummation of the ages but to their restoration; it no longer looked forwards but backwards. Had not the Renaissance taught the Christian to read his Bible in Hebrew again, instead of in Greek or in Latin? Now, Hebrew is not read from left to right but from right to left, not from West to East but from East to West. The true sunrise is to be found in the place of its setting. It was there on the routes to the West that they would find the worlds which had disappeared into the unattainable past. Since the swords of the cherubim barred the way to the Lost Paradise to the East (Genesis 3: 24), one would return to Paradise through the open doors to the west. By this simple stratagem of a change of direction man would thus override the will of God and elude the vigilance of the angels. It was from the place of the setting sun, where Eden had literally slept a sleep several millennia long, that it was now to be restored to man.[3]

THE YEARNING FOR ATLANTIS

It would be restored, first of all, to the man who knew the Bible, but on this point the boundaries were fast being effaced between Bible-reading man and man as such. For what the clerics now read in the Bible with a new understanding, the secular humanists read in those texts which had been overlooked by the Middle Ages or were unknown to them, but which the fall of Byzantium had now dropped first into Italy and then into France, England, the Holy Roman Empire, and the Iberian Peninsula—Homer, Diodorus Siculus, Strabo, Plutarch, and all the countless authors who spoke in more or less veiled terms of a secret which Plato, now read at last in the original, revealed in a dazzling synthesis—the myth of Atlantis, that vast isle of fantastic riches sunk into the ocean

---

[3] On the Messianic themes common to Christians and Jews in connection with the discovery of the New World, see Jacques Lafaye, *Quetzalcoatl et Guadalupe, La formation de la conscience nationale au Mexique* (Paris, 1974), Marcel Bataillon's striking and frequently-recurring phrase: 'the immense discovery became part of the theology of history before assuming an ethnographical form'.

through the will of the jealous gods. Neither the Pillars of Hercules nor *ultima Thule*, then, were the end of the earth. Far away to the West in the depths of the terrible Ocean there lay a sunken kingdom which had waited like Eden for millennia for men to bring back in its state of abundance the former City of Human Happiness.

Here we see the second mutation in the soul of sixteenth-century man. The nostalgia for the Lost Paradise had reversed a view of history of which man now felt himself to have been captive, and whose chains he wished to break asunder. It was a return to man as he was when he left the hands of God, before the Fall and the Exile. The yearning for Atlantis, on the other hand, directed men forward towards the future, towards a new historical perspective where man could begin to remake his own happiness and enjoy it to the full. The return to Eden was a renewal of man's original alliance with the Creator: the rediscovery of Atlantis was a release of man's creative potential, confronting the Creator with the challenge of Prometheus.

Was this a contradiction? Was it a tension between two contrary forces? Undoubtedly, but neither polarity was felt to be unbearable. Lucien Febvre has well described the sixteenth century as the century 'that wanted to believe',[4] which wanted to believe the unbelievable, both a fact and its negation, a faith which was doubted and a doubt made into a faith—the century that wanted to believe that man, newly liberated from the shackles of religion, remained the creature of God, just as man, while remaining the servant of God, had no accounts to render to anyone but himself.

THE EXODUS TOWARDS INFINITY

And so—lost sheep returning to the fold of its infancy or new-born eagle learning the use of its wings—the man of the sixteenth century could be compared to both at once, since the way of return was also that of departure, and one had to plunge into the Atlantic both to be born and to be reborn. To return to the divine Palace of Eden or to rebuild the human City of Atlantis was, despite the apparent incompatibility of intentions (one directed to the future and the other to the past), one and the same enterprise: leaping

---

[4] Lucien Febvre, *Le problème de l'incroyance au XVIᵉ siècle: la religion de Rabelais* (Paris, 1962); *Au cœur religieux du XVIᵉ siècle* (Paris, 1957).

over the boundaries which hitherto had defined man and hedged him in. No matter if the leap were backwards or forwards, but it had to take man out of his finite and bring him into his infinite condition, to place him in an absolute 'beyond' and provide the human horizontality with an illimitable 'meta'. And it is perhaps here that the real meaning of the term 'humanism' is revealed. The discovery of America, because in every sense it was a meta-physical adventure—breaking through the physical dimensions of the globe, but at the same time breaking through the physical dimensions of man—the discovery of the New World was, I say, for sixteenth-century man an Exodus towards Infinity.

2

The reality of the New World in the Jewish consciousness: scholars and Marranos

IF we now try to evaluate the Jewish presence in the two aspects of this Exodus, in its reality and in the myth, we shall be pleasantly surprised to discover that we are able to do so if we allow ourselves to be guided by David Gans: by the historian of *Zemaḥ David* no less than by the astronomer of *Neḥmad ve-Na'im*. Living at the end of the sixteenth century, he looked back upon an evolution which was now in its final phases. All the problems were not yet solved: by no means. But at least David Gans knew how to state the problems and, where necessary, to decide courageously in favour of one solution or another. He gives a list of names which, simply in itself, allows us to trace the Jewish contribution to this great event of the discovery of the New World: i.e., the Talmud, the *Zohar*, the medieval Jewish astronomers in France and Spain, and then the great Jewish contemporaries of Columbus and Vespucci—Abraham Zacuto and Isaac Abravanel—and finally, in the sixteenth century, the Jewish chroniclers who recorded the event: Abraham Farissol, Joseph Ha-Kohen, Solomon Ibn Verga, Gedaliah Ibn Yaḥya, and Azariah dei Rossi.

Let us now take our place at the observation post next to David Gans, and before we begin to share his bread, his joys, and his troubles, let us join him in seeing the reaction of those Jews who came before him and whose echo he faithfully captures, now fleetingly, now in a more discernible manner.

One clear line of demarcation immediately becomes apparent: that between the periods previous to the sixteenth century and the sixteenth century itself. Previous to the sixteenth century the enormous, vital Jewish contribution to the discoveries was of a purely rational and scientific nature: it related only to the real aspect of the enterprise. But in the sixteenth century we find the Jewish version of its mythical, mystical dimension. It will soon be quite clear to us why this should have been the case. We shall begin by looking at the first part of the picture.

If the Jewish part in the preparations for the discovery of the New World was of an almost exclusively rational and scientific nature, it was because it was intimately connected with the important role of astronomy in ancient and medieval Jewish science.

We shall examine astronomy as a subject in its own right when we come upon David Gans spying out the consequences of the Copernican revolution in the team of Tycho Brahe and Johannes Kepler. In the American adventure, however, astronomy played only a subsidiary role, although a very valuable one, for, without it, seafaring in the fifteenth century would never have developed on the scale it did, ending with the discovery of America and the circumnavigation of the globe. Nautical astronomy provided Columbus and Magellan with their intuitions, their information and, above all, their instruments.

Of course, the Jews were not always the inventors, and in many cases they applied knowledge inherited from the Greeks or acquired from the Arabs. But there were certain areas in which the Jews took the lead and in which their influence was original, decisive, and clear.

THE CONCEPTION OF THE EARTH AS ROUND: THE ZOHAR

There was first of all the idea that the earth was round, essential for a voyage that would circumnavigate the globe and not merely travel across it. This ancient Greek hypothesis expressed by Parmenides had been rejected by Ptolemy, and in the medieval Western world, dogmatically attached to Ptolemaic doctrine, it was consequently completely forgotten. Yet the Talmud had retained this idea, stating on several occasions that the earth was a globe. *Kadur*, the Hebrew term that was used, could mean a round ball (this was the original meaning of the term), but also a flat surface, and the Talmudist rabbis of the Middle Ages, especially Maimonides, supported this latter interpretation in order that the Talmud should not be suspected of containing a statement incompatible with the Aristotelian system which inspired Ptolemy.

But the idea of a round globe nevertheless remained alive to the readers of the Talmud: more, perhaps, to the ordinary man reading

his daily page of Talmud without concerning himself about the
scientific problems it might raise than to the scholars. It is by no
means surprising that it is in the *Zohar* which, as we know, came out
of the popular layers of the Jewish tradition in protest against the
excessive intellectualism of the 'philosophers', that one finds a
famous empirical statement (the *Zohar* was written around 1300)
implying the scientific theory of the roundness of the earth: 'In the
book of Rav Hamnuna the Elder we are told, moreover, that the
earth is round as a globe and its inhabitants differ according to
climatic conditions. These revolutions have the consequence that
when it is daytime in one half of the globe it is night in the other
half, and that when part of the inhabitants of the earth have light,
the other part is in darkness. Moreover, there are places where
there is perpetual daylight and night only lasts for a few moments'
(III 10a).

I think it is no exaggeration to say, with Adolphe Franck, that one
could imagine this text was written by a pupil of Copernicus,[1] for
the word *mitgalgelet* which is used here can only be understood as
referring to the rotation of the earth upon its axis. Thus, three
centuries before Copernicus, the Kabbalists rediscovered the
heliocentric system of Aristarchus of Samos. It is true that Duhem,
the learned historian of cosmological doctrines, devotes five long
pages to an attempt to prove that this is not so at all, and that 'in the
stars and heavens the Kabbalists only sought suitable symbols for
their theological and mystical doctrines'.[2] But, quite apart from the
fact that the Aramaic terms of the *Zohar* only admit of a
'Copernican' interpretation,[3] it may be objected that in the Middle
Ages the Kabbalists were not alone in confusing theology,
mysticism, and astronomy, and, on the contrary, it would be
difficult to find any medieval thinker, Jewish, Christian, or Muslim,
who was not guilty of such a confusion, an almost automatic
concomitant of a biblical way of thinking which continued (it cannot
be stressed sufficiently) right into the Renaissance, up to Descartes,
and even to Leibniz and Newton. Were not Copernicus himself
and Tycho Brahe, Kepler, Galileo, and Pascal willing or unconscious
captives, as we shall see, of this understanding—at once religious
and secular, mystical and scientific, 'geometrical' and metaphysical

[1] Adolphe Franck, *La Kabbale*, third edn., p. 75.
[2] P. Duhem, *Le système du monde*, vol. 5, pp. 143–7.
[3] See S. W. Baron, *History and Jewish Historians*, pp. 179–81, n. 35.

—of a universe in which a dividing-line between reason and faith was simply inconceivable?

Moreover, even if this passage in the *Zohar* is not regarded as 'Copernican', it still deserves some credit for originality: a point to which Duhem does not give sufficient emphasis. For even if we admit that the *Zohar* does not mention the rotation of the earth on its axis, at least it states unambiguously not only that the earth is round, as had been timidly suggested by previous medieval thinkers (the Venerable Bede in the eighth century and, later, Gerbert who ascended the papal throne as Sylvester II around the year 1000), but also that the roundness of the earth implies that the antipodes are inhabited for 'when it is daytime in one half of the globe it is night in the other half, and when part of the inhabitants of the earth have light, the other part is in darkness'—an idea which Bede categorically rejected and Gerbert did not mention. Thus, disregarding the old rationalistic objections to the idea of an inhabited antipodes (Lactantius' objection, for example, that people would have to walk upside down!), and Bede's theological objections (as the antipodes are unreachable, their supposed inhabitants could not be descendants of Adam), the *Zohar* gives a description of the roundness of the earth which, set though it is against a background which is obviously mystical and irrational (the myth of vanished worlds, probably identical with the myth of Atlantis), nevertheless possesses a character which is singularly rational and modern, and, in any case, quite contrary to the Aristotelianism dominant at the end of the thirteenth century, and several centuries in advance of the ideas of the cosmos current at that period.

INVENTIONS: THE ALPHONSINE TABLES, THE QUADRANT, JACOB'S STAFF

Concurrently with this mention of the roundness of the earth and the existence of the antipodes in a mystical work, there were the practical instruments invented through the mathematical and technical ingenuity of medieval Jewish brains: i.e., the astronomical tables and the ancestors of the compass.

With regard to the Tables, indispensable to the navigator, Columbus used those of his contemporary Joseph Vecinho, disciple of Rabbi Abraham Zacuto, professor at the University of Salamanca and subsequently associated with the court of Portugal, but the Alphonsine Tables were still in use and would still for a long time be one of the documents which shipowners and *conquistadores* would consult in order to chart the unknown seas for which they set sail. The Alphonsine Tables were compiled in 1252, two and a half centuries before Christopher Columbus, by a mixed commission of Jewish and Arab scholars brought together by Alfonso X the Wise, King of Castile. At the end of the sixteenth century the great Tycho Brahe remembered the labours of this learned company presided over by Rabbi Isaac Ibn Sid of Toledo, and the subsequent history of the Alphonsine Tables. He knew that they had been updated and corrected by a new commission assembled by Pedro the son of Alfonso, but he was unable to consult these Tables of Pedro because they existed only in Spanish or Hebrew, languages with which the Danish astronomer was unacquainted. It was one of the claims to fame of his Jewish disciple David Gans and one of his noteworthy contributions to the work of Tycho Brahe and Johannes Kepler that he translated for Brahe what he continued to call the 'Alphonsine' Tables from Hebrew to German.[4]

As for the instruments of orientation—in medieval times generally known by the vague name of astrolabe before the invention of the compass as late as the fifteenth century—one, a quadrant known only by its Hebrew name of *Rova Yisrael* ('Jewish quadrant') was invented by Rabbi Jacob ben Makir—who taught at the University of Montpellier—in 1300, and another thirty years later, again by a Jew, Levi ben Gerson or the great Gersonides, known in rabbinical tradition as Ralbag; but in that case the accounts of both the instrument and the inventor have been so garbled and full of errors, right down to our own day, that in order to obtain a more specific account we have to wait for David Gans to speak of Ralbag, not in a cosmographical context but in the astronomical part of his book.[5]

CHRISTOPHER COLUMBUS AND THE MARRANOS

We now turn to the world of the end of the fifteenth century, beginning, of course, with the first voyage of Christopher Columbus in 1492. Here we come upon a man and a date which,

[4] See below III. 1.   [5] See below III. 2.

from the Jewish point of view, are both equally remarkable, for both of them gave rise, in Jewish thinking as well, to a characteristic cleavage between myth and reality.

The man is Christopher Columbus whose origins are still wrapped in such mystery that the idea that he was Jewish has been argued so persuasively that some writers have not hesitated to turn it into a fact.[6] What is certain, at any rate, is that this man, to carry out this enterprise, surrounded himself with a group of men among whom Jews were notable both for their numbers and for the moral, material, and technical aid which they provided for Columbus, without which he would never have succeeded in his fantastic projects. The biographies of Columbus, as well as his own writings and correspondence, abound in names of people known to have been Jews: Luis de Santangel and Gabriel Sanchez, who provided the funds and equipment: Joseph Vecinho who drew up the tables and charts; Rodrigo de Jerez, Luis de Torres, and Bernal who accompanied him on his voyage as interpreters or physicians for, in his passionate desire to find the Lost Paradise, in order to discern the biblical potentialities of the route, Columbus had to have with him on his journey some companions who were conversant with Hebrew.

But a fact often overlooked in connection with these Jews who joined Columbus is that all were *converted* Jews. The same may also have been true of the Franciscan prior to the Convent de la Rabida, Juan Perez de la Marchena, without whose assistance Christopher Columbus and his son would have died of hunger in 1485.

They were converted Jews, which was natural enough at a period when the intolerance of the Catholic Sovereigns was reaching its height. How could Columbus have obtained their support if he had not presented himself to them as a fervent Catholic surrounded by Catholic protectors: he who attempted to win over Ferdinand and Isabella with the persuasive argument that the massive gold bullion he would bring back from India reached from the West would be used to deliver the Holy Places in Jerusalem? Where so many medieval sovereigns had failed, this couple, Catholic *par excellence*, would finally succeed in an ultimate crusade furnished with the treasures of Ophir which their humble Catholic servant would lay at their feet.

---

[6] See bibliography.

It was natural enough, but it seems to me that a recognition of this fact is all-important for an understanding of the impact of the discovery of the New World on the Jews of the sixteenth century. These converted Jews, to be sure, companions of Columbus— Columbus himself, perhaps—were good Catholics, but who knows if some of them did not retain in some corner of their Christian soul a yearning for their former Jewish identity?

Nearly two and a half centuries previously, from the year of the reconquest of Seville from the Moors in 1248, the Jews had begun their grim Calvary in Castile and in all those provinces already reconquered or which were destined to be progressively reconquered in accordance with a strategy fatal for the Arabs, but equally for the Jews. The crucial year in this process was 1391, whose repercussions were felt even in France where the Jews were definitively expelled from the kingdom three years later in 1394. A series of massacres in Seville inspired by the Catholic clergy and bourgeoisie for both religious and economic motives resulted in a choice weighty in consequences for the Jewish people: 'death or conversion'. It was the beginning of the Marranos. Those Jews who remained loyal, forced to emigrate to provinces more tolerant than Castile and received particularly graciously by the Kingdom of Portugal, naturally regarded the converted Jews, at first at least, as traitors and cowards; but the Christians themselves were amazed by the number of Jews who preferred to renounce their faith rather than to undergo exile or martyrdom. And soon there grew up a general—and generally justified—suspicion of these new Christians in whom it was felt that, in some more or less surreptitious manner, some Jewish spark, whether religious or social, was still alive.

In Spain, the fifteenth century was to be the tragic period of the persecution of the Marranos. These, since their conversion, had massively penetrated Christian society, offering the Catholic kingdoms their loyalty and intelligence, scaling the upper ranks of the bourgeoisie and clergy to such a degree that the high civil, military and ecclesiastical dignitaries of Jewish origin could no longer be counted. However, cut off from their society of origin, they were at the same time suspected by the society which received them, and the slightest real or imaginary sign of 'Judaization' was tracked down, suppressed, and punished with a zeal which the basest motives—jealousy, competition, regret at having opened a gate of salvation where straightforward condemnation would have provided a 'final solution'—made more bitter and cruel with every passing year. The setting up of the Inquisition was only the culmination of this process which each successive stage of the Reconquista took a step further, and the die, so to speak, was cast, the fate of the Marranos definitely sealed in 1481, towards the end of the fifteenth century, when the first tribunal of the Inquisition began to function in Seville, the very spot where the decisive turn of events had taken place a century earlier.

In 1481 Christopher Columbus was already dreaming his dreams. The years were already drawing nigh when, like some wandering beggar, he set them out in Italy, in Portugal, and finally in Spain where he found his travelling companions, his friends to whom he sent the fantastic accounts of his first voyage: those men who were his spokesmen and his mentors with the Most Catholic Royal Couple, and who convinced them of the seriousness of his schemes, informed them about his achievements, and persuaded them to follow this first undertaking with a second and then a third voyage.

Among the people we mentioned surrounding Columbus, without whose support and constancy the wandering beggar would never have been transformed into a triumphant admiral, most, if not all had, long before they met him, been the object of investigations, prosecutions, and condemnations—a persecution which was to continue until after the death of Columbus in 1506. All these converted Jews were regarded as Marranos by the Inquisition, and indeed, from the end of the fifteenth century and the beginning of the sixteenth, 'marranism' was to develop amongst them on a considerable scale.

Maestro Bernal, the physician who travelled with Columbus on his first voyage, had been accused of Judaizing in 1490. Even earlier, the Inquisition had so persecuted the Santangels that in 1485 some members of that illustrious Catholic family had helped to bring about the assassination of the Inquisitor Pedro Arbues, right-hand man of Torquemada,[7] for which Martin de Santangel was burnt on 28 July 1486 and his brother Luis de Santangel was also burnt in the auto-da-fé at Saragossa on 18 August 1487. This Luis de Santangel was the father-in-law of Gabriel Sanchez and the uncle of the Luis de Santangel who, as we said, provided

[7] We should note in passing that Pedro Arbues, one of the cruellest inquisitors in history, was canonized by Pius IX (the pope of the Mortara affair!) in 1867.

Columbus with the funds for the equipment of his armada. But one should not suppose that it was in an atmosphere of serenity that these two men negotiated with Columbus and the royal couple. If some members of the Santangel and Sanchez families gained their safety by fleeing to France or were burnt only in effigy (the brother of Santangel in 1492 and the father of Sanchez in 1493), others—brothers and sisters of Sanchez—were burnt at the stake in 1493. As for Columbus's two associates themselves, in Saragossa, dressed in the sanbenito, on 17 July 1491 they solemnly denied any connection with Judaism, but that by no means guaranteed them against the harassment of Torquemada. For that there had to be a royal decree in 1497, protecting Luis de Santangel and Gabriel Sanchez against the Inquisition until their death in 1505, one year before that of Columbus, who had sent them his first letters dealing with his epoch-making discoveries.

We should note that Christopher Columbus was not the only navigator of that heroic period to be intimately associated with the phenomenon of 'marranism'. So also were Vasco da Gama, Amerigo Vespucci and Pedro Alvares Cabral, through the celebrated Gaspar, who was as well known for his skill as a pilot as for his deep familiarity with the Indies, which they were attempting to reach from the West. Gaspar was a good, worthy Jew from Goa, faithful to his religion and his people. When Vasco da Gama arrived in Goa, he was so amazed by the amount of information which this Jew provided him about the country, its inhabitants, and the routes into the interior that he accused him of spying and submitted him to the most terrible tortures from which he was only delivered by attesting to two things: first—and less important—that he was innocent, and second—which alone could furnish the proof of the first—that he was ready to abjure the abominable religion of his ancestors and accept Christianity. Vasco da Gama was his god-father, and from that time (December 1498) the new Christian entered into history under the name of Gaspar da Gama. In 1500 he was a pilot in the service of Cabral in the expedition in which he discovered Brazil. On his way back, Cabral's fleet met that of Amerigo Vespucci, in search of Brazil which had just been discovered. Vespucci, in turn, made use of Gaspar's ingenuity and intelligence, and the latter finally returned to Goa, where he rejoined his wife who had remained Jewish. One must suppose that Gaspar's conversion, extracted under torture, was hardly sincere, and that he was one of the first Marranos of the region of Goa where the Inquisition was soon to stage some of its most sinisterly sumptuous autos-da-fé. Thus, the theme of 'marranism' envelops, so to speak, the discovery of the New World, and it was precisely 'marranism' which, as we shall see, was one of the first consequences, unexpected but spectacular, of the discovery of America for the spiritual and historical destiny of the Jews in the sixteenth century.[8]

The sole exception to the company of converted Jews surrounding Columbus was Don Isaac Abravanel. He, the master of rabbinical scholarship of his period, did not convert and remained steadfast in his Jewish faith,[9] but his prestige as a statesman and economist was such that the Catholic Monarchs could not dispense with his services. He was minister of finance in Aragon and Castile as he had previously been in Portugal and was later to become in Naples, and it was his support of the schemes of Christopher Columbus which made them acceptable to the Most Catholic Sovereigns through the recommendation of their Jewish minister, Rabbi Don Isaac Abravanel.

He was the exception, then, which confirmed the rule. And now, with the mention of Abravanel, we come upon the second factor in the part played by Columbus's adventure in the Jewish adventure in the sixteenth century. Side by side with the man, Christopher Columbus, we now find the date: 1492.

THE AMBIVALENCE OF THE SUMMER OF 1492: THE DEPARTURE OF COLUMBUS AND THE EXPULSION OF THE JEWS FROM SPAIN

There can be nothing more impressive for the Jewish reader than

[8] Among the Marranos who fell victim to the Inquisition in the seventeenth century there were several descendants of Petrus Nonius (Pedro Nunes), the famous cosmographer mentioned in I. 2. See Cecil Roth, 'Abraham Nunez Bernal et autres martyres contemporains de l'Inquisition', *REJ*, C bis (Jan.–June 1939), pp. 38–51.

[9] Abraham Zacuto also refused to convert, and when the Infanta Isabella II (daughter of Isabella the Catholic), who had become Queen of Portugal in 1496, forced him to choose between conversion and expulsion in 1498, he chose to follow his teacher Isaac Aboab into exile, going first to Tunis where he wrote his chronicle *Yuḥasin*, and then to Smyrna where he died in 1510. If Columbus used Zacuto's Tables, that does not mean that he can be regarded as one of Columbus's 'supporters'. On the contrary: in a meeting held by King João II of Portugal in 1481, he had advised against the expedition, with the result that Columbus turned towards Spain, where Isaac Abravanel supported him.

the opening pages of the Journal of Christopher Columbus. What secret need prompted this man to establish from the beginning a fatal connection between two events which took place in the spring and summer of 1492: his own expedition and the expulsion of the Jews from Spain?

The Journal reads as follows:

Most exalted, Christian, excellent and very mighty princes, King and Queen of Spain and of the Isles of the Sea, our lord and sovereign: in this present year 1492, when Your Highnesses had ended the war against the Moors who reigned in Europe and concluded this war in the great city of Granada where, this present year, on the second day of the month of January I saw the royal standards of Your Highnesses raised by the force of arms on the towers of the Alhambra... Your Highnesses, as Christian Catholics and princes devoted to the propagation of the holy Christian faith and hostile to the sect of Mohammed and all idolatries and heresies, thought fit to send me, Christopher Columbus, to these countries of the Indies... They commanded me not to go overland to the East as is customary, but to take, on the contrary, the route to the West which, until today, we do not definitely know that anyone has ever taken. In consequence, after having expelled all the Jews from your kingdoms and domains, Your Highnesses commanded me, that same month of January, to leave with an adequate fleet for the said lands of the Indies. And on that occasion they bestowed on me great benefits and ennobled me, so that henceforth I bore the title of Don and was Great Admiral of the Ocean and Viceroy and perpetual governor of all the isles and continents which I was to discover and conquer in that Ocean... I left the city of Granada on the twelfth of the month of May in that same year 1492; I came to the town of Palos, which is a seaport, where I equipped three very suitable ships for such an enterprise, and I left that port well provided with victuals and seamen on Friday, the third day of the month of August of that year (1492), a half-hour before sunrise, and I followed the route of the Canary Islands which belong to Your Highnesses and are situated in the said Ocean, intending to sail from there until I reached the Indies ...[10]

Let us restate the facts, which are of an extraordinary chronological simplicity despite the slight confusion voluntarily created, no doubt, by Columbus himself. On 31 March 1492, Ferdinand and Isabella signed the decree obliging the Jews either to convert or to leave Spain within four months. This decree was published on 30 April, the very day that another decree was published commanding Christopher Columbus to equip a fleet

---

[10] See Jean Cassou, *Sommets de la Littérature Espagnole* (Paris), pp. 335–7.

with the purpose of sailing to the Indies. On 2 August, 300,000 Jews left Spain in the most tragic circumstances, and the next day, the third of August, Admiral Columbus's fleet put out to sea.

From a Jewish point of view these were extraordinary coincidences, but why did Columbus draw attention to these coincidences as if he wanted them never to be forgotten? One man, however, did forget them, or rather deliberately blotted them out of his memory, for reasons that we shall duly examine. That man was Don Isaac Abravanel, the only authentic Jew among the architects of Columbus's expedition.

If we wish to understand why this learned rabbi, interested in all new developments right up to his death in 1509, why this chronicler with an already very modern sense of history who in Italy absorbed the political and social ideas of Savonarola, the Medicis, and the Doges of Venice ... if we wish to understand why Don Isaac Abravanel did not devote a single line or word to the discovery of the New World by Christopher Columbus, we must place him within the fabric of events of the spring and summer of 1492 which contains, as its warp and woof, the expedition of Columbus and the expulsion of the Jews.

Don Isaac Abravanel had fought with all his might against this plan of expulsion which the Sovereigns had already been considering for a number of years. Immediately before the signing of the decree, he was admitted to plead once more the cause of the Jews before Ferdinand and Isabella who allowed themselves to be swayed when the Grand Inquisitor Torquemada came forward and reminded the Most Catholic Sovereigns of the fundamental obligations of the faith: there were to be no more infidels within the boundaries of the reconquered kingdom. The Muslims had been vanquished; the Jews ought now to be expelled.

The scene has been immortalized by Victor Hugo who omitted, however, one important historical detail.[11] Isaac Abravanel did not

---

[11] Victor Hugo, *Torquemada*, II. iii. This scene is undoubtedly 'philosemitic', but when Léon Poliakov claims that, by writing *Torquemada* (in 1882, three years before his death), 'Victor Hugo made amends towards the Jews' (*De Voltaire à Wagner* (Paris, 1968), p. 369), he forgives him rather too easily. In his fiercely anti-Semitic *Cromwell*, Victor Hugo called the rabbi thirsty for Christian blood by the name he really carried in history: Manasseh ben Israel. In *Torquemada*, on the other hand, Victor Hugo does not present Isaac Abravanel as the 'representative of the frightened and ragged crowd' of Jews, but a fictitious rabbi, Moses ben Habib, who never existed and was entirely invented by the poet: a fact which provides food for thought on the proportion of reality and fiction in literary philo- and anti-Semitism.

stand alone before the Sovereigns when he attempted, for one last time, to obtain mercy for his people. He was accompanied by two other eminent Jews: Abraham Senior, treasurer of the Kingdom of Castile, and his son-in-law Rabbi Meir, farmer-general of the Kingdom. It was an impressive delegation, made up of people so indispensable to the Castilian economy that a special proposition was suddenly made to them: an extra period of grace would be granted to them on a strictly personal basis. While continuing to occupy themselves with the affairs of the Kingdom, they could prepare for their inevitable conversion and thus escape the fate in store for the masses obstinate in faith.

Abraham Senior and Rabbi Meir, like so many others before them, clutched at this last hope. On 16 June 1492, six weeks before the decree of expulsion came into effect, their conversion was celebrated in Valladolid with a solemn procession, accompanied by the victorious sound of bells. Don Isaac Abravanel, however, refused the offer with dignity and nobility. He was never to convert. He needed no further time to consider: he refused to abandon his people. On 2 August 1492 Isaac Abravanel embarked with his brothers and sisters on one of the innumerable vessels which were to carry them away from the Spanish Eldorado for good. Some of these boats, water-borne coffins, sank in the open sea, while others reached various shores: some hostile, others more welcoming.

While the fleet of Christopher Columbus had set out to reach Eldorado by the western route on 3 August 1492, the previous day the ship of Don Isaac Abravanel had set sail towards the East. It came to land a few weeks later near Naples.

THE AMBIVALENCE OF ISAAC ABRAVANEL: HISTORY AND ESCHATOLOGY

Almost as soon as he reached Naples, Abravanel returned to his literary activities from which his political occupations had kept him for many years against his will. He prefaced his commentary on the Book of Kings in the Bible with a brief and poignant description of the dramatic days which he and his people had just lived through. He made some biting comments on the ingratitude of kings and then began his commentary in which, as we said, there is not a single line about Columbus, although it contains a real philosophy of history and a theory of politics, full of allusions to contemporary events. But Abravanel wrote as if no word about Christopher

Columbus, his voyage, or his discoveries, had ever reached his ears.

There is another indication of Abravanel's deliberate silence about Columbus: his commentary on verse 18 of chapter 3 of the Book of Jeremiah. This is the only place in the voluminous works of Abravanel where he mentions the Portuguese discoveries, but he does so without any reference to the Spanish voyages which preceded and accompanied them.

Let us now look at Abravanel's interpretation of this verse, which he describes as difficult: 'In those days [the times of the Messiah] the house of Judah shall be joined to the house of Israel, and they shall come together out of the land of the north to the land that I have given for an inheritance unto your fathers.' Abravanel comments:

And now, in these very days when I am writing this commentary, I have read in a true account by Westerners who now go from the Kingdom of Portugal to the Indies to bring back spices, their testimony concerning the many Jews they have seen there; they even brought back letters from one of them. They claim to be descended from the children of Judah and Benjamin whom Sennacherib had exiled from the towns of Judah before Jerusalem fell to Nebuchadnezzar, as is stated in the *Seder Olam*. He settled them beyond the Mountains of Darkness; they did not return in the time of the Second Temple.

I think, therefore, that since their dwelling-place is close to that of the ten tribes exiled by Sennacherib, it is for that reason that Jeremiah prophesies here that at the time of the Great Return the former will join the latter and they shall come together from the North to the Holy Land.

Everything becomes clear when one examines the first words of this passage: 'And now, in these very days when I am writing this commentary. . .'. The care which Isaac Abravanel took in dating his manuscripts permits us to date 'these very days' precisely. The commentary on Jeremiah was finished on the eve of Shavuot [Pentecost] 1504. Abravanel was no longer living in the Kingdom of Naples but in Venice, where he arrived in December 1502 on the invitation of his son Joseph who had a good reputation as a doctor there. If he had devoted the year 1503 and part of 1504 to writing his commentaries on the major prophets, this literary work had been accompanied by considerable political and economic activity whose reflection is to be found precisely in these few lines of commentary on a difficult verse of Jeremiah. From 1498 onwards, the Portuguese had begun to take part in the great voyages of discovery. Vasco da Gama's first voyages took place in

1498, Cabral's expedition in 1500, Vasco da Gama's second voyage in 1502. In those few years, the Portuguese had taken possession of the Spice Islands (the Moluccas). There was much anxiety in Venice, which was seriously threatened by this competitor in the spice trade. The long route from Venice to the Indies via Arabia was short-circuited by the direct Lisbon–Calicut return route via the Cape of Good Hope.

When Joseph invited his father to settle in Venice, he was fully aware of Don Isaac's remarkable diplomatic capabilities. Had he not, until 1484, been counsellor to the Kings of Portugal, and later to the Kings of Castile and Aragon, and then to the King of Naples? The time now seemed to be ripe to place these talents at the disposal of the Republic of Venice, and, indeed, he did his very best to try to bring about a commercial agreement between Venice and Portugal, a kind of treaty of division of the seas allowing each of these two powers to extract the maximum benefit from the discovery of the new sea-routes. The Venetians, who were obviously the party most interested in signing such a treaty, soon gave a sympathetic hearing to Isaac Abravanel's ideas, and on 12 August 1503 the Council of Ten entrusted him in writing with the delicate mission of entering into negotiations with the Portuguese. The latter, however, were more cautious. What had they to gain from this partition? Yet, for all that, King Manuel of Portugal nevertheless agreed to receive Joseph Abravanel, a nephew of Don Isaac, invested with full diplomatic powers by his uncle, just as he himself had received them from the Doge of Venice.

Such were the memorable 'days' of 1503 and 1504 when Don Isaac Abravanel was deeply engaged in his last diplomatic battle while writing his commentary on the prophets.[12]

Once again, this might have been a suitable occasion to mention in his commentary, side by side with the Portuguese discoveries, those of Christopher Columbus, the first to open up the 'spice route' concerning which Abravanel was then trying to secure a commercial agreement between Venice and Portugal. But Spain was just left out of the picture, in the same way as it had been on a recent occasion in Isaac Abravanel's life. In the period between his

---

[12] See D. Kaufmann, 'Don Isaac Abravanel et le commerce des épices avec Calicut', *REJ*, xxxviii, pp. 145–8. See also B. Netanyahu, *Don Isaac Abravanel* (Philadelphia, 1953), p. 6, which calls attention to another 'obliteration' on Abravanel's part: his suppression of all reference to the conversion of his grandfather Samuel.

arrival in Naples in 1492 following his expulsion from Spain and his settlement—at the end of 1502—in Venice, where he was to remain until his death in 1508, his existence had been full of vicissitudes. The King of Naples, Ferrante, had received the Jews graciously, but he himself had been forced to flee from Naples before a French offensive. Abravanel and his family followed the king first to Sicily and then to Monopoli, a little port on the Adriatic, midway between Brindisi and Bari. Politically, Monopoli was soon to be swept into the Venetian sphere of influence, but the town remained legally attached to the Kingdom of Naples which Federigo, the grandson of Ferrante, took over in 1501. Meanwhile the Spanish, allied to the Venetians, had laid their hands on Sicily, whose governor, Gonsalvo de Castille, re-entered into contact with the Abravanels; and when he seized Naples with the aid of the armies of Louis XII in 1501, he sent Abravanel a carefully drawn-up proposition, giving him the option either of returning to Naples under Spanish authority or of remaining in Monopoli, which the French and Spanish had left to the Venetians. Peace having returned, Naples, the capital, had again become accessible to Don Isaac Abravanel. A nephew of Abravanel had already prepared the way, but Don Isaac chose to remain in Monopoli which, as we have seen, he was to leave only in 1503 when he was given the opportunity to settle in Venice.

Thus, 'noes to Spain' multiplied both in the life and in the work of Isaac Abravanel, and these were paralleled by his 'yeses' to Portugal. There is no doubt that this was a matter of systematic and deliberate choice. Both in thought and in life, we see here a process of deliberate obliteration. Abravanel, of his own free will, attempted to expunge Spain from his life and thought.

However, in so far as Spain was rapidly losing the privilege of being the only maritime power to engage in the discovery of new sea-routes to India, Abravanel was led to take a lively interest in that process with which he was one of the Jews to be most closely associated, first as a reality experienced in his own flesh and blood, and then as a *sign* of eschatological significance.

It was a completely transformed Isaac Abravanel who set foot on Italian soil. He immediately felt that the expulsion of which he and his people had been the victims was an event of a different kind from the expulsion of the Jews from England in 1290 or from France in 1394. Isaac Abravanel was one of the first contemporaries of the second of August 1492—a date which coincided in the Jewish calendar with the ninth of Ab, date of the fall of the First Temple in 568 BCE and the fall of the Second Temple in 70 CE; he was one of the first contemporaries to see it as the date of the fall of the Third Temple.

Besides his commentary on the Book of Kings in the preface of which he expounded this idea, Abravanel devoted his first years of exile to the frenzied writing of a Messianic trilogy, one of whose original features was to bring back into the foreground of history a theme which at that period had only a purely formal significance, but which, thanks to him, became a factor to be reckoned with: the Lost Ten Tribes. This became a factor not only of eschatological but of real history, for Abravanel was convinced that the days of the Messiah were at hand: he calculated the date of his coming as 1503. It has often been pointed out that in giving his people this trilogy, Abravanel was offering it something more than simply an original work: he was giving it new hope. Out of the greatest depths of the catastrophe, Don Isaac Abravanel, like the great biblical prophets of old, perceived the vision of salvation and redemption for which he sought to gain acceptance by his people. Thus, within that general picture in which one may find the most stubbornly optimistic and, for that period, most absurd ideas, a connection was established between the Lost Ten Tribes and the discovery of the New World: a kind of intuition, to which the commentary on Jeremiah 3:18 bears witness, that Providence had prepared a route which would sooner or later provide some answer to the tragedy of 1492. Abravanel situated the Lost Ten Tribes in Central Asia in accordance with the account in the Bible which the discovery of the New World had not yet displaced by one iota.

But here they appear, after a long eclipse, in association with a group of Judean tribes which had also been lost and were rediscovered through the opening-up of the new sea-routes. Thus the work of Isaac Abravanel constitutes a turning-point.

Behind the historical fabric in which the Jews were so intimately and dramatically associated with the discovery of the New World, we now discern the mythical backing. Side by side with the biblical and apocalyptic prophecies of Christopher Columbus, which could certainly leave no Jew indifferent but were generally inspired by Christian ideas of redemption, there appears a specifically Jewish theme of redemption: the Lost Ten Tribes.

3

The myth of the New World in the Jewish consciousness: the Ten Tribes lost and rediscovered

THE MYTH OF THE LOST TEN TRIBES BEFORE THE SIXTEENTH CENTURY

IN the same way as the loss of Paradise, for the Christians, was an obsession for which the discovery of the New World was able to provide a catharsis, so the question of the Lost Ten Tribes periodically rose up in the Jewish consciousness associated with the Messianic dreams of which it was one of the negative constituent elements. For the Sambatyon, that impassable river which separated the lost Israel from the remnants of Judah in exile, was not only a geographical boundary: it was an obstacle, one of the most unsurmountable obstacles to the coming of the Messiah. The realization of the moving prophecy of Ezekiel 37: 16–17 concerning the reunion of Judah and Joseph would be the essential prelude to the reunion of the entire Jewish people in its own land. As long as the Ten Tribes were separated from the body of Israel, Israel's soul remained defective.

Would the discovery of the New World with its previously unknown inhabitants restore the body and soul of Israel to a pre-Messianic condition of wholeness? That was the question which the train of events beginning in 1492 raised all the more insistently in that the first to ask it were non-Jews, struck by the affinity between the ancient Hebrew culture and the language, customs, beliefs, and physical characteristics of the new populations which were being discovered (and which were also being annihilated at such a rate that soon this 'Night and Fog' operation, tragic forerunner of the twentieth-century Holocaust, made any serious scientific investigation impossible).

To find a Jewish reaction to the theme of the Lost Ten Tribes one would have, indeed, to go back as far as the account of Eldad the Danite in the ninth century. The sudden appearance of this adventurer upon the scene of history, coinciding, to within a few years, with the appearance of the narratives relating the conversion of the Khazars, had a profound, if short-lived effect.[1] From the tenth century, when the Jews moved towards a preoccupation, in the Sephardic world, with philosophy and, in the Ashkenazic world, with Talmudic commentary—or, if one prefers, from the time of Saadiah Gaon and Rashi—the theme of the Lost Ten Tribes had ceased to have any real existence for the Jews. In the golden age of Spanish Jewry and the period of the Crusades it had become a purely abstract item comparable to a bibliographical reference which no philosopher or serious commentator would dare to omit, but which is not given the importance due only to a theme of vital interest. There was no longer any emphasis on the idea of loss and separation implicit in the theme of the Lost Ten Tribes, no doubt because the general concept of Messianism (of which the Ten Tribes were only one element among many) was being increasingly rationalized, and in a system like that of Maimonides had become a belief which exists in the mind without affecting the soul. In the Middle Ages, Jewish eschatology had become an abstraction without a historical substructure, without vital emotional associations even for the *Kabbalah*, which like Christian mysticism operated in the cosmos rather than in history.

It was only the sixteenth century which provided the shock that set loose Jewish Messianism which, like the Sleeping Beauty, was suddenly to be rudely awakened; and at the same time the Lost Ten Tribes were to find their place again in history.

In our *Puits de l'Exil*[2] we spoke at length of the importance of the year 1492 for the awakening of Jewish Messianism. The expulsion from Spain, experienced right from the start by the victims themselves as an event of eschatological importance, explained the series of Messianic explosions which rocked sixteenth-century Jewry. Extending from the time of Isaac Abravanel who witnessed the expulsion to that of the Maharal of Prague, embracing in one comprehensive sweep the whole of the sixteenth century from 1492 to 1592, the impressive series of flesh-and-blood Messiahs

---

[1] It had its deepest effect upon the Christians who, as a response to the story of Eldad, invented the myth of Prester John (see pp. 139 ff.).

[2] Pp. 78 ff.

appearing every twenty or thirty years, none of whom—it cannot be overstressed—was ever regarded or treated as a false Messiah, and the equally impressive series of Messianic theories which, especially in Safed, were tested against historico-mystical reality: all this was a direct result of the trauma of the expulsion of 1492.

This Messianic awakening obviously embraced, among many other themes, that of the Lost Ten Tribes. But we feel it is even more obvious that the Ten Tribes should have come to the forefront of Jewish history on account of the other event for which the ambivalent year 1492 is celebrated: not the expulsion of the Jews from Spain, but the discovery of the New World. This is to be plainly seen—as we shall discover—in the association of the theme of the Lost Ten Tribes with America in the Maharal of Prague; but we feel that a logical chain of development leads from the beginning of the sixteenth century to its end, from Columbus to the Maharal of Prague. We shall try to reconstruct the links in this chain in attempting to describe the internal evolution of what appears to have been a real psychosis, whereas our predecessors have offered us only a list of texts without any apparent logical connection between them.

Looking at the material in hand, we find that our predecessors seem to have bequeathed us a kind of bibliographical card index in which the theme of the Lost Ten Tribes appears periodically among the Jewish accounts of the discovery of America in the sixteenth century, but that this theme has not been studied as something in itself. It often even happens that because the texts have not been placed in their correct context, their associations with this theme which gave a meaning to certain passages, otherwise incomprehensible or absurd, went completely unnoticed.

We are thus going to change the general understanding of the subject, always bearing in mind something that we had occasion to mention before: namely, that the men of the sixteenth century gained their knowledge of the voyages of Columbus, Vespucci, Magellan, Vasco da Gama, and so many others in successive waves, one superimposed upon the other, and that the fragmentary descriptions they left owe as much to the mythical, subjective imagination as to objective, scientific reality.

THE IMAGE OF THE NEW WORLD BEFORE DAVID GANS:
ABRAHAM FARISSOL, JOSEPH HA-KOHEN,
GEDALIAH IBN YAḤYA

There is not a great deal about the discovery and the reality of the New World in Jewish sources before David Gans. He was both the first Jewish cosmographer and the first Jewish historian to offer a really new and complete account of the known world. We have no names to add to the list drawn up by Mendel Silber in his book *American Jewish Literature* (New Orleans, 1928), and in his article 'America (Discovery of), in Jewish Literature' in the *Universal Jewish Encyclopaedia* (New York, 1940).

The titles listed are *Iggeret Orḥot Olam* by Abraham ben Mordecai Farissol (Ferrara, 1524); *Sefer Divrei ha-Yamim* by Joseph Ha-Kohen (Sabionetta, 1554) and the manuscript by the same author entitled *Maẓiv Gevulot Ammim* and dated 1557; and *Shalshelet ha-Kabbalah* by Gedaliah ibn Yaḥya (Venice, 1587). By that date, one has already reached the period when Azariah dei Rossi and David Gans were publishing their own works.

All these Jewish authors were mentioned by David Gans himself. Through them, he also gained knowledge of a certain number of geographical works by non-Jewish cosmographers and particularly those which Joseph Ha-Kohen quoted in translation in his *Maẓiv Gevulot Ammim*: namely, *Omnium Gentium Mores Leges et Ritus* by Jan Boemus (Augsburg, 1520) and the two volumes of the *Historia general de las Indias* by Francisco Lopez de Gomara (Antwerp, 1554).[3] To these two sources one must naturally add the letters of Amerigo Vespucci, quoted by Abraham Farissol. Several were published before 1512 in Vespucci's lifetime; others, authentic or apocryphal, were circulated throughout Europe in the first half of the sixteenth century.[4]

We concur with Mendel Silber's opinion that the geographical description of the New World in Jewish writers before David Gans

[3] Joseph Ha-Kohen's manuscript is to be found in the library of the Alliance Israélite Universelle in Paris. It has been described by Isidore Loeb in 'Joseph Hacohen et les chroniqueurs juifs', *REJ*, xvi, 31 (1888), pp. 29–32. It is a pity that Loeb did not extend this admirable study (*REJ*, xvi, 31 pp. 28–56; 32, pp. 211–35; 33, pp. 74–95; 34, pp. 247–71) to include David Gans.

[4] Cf. F. A. de Varnhagen, *Amerigo Vespucci, son caractère, ses écrits (même les moins authentiques), sa vie et ses navigations* (Lima, 1865), and C. H. Coote, *The voyage from Lisbon to India 1505–6, being an Account and Journal by Albertus Vespuccius* (London, 1894).

as well as in their sources is naïve, fantastic, and incomplete. The terminology of Joseph Ha-Kohen, to take only one example, is still primitive: he does not refer to America but to the Spanish Indies or the New Indies. We shall see that David Gans was greatly indebted to the posthumous editions of Sebastian Munster's *Cosmography*, and especially to the world maps of Gerard Mercator and Abraham Ortelius which appeared from 1570 onwards.[5]

But we disagree totally with Silber when he attempts to separate this distortion of reality from the theme of the Lost Ten Tribes. In Farissol or Joseph Ha-kohen this theme is not something separate from that of America, as Silber suggests, but on the contrary is one of the principal reasons for this distortion in the description of the New World. It was not due solely to a pure and simple lack of information, but also to a certain psychological orientation in the minds of these Jewish writers produced by the fascination of the Messianic myth of the Lost Ten Tribes.

We shall attempt to demonstrate this fact with regard to Abraham Farissol, taken as an example because David Gans himself misunderstood his intentions. He said he failed to understand a gross error of geography committed by Farissol in 1524.[6] He was no longer able to understand it, we should explain, because in 1592, when he published his *Zemah David* which contains this criticism of Farissol, David Gans could no longer fathom why or how the theme of the Lost Ten Tribes could fascinate a Jewish writer to such a degree as to completely obliterate the frontiers between myth and reality.

THE APPEARANCE OF THE LOST TEN TRIBES IN AMERICA AT THE BEGINNING OF THE SIXTEENTH CENTURY

We shall began by noting certain facts which will enable us to grasp the evolution of the theme of the Lost Ten Tribes at its two extremities in time and help us to discover its inner relationship with the discovery of the New World.

At the beginning, we have a Spanish manuscript from Seville quoted in full by Kayserling,[7] which begins with a clear affirmation that the American Indians and the Lost Ten Tribes are one and the

---

[5] See Chap. II. 5.   [6] *Zemah David*, 32b.   [7] See bibliography.

same. The manuscript reads: 'The Indians of the Isles and mainland of the Oceanic Sea which are now under the suzerainty of the Royal Crown of Castile are Hebrews, descended from the Lost Ten Tribes of Israel.' I shall pass over the continuation which in four long pages explains the reasons for this identity: the similarity of the language (the Indian *caciq* is the Hebrew *qatsin*), of certain rites (circumcision, ablutions, the levirate marriage, fasts, abstention from blood), and the bastardized character of a religion associating the adoration of a supreme Divinity with the grossest idolatry such as the Bible attributes to the Lost Ten Tribes exiled by Shalmaneser. Such, at any rate, are the foundations on which until our days have been constructed the serious or ludicrous theories of the supposed identity of the American Indians with the Tribes of Israel.

A remarkable and, in a way, disappointing fact is that this manuscript cannot be precisely dated. It is undoubtedly of the sixteenth century, but there is nothing which allows it to be dated with exactitude; it is also impossible to date with precision another source, the writings of the Bishop of Quito, Luis Lopez, in which a certain Antonio Montezino of Lima is quoted as making similar assertions. We therefore have at least two sources, both non-Jewish (unless Montezino was a Marrano, which is probable), running across the sixteenth century in a chronologically untraceable manner and culminating in a work which appeared in Valencia in 1607 at the beginning of the seventeenth century, *Origen de los Indios del Nuevo Mundo*. The author, Gregorio Garcia, also a Christian, claimed categorically: the natives of America are the descendants of the Tribes of Israel.

It was the outcome of a discovery as amazing as the discovery of America itself. Upon the geographical revelation there was superimposed an anthropological revelation of an obviously Messianic and even apocalyptic character.

It should be pointed out that this discovery of what I might call a 'Jewish Atlantis' first traumatized the Christian consciousness, or, at any rate, traumatized it more deeply than the Jewish consciousness. One can easily discern two opposite tendencies in the Spanish Christian writings on the subject. One saw the discovery of Jews in America as a positive element on the path to Salvation: Las Casas, Sahagun, Garcia himself take this point of view. On the other hand, Torquemada, Gomara, Cortez, Diaz saw this discovery as the work

of Satan, an obstacle to redemption and to the conversion of the
New World to Christianity (the missionaries were sent to Mexico
only after a certain lapse of time, precisely because of this
unexpected presence of Jews in the new territories!). This whole
controversy was steeped in the atmosphere, charged with providential
and Messianic electricity, characteristic of the historiography of the
West Indies in the sixteenth century. Columbus and Cortez were
regarded as apostles appointed to bring the Word to the Gentiles of
the New World; but what should one do with the Jews mingled with
these Gentiles? A real debate began, comparable to the one of the
period of the Apostle Paul. Which was the True Israel? The
Church, alighting in full sail upon a continent still innocent of
evangelization, or this Remnant of Israel obstinately embedded in
that continent which claimed to be the spokesman of the God of the
Bible?

Jacques Lafaye has given a brilliant impression of this seething
cauldron of ideas and of the ideological and sociological problems
which it raised in the Christian mind, and we refer the interested
reader to his text and bibliographical notes and to the references in
the bibliography at the end of this book.

1648: THE MYTH BECOMES HISTORICAL REALITY

To grasp the repercussions of this theme for the sixteenth-century
Jewish consciousness, let us examine it at the end of the period. It
first made its appearance about the first third of the sixteenth
century, and in the middle of the seventeenth century we find it
again, this time in a source that is unquestionably Jewish.

In the full light of day and with a meticulous chronological
precision, the Lost Ten Tribes were situated in America in the
celebrated testimony of another Antonio de Montezinos who *was* a
Marrano and had returned to Judaism under the name of Aaron
Levi. On 18 August 1644, Aaron Levi solemnly assured the
rabbinical tribunal in Amsterdam that while staying in the
equatorial regions near Quito he met Indians who practised Jewish
religious ceremonies, recited the Shema and claimed to belong to
the tribe of Reuben, and other Indians who claimed to be Levites
and embraced Montezinos warmly when he said he was not a
Christian but a member of the tribe of Levi, just as they were.

Menasseh ben Israel used this testimony of Aaron Levi as an

introduction to his *Sefer Mikveh Israel* (*The Book of the Hope of Israel*) which he published six years later in 1650, with the intention of presenting to Cromwell and his entourage his great idea of Jewish 'resettlement' in England for the purpose of hastening the coming of the Messiah—an event as eagerly awaited by the Puritans as by the Jews. Did not this event have as its essential precondition the dispersion of the Jews to the four corners of the earth (an idea which Menasseh ben Israel had gathered from the mystics of Safed and had transposed into political terms), and was not the existence of Jews in the New World, *finis terrae incognitae* (the end of the unknown world) an important milestone in this dispersion, of which another important milestone would be the presence of Jews in England, *finis terrae cognitae* (the end of the known world)?

We should at any rate carefully note the following fact: the theme of the exile of the Lost Ten Tribes in America gained its importance in Jewish history for Messianic reasons and at a Messianic moment: 1648, the date predicted by the *Zohar* for the coming of the Messiah, the date of the first premature 'revelation' of Shabbetai Zevi at Smyrna, and finally the time when Cromwell's accession to power presented an unhoped-for historic opportunity for the return, for Messianic reasons, of the Jews expelled from England.

Does not all this suggest to us that this whole theme of the Lost Ten Tribes rediscovered in the New World from the sixteenth century onwards should be placed in a Messianic context? We feel that Abraham Farissol's *Iggeret Orḥot Olam*, so ill-understood by David Gans, provides an outstanding proof of it. This book binds together into one the three themes: America, the Lost Ten Tribes, and the Messiah.

This interconnection is so blatantly obvious that I am surprised that no one has yet noticed it. And yet Farissol was by no means unknown, and some slight investigation of his psychology could long ago have brought his particular preoccupation to light.

THE INTERLUDE OF MYTH IN ABRAHAM FARISSOL: ITS PART IN THE HISTORICAL EPISODE OF DAVID REUBENI AND SOLOMON MOLCHO (1524-33)

In his Preface, Farissol presents his *Iggeret Orḥot Olam* (Epistle Concerning the Routes of the World) as a modest cosmography:

modest in scale (thirty chapters consisting of seventy-two quarto pages) and modest in its intentions. If there are so many books about wars or romances, he asks, why not entertain readers by a description of the world? And if astronomy is so esteemed which gives a picture of the routes of the heavens, why should geography be less so, which traces maps of the routes of the earth?

Already on the title-page, however, we are informed that this cosmography deals with the three known continents, Asia, Africa, and Europe, and with 'distant islands, recently discovered by the Portuguese fleets in the southern hemisphere', and also contains information 'on the river Sambatyon, on the territories where the captive Jews may be found, on the frontiers of the Land of Israel, and on the location of the earthly paradise'.

These few lines are enough to give us an idea of the tone of the book in which ancient and modern geographical facts are intermingled with myths and legends. This simple juxtaposition of elements should no doubt be sufficient to alert us and to convince us that in this little book we possess a most valuable testimony of the mentality of a learned Jew of that period and his reaction to the new maritime discoveries.

We feel it is precisely because they have seen it simply as a juxtaposition and not as a construction that historians have failed to understand the chief point of interest of this little book—the first, we repeat, to give an account of the discovery of America in Hebrew.

This occurs in the last chapter but one, the twenty-ninth, immediately followed by the concluding chapter, devoted to the hypothetical location of the earthly paradise. If this twenty-ninth chapter is isolated and disconnected from its context, it can be seen as a parenthesis: interesting, certainly, but apparently unrelated to all that precedes and follows it. In it the author seems to relate in passing all that he knows by hearsay about the discovery of the Great New World (*Olam Ḥadash ha-Gadol*):

About twenty years ago now, this discovery was made by explorers in the service of the King of Portugal. I was fortunate enough to be in Florence in the period of Prince Lorenzo de Medici when the Sovereign the Sultan of Egypt sent him a gift consisting of a giraffe, spices and balm, and when a long account was given in the presence of his son Pietro of the existence of a vast continent to the south of the equator. Similarly, I have seen with my own eyes here in Ferrara in the period of Duke Ercole a navigator who sailed on this southern Ocean for nearly twenty years and confirmed the discovery of this great southern continent . . .[8]

The description he gives of it is realistic and objective in character. Except in the last lines, where the believer's admiration for the amazing works of the Creator expresses itself, we hardly sense the involvement of a man who has a subjective interest in the subject, still less of a Jew who is personally concerned. And yet, how alive and poignant this chapter becomes, how it appears to spring up out of the depths of the author's Jewish soul, when it is connected to the rest of the book!

One has only to replace this 'New World'—which is wild and to some degree meta-human and in any case devoid of any special Jewish significance—within the context of Abraham Farissol's cosmography, and several points of equal importance immediately come to light. The first is that chapter 29, the one on the 'New World', is the last but one of Farissol's book. It is followed by a final chapter devoted to the problem of the location of the biblical Paradise. This *Gan Eden* (Garden of Eden), concerning which Jewish tradition was divided, some sages believing that it was locatable on the earth and others that its location was purely allegorical, had ceased to be merely a Utopia. With the discovery of the New World, the gates had been opened on a real Paradise, on an Eden situated in one of the continents recently discovered, or one of those which still would be. It was the transition from the hope to the reality of Paradise which Christopher Columbus had dreamt of. Our Jewish writer readopted this dream: the architecture of his book makes this sufficiently clear since it makes the discovery or rather the rediscovery of the Lost Paradise to be the logical and ultimate consequence of the discovery of the New World. But Farissol gave this theme of universal significance a purely Jewish interpretation, and this is the second point that arises from a study of his book.

In the chapters one might describe as 'classical'—that is to say, those in which Farissol seems to be content to recall the fundamental known facts about the geography of the continents— the writer piles up numbers of 'confusions' which, if one looks

---

[8] The event in Florence must have taken place in the reign of Lorenzo II de Medici (1492–1519). Ercole was Duke of Ferrara from 1471 to 1505. See David B. Ruderman, *The World of a Renaissance Jew: The Life and Thought of Abraham ben Mordecai Farissol* (Cincinnati, 1981).

closely, are really vistas of new horizons, a broadening-out of territories which were vaster, more interrelated than was thought hitherto. It was as if Farissol had sought to break the feeling of constriction, almost of suffocation, produced by the classical division of the world into the three continents of Europe, Asia, and Africa, opening windows, imagining routes by sea and land which enabled these continents to be circumvented or reached by new ways. The classical medieval map of the world had become a puzzle.

It is to be regretted that Farissol did not attempt the cartography of that puzzle. His little book does contain a map: the very clumsy one of the 'New World' described in chapter 29 which gives some sort of account of Farissol's idea of South America; but, reading between the lines of the chapters devoted to the recent voyages of discovery of the Spanish and Portuguese, it would not be too difficult to draw a map of what in 1524 might have been called 'The Old World reconstituted'. And one can also follow the complex pattern of the events which Farissol refers to, basing himself largely on 'the new maps of the world drawn up with so much artistry in Germany, Venice, and Florence' (end of chapter fifteen), and, above all, on a source which he often mentions, *Olam Ḥadash* (New World), which, he said, had appeared a few years before in Vicenza (the Venetian edition of 1586 wrongly states Venice instead of Vicenza).[9] This could only be the *Novus Mundus* of Amerigo Vespucci, the famous letters of the 'inventor' of America which appeared in Italian in *Paesi novamente retrovati*, published in Vicenza in 1507. It is likely that Farissol had this work in front of him and extracted from it (we shall soon understand why) the elements of his reconstruction of the world.

From the historical point of view, it was Vespucci's second voyage (in September 1500) which particularly interested him: the one which led to the *re*discovery of Brazil, for Brazil had already been discovered in the spring of that year by Cabral. The two fleets met in mid-ocean, and Vespucci enthusiastically described how, thanks to his conversations with Cabral's pilot Gaspar, he came to learn of the existence of the peninsula of Malacca, the farthest point of that immense Empire of the Indies, replete with gold, pearls, spices, and Muslim and Jewish populations, the latter of

---

[9] *Olam Ḥadash* by the 'great Christian scholar' is referred to in several places in chapters fifteen and twenty-four.

whom were rich and opulent. Geographically, Brazil was then regarded as part of that Empire of the Indies: it was the eastern part, while the western part, still as little known and exploited as the eastern, extended 'from Calicut to Lamic', to use Farissol's favourite expression. Here, in fact, we have a remarkable example of the new picture of the world which a learned Italian rabbi could have had, or perhaps wanted to have, after the great maritime discoveries of a quarter of a century previously. Everything, for him, centred on the Indies, which had now been reached by the western route. The crucial event, to which Farissol returns continually, was the discovery of the route along the east coast of Ethiopia and Arabia Felix to the Indies, whose area increased as the explorers penetrated further and further.

Farissol did not mention Bartolomeo Diaz, Vasco da Gama, and Cabral in this connection, but he was convinced that Amerigo Vespucci had made the same voyage as they had, and that he, too, had rounded the Cape of Good Hope and reached the Indies where there floated the Portuguese standard planted by Albuquerque.

Where did Farissol get what one might almost call this obsession with the route round the Cape of Good Hope? From several causes of mounting importance which we should have no difficulty in understanding if we only take the trouble to read Farissol's cosmography with the eyes of the author: that is to say, with the eyes of a Jew living in Ferrara in Italy in the year 1524. And this is our third and most crucial point.

We should begin with the short chapter (number ten) which describes the geographical frontiers of the Land eternally dear to Jewish hearts: the Land *par excellence*, Erez Israel. In this geography of the Holy Land, which could obviously not be omitted in a cosmography written by a Jew, the 'restoration' took on extraordinary proportions, as if the writer were making a new version, with new colours and dimensions, of some classic painting by an old master. If there has ever been an expansive physical description of the Greater Israel of the age of Solomon and of biblical prophetic visions, it is in this miniature by Abraham Farissol. Everything is bursting apart and overflowing: the Jordan and the Red Sea, naturally, but also the Euphrates, the Mediterranean, Asia, Africa . . . The frontiers of the Holy Land are not limits but indicative arrows running across deserts and oceans. They indicate the great route 'from Lamic to Calicut', towards regions which bear the fascinating names of the East and West Indies.[10]

Such are the frontiers of Ereẓ Israel. It should be understood: the ultimate, Messianic frontiers within which the exiled and dispersed shall be gathered in. This brief chapter ends with the prophetic declaration that the Jews will return by way of the sea (Isaiah 18: 1–2): or, that is to say, by way of the neck of the Red Sea which had now become available through the great route to the Indies round the bottom of Africa. The fleets of the exiles of Europe, Asia, and Africa will meet somewhere (like the fleets of Cabral and Vespucci!) and enter triumphally into the home port, not by way of the Mediterranean but by the great trans-Ocean route.

In the midst of these vast lands, within the maze of continents and oceans, live Jews: innumerable, mighty, strong Jews such as have never been known, and whose existence had now been revealed by the accounts of Vespucci.

Did Farissol know that Gaspar, the man from whom Amerigo Vespucci received all his information, was the Jew we described earlier who had been forced to convert by Vasco da Gama, rendered him enormous services, and then took part in Cabral's expedition of 1500 and thus entered into contact with Vespucci? This would mean introducing a Marrano element into Farissol's cosmography: one finds it difficult to understand what could have prevented him from speaking about it openly. Let us assume, then, that it is more probable that Farissol was unaware of the Jewish origins of the pilot Gaspar, but that the information supplied by

[10] The term *Lamic* which Farissol always uses together with *Calicut* is an enigma whose solution seems to me to lie in an intentional confusion in Farissol's mind. The simplest interpretation of Lamic is Mecca, but Farissol specifically gives it this identification only once in his book (this was already pointed out by Thomas Hyde, the learned librarian of the Bodleian Library, who published a Latin translation of the book of Abraham Peritsol (*sic*) in Oxford in 1691, with many instructive notes). Elsewhere, the term is ambiguous. Sometimes it refers to a Mecca which stretches towards the Persian Gulf, in which case the expression 'from Mecca to Calicut' indicates the last lap of the sea-route from Portugal to the Indies via the Cape of Good Hope, and sometimes—as is obviously the case in chapter twenty-four—Lamic is situated beyond Calicut in those parts of Asia which extend to the areas where the East Indies become confused with the West Indies. In this case, I think that the term Lamic as used by Farissol is a deformation either of the Moluccas or, more likely, of the Malacca peninsula, often mentioned by Vespucci in relation with Calicut (see Varnhagen, p. 62 and especially Coote, p. xi, who noticed the same ambiguity in Vespucci himself, who sometimes correctly sited 'Melaccha' to the east of Calicut and sometimes sited it to its west!) Once again, there is a psychologically intentional ambivalence. The expansion of the frontiers of the Holy Land had a similar effect upon those of Arabia, and both were the result of the volcanic eruption of the whole earth caused by the recent discoveries of the new continents.

Gaspar to Vespucci contributed to an idea which in Farissol's cosmography was not a mere parenthesis, like the geography of the Holy Land or the account of the Portuguese voyages, but runs through it from end to end.

This idea is the theme of the Lost Ten Tribes: a myth which, as we said, is the Jewish version of the myth of Atlantis and which came back to life with the great maritime discoveries of the fifteenth and sixteenth centuries.

Farissol first introduced the theme of the Lost Ten Tribes in chapter 14 of his cosmography, for reasons which will soon become clear to us. From that point onwards, he no longer left it: traces of it remain in his description of recent discoveries, and it occupies the foreground in chapter 24 and the following chapters which are devoted once more to a geographical 'restoration'. The site of the Kingdom of the Lost Ten Tribes and the River Sambatyon which divides it from the known world, and the sociological character of that kingdom, are described with an exactitude which admits no contradiction. These Jews whose existence Gaspar revealed to Amerigo Vespucci, these powerful, noble Jews who walk upright and not with bowed head in the midst of Muslims and Christians, these Jews of the New Indies 'beyond Calicut and Lamic' are the Jews of the Kingdom of Israel. They are not mythical; their land is not a Utopia. Here they are in flesh and blood with their precious River Sambatyon on the map of the New Indies extending as far as Tibet, as Siberia, as those arctic regions which have remained unexplored until this very day, but where there are also masses of Jews 'enclosed' in their solitude.

These Jews who were 'closed in' or rather 'prisoners' (*segurim*) were the Lost Ten Tribes before whom Alexander the Great had already trembled, constructing a Great Wall (the Great Wall of China?) to prevent them from invading the pagan, or, rather, the Christian world, for here we are dealing not with the historical Alexander but with Alexander as a pagan converted to Christianity, as he appears in the romances woven around him in the Middle Ages. In medieval maps and even many maps of the sixteenth century we see this Wall of Alexander with the territories of the Danites and Gadites beyond it: i.e., the territories of the Jewish tribes of Dan and Gad.[11]

[11] See Oscar Peschel, *Geschichte der Erdkunde bis auf A. V. Humbolt und Carl Ritter* (Munich, 1865).

Prague: General view in the sixteenth century   *A. Neher Collection*

Statue erected in 1912 by Ladislas Salun (a non-Jewish sculptor) in tribute to the
Maharal of Prague, at the Prague Town Hall. This statue is no longer in existence

Nicholas Copernicus (1475–1543)   *National and University Library, Jerusalem*

IOANNIS KEPPLERI,
Mathematici Cæsarei,
hanc Imaginem.

ARGENTORATENSI BIBLIOTHECÆ
Conficr.

MATTHIAS BERNECCERVS.
Kal. Ianuar. Anno Chr.

M DC. XXVII

Johannes Kepler, the only authentic portrait (1627), dedicated to his friend
Mathias Bernegger of the Fondation Saint Thomas at Strasburg, where it still is
Fondation Saint Thomas, Strasburg

Tycho Brahe: Sovereign of his observatory *A. Neher Collection*

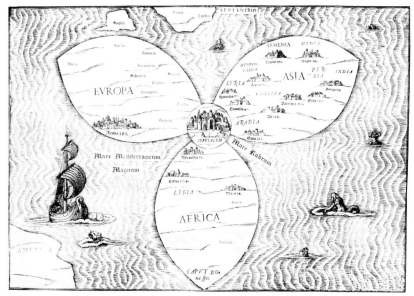

(*a*) Jerusalem as centre of the world: Map in trefoil shape, by Heinrich Buenting, Helmstedt (1581). The tip of the American continent is shown *A. Neher Collection*

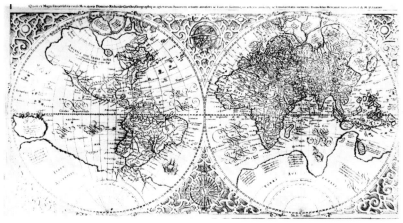

(*b*) *Mappa Mundi*: From the *Theatrum orbis terrarum* of Abraham Ortelius, ed. princeps, Antwerp (1570). One of David Gans's constant works of reference *A. Neher Collection*

שהגל קו א"ב גבר ע"ג ותאחר חלקים בטובך הם
ם"ם בכ"ב בשבעל הקטן תר"ף פסיעות בקו הטובך
ממטולג הגדול כמה הם גגיבב מטטולם כנגדן הם וינח
לך פות הכ בב גגדול ש"ע פסיעות ולדעת נ בה המגדול
בעומד בבתוך תהיה מקף ט מלכב הרשיין וזנקוידים ח' עד
נקודת ה' וזה מד שחתך הבריח נ ו"ז חלקם מתא"ף והנה
יתהנו נדה כ' מטולבים מד בתים ה'ל' ככלי ובב' חלבה לב
ע"ב תיהם ותתאור תל"ף ה-לקים בטובך הב ל"ם בכלב
תר"ף פסיע'כטובע'כטובב הב בגגיבב ונלא ל' רכ"ו פסיע'
וכ' טלישית ממשבר זה תאחר ממטבר פטיעות גובה סהר
שהגל קו א"ב בבבר בלחת אותו ט"מ פסיעות יטאר לך
מדת נוטב המגדול קל"ג פסיעותא' פסיעות :

סימן רפ"א
יתבאר בו המדידה כאשר לא תוכל
לילך אחר כ כמו למדוד מן המגדול לעומק :

לעמוד   במגדל ח' העומד על בגגד ולמדד בו עומק
הבקעה ונכה בגגד העומד בבכאב תחזה
מתיחתיות המגדל מנקודת פ' אל   נקודת ב' טטארה

ולהומר שחתך הבריח הכלי לשנים שהם תל"ך חלקים אח"כ
תעלה על ראש המגדול ותחזה סם חנק דת ג' עד נק דת
ב' וסם יחתוך הבריח ע'ל"מ ה"ר חלקים אל"ב המספר
הממדע שטין ב'המספרים הם קכ"ח חלקים ונאמר שגובה
המגדול כנכותם ח' עד נקודת ג' עד ט' חאם מלעדים וכבר
תבאר בשער' רפטקר מקטר המגונד שהגל ק"ן סלקים למקטר

סימן רפ"ב
יתבאר בו הדרושי הבדידות ע"י נלי
מהזים כאשר הם שוכבים עס רב תועלתם :

ואתה   הקורא ידוע תדע לך שכל המדידות שבאחרנו
למעלה כולם הם ע"י כלי מהזים כאשר פם
זקופים ועתה אבחר לך מדידות הורגגיבה ועשב ע"י כלי
מש'ים כאשר הם שוכבים ות'ע'פ שהמדיד' הם הוא מעט
יותר סודד מכללים וזקופים מ"מ תזע בקטמדיה הכ בהם יותר
מעולים ומשובחים יקרים וכטובדים ובונקדקים
יותר במדדות ע"י כל כל מחזים זקופ'כזה מטע מי'
רבים הם' שע"י לימודים אלו שלפנינו יתבאר
לתלמידים חוסקוי מכמאה זו טעם כל דבר וירגלה לב
שב' מלביט זה אחד וה אז זה למעלה מזה לו אז בבד
זה הכל ש ר רם וע קר אל'הם סבית בכתור תבקף לדישת
גובה המגדול חו רותב סנבר או שרד סעה ובלא תוכל
לקרב אליו ונם בלא תוכל לילך מאחרין לעטל"פ תוכל
למדוד נבכו או רחבו ע"י' מ' ביב זה בבד זה אסר
דכר זה טדין לא כתבאר למעלה בליטדים וטלישית
סעה המדידה זה בכתדבה יותר יתבאר לך נם בידת
הבתרמק סמין כ'מגדל ם אף רם אז הקרב לטוש א'
פטי רביעית בה'יית כאשר הם בטובך הבמרחק וזגוך
מקן הכילב מרחק רב ר'ל' ש'ר'מהם במם ובנם פעמי'
יותר ויותר עד ל' מבהאת 'ס אז אין הבדירה בככ כ"כ
הבומל'את ע"ב כמד'דה ל' שלפנינו תוכל לבאריך
ולהרחיב קו טבוכב כפי רגונך ונתמיל בבדידת הארוך
ב' או סרוחב פהיה המדידות ברדהו ויקרה שבכלב הכה
מגדול ח' טובב בהפירת או ל' וטקטן מנדון על אי חו
ט'לל ח' נקורין בכ"אם דל"ם בחומך כלא מוכל לילך
אחריך חו תעשה סימטי' ע'על בארך ח נך חקף בו 'טולבמת
ותעטיעדים על בטובל ט'ם ה'לוות אך מזה וגריך שעמדו על
קן הטוב שכלאם סטעם בבר ט'ם טיינך ובקר ' סלטן הכ' ותראה על
שולי או שפטם שלמן ב'טבוג סיבו' מנידם על קן יטר גטוה
כאלו היה מבניבם מניבם בלמן ח' סמא חקר הכלי ח'ונת תבנתו על
גכו בקנכם סלמן הרטון ונברים וכלל תם'ם אל קלהא
יתרטקב דרך חורי חורי הבנטטב סון טאונלא ה-רטאון טל מוחת
הבגדול

A diagram from *Neḥmad ve-Na'im*, Brno Manuscript   G. Alter—A. Neher

Tombstone of David Gans, Old Jewish Cemetery, Prague   *A. Neher Collection*

Was there a confusion with the Cochin Jews? Quite possibly. But there was undoubtedly a connection with the idea of a 'Kingdom of Prester John' in Asia, as distinct from the Kingdom of Prester John in Africa.[12] It is known that the myth of Prester John was invented in the twelfth century as a Christian answer to the Jew Eldad the Danite in the eleventh century. Eldad the Danite had claimed that the Kingdom of Ethiopia was ruled by a Jewish sovereign, his brother, and so there appeared the legend of Prester John, a good Christian, slightly given to Judaizing but perfectly submissive to the Pope and, above all, uncontested master of the Jews in his country whom he kept firmly under his control.

In Africa, then, the Jews were the slaves of the Christians when they were not the slaves of the Muslims. But in Asia 'from Calicut to Lamic' and as far as those distant regions where the 'captive' Jews awaited their deliverance, there was another 'Kingdom of Prester John' where the Jews were in effect masters of the Muslims and Christians and where their numbers included not only the rich merchants described by Gaspar to Vespucci and Vasco da Gama, but high dignitaries, diplomats, kings. . .

And, that being the case, everything now becomes comprehensible, everything now comes together in Farissol's book in the light of an event which he witnessed in Italy in 1524 and which he relates in chapter 14, the turning-point of the book: the appearance of David Reuveni, the new Eldad, a true sovereign sent by the Lost Ten Tribes to negotiate with Pope Clement and to propose a kind of crusade in which Christians and Jews, uniting their forces, would overcome the Muslims. The prize that the victory would secure would be rule over Arabia for the Christians, and, for the Jews, the reconquest of the Holy Land, which was theirs by Divine Promise.

While pretending to be neutral in the matter ('I am sceptical by nature and cannot give an opinion concerning the truth of the assertions of this David'), Abraham Farissol could not avoid glowing with pride when, towards the end of the chapter, he related how David Reuveni rode about the streets of Rome on a donkey, preceded and followed by an enthusiastic throng of Jews and Christians, how he entered at all hours and always on donkey-back into the Basilica of St Peter's, and how he was received by Pope Clement VII who gave him letters of recommendation to the King

[12] See Oscar Peschel, pp. 153 ff.

of Portugal so that he could recruit the arms and men for this imminent Judeo-Christian crusade.

At this point, Farissol became so taken up with his theme and so devoid of any 'scepticism' that he decided to intervene, ending chapter 14 by advising David Reuveni not to use the old Mediterranean routes for the conquest of Arabia and the Holy Land, but to take the new routes discovered by the Portuguese navigators, skirting Africa by the Cape of Good Hope and taking Arabia and the Holy Land from behind, from the area of the seas and continents which extend from Lamic to Calicut and from Calicut to Lamic, where there are so many Jews who would doubtless swell the ranks of the expedition.

It is clear that it was the word 'Portugal' which started up this train of thought in Farissol's mind. To his way of thinking, as soon as David Reuveni was sent by the Pope to Portugal, he was necessarily engaged in the process of the revolutionary new discoveries. He would have to pass through 'India', or rather, 'the Indies', through those new-found lands where the union was to take place of the Jews of the Old World and the Jews of the New World, those Jews of the Lost Ten Tribes whom the Portuguese navigators had rediscovered and to whom David Reuveni himself no doubt belonged,[13] to whom he had to belong if his expedition was to have the character—the Messianic character—which he wished to give it and which was hoped for by every Jew on earth.

David Reuveni was definitely to confirm its Messianic character from the time of his meeting, precisely in Portugal, with Solomon Molcho. Molcho, a Marrano originally called Diego Pires, attracted to Reuveni, fled from Portugal, returned openly to the Jewish religion and proclaimed the imminent coming of the Messiah. Everywhere—first in Turkey, then in Safed in the Holy Land, and finally in Italy, where he rejoined David Reuveni—he aroused hope, enthusiasm, and finally belief in his own Messianic vocation. The two men were protected and saved from the Inquisition by

---

[13] Perhaps Joseph Ha-Kohen wished to express this same idea in *Divrei ha-Yamim*, II, 206b (Sabionetta, 1554) when he introduced the story of David Reuveni by saying 'A Jew called David, come from the distant lands of India. . .'. In his famous 'letter of credit', however, David simply said that he had come from Habor and made no mention of India. On Abraham Farissol's lack of scepticism where Messianic matters were concerned, see H. H. Ben-Sasson, 'The Reformation in contemporary Jewish Eyes', *The Israel Academy of Sciences and Humanities Proceedings*, iv (12) (Jerusalem, 1970), pp. 249, 255 ff.

Pope Clement VII, but they failed when they attempted to draw the mighty Emperor Charles V into the adventure. When they came to Ratisbon carrying the standard of the Maccabees, Charles V had them arrested and handed them over to the Inquisition. Solomon Molcho was burned at Mantua as a 'relapsed' heretic in 1532, and David Reuveni probably perished at the stake in Portugal.

Like two great statues, linked by a single Messianic pact of alliance, these two men dominated Jewish history in the sixteenth century. When, within the space of a few months, the flames of the Inquisition consumed them both, Christian Europe had carried out on the very soil of Europe a fragment of that genocide which it was executing at the same time on the soil of the Americas. It had attempted unsuccessfully to nip in the bud the spiritual and historical association which since 1492 had linked Jewish history with that of the Americas.

The episode of David Reuveni and Solomon Molcho took place between 1524 and 1532. Abraham Farissol did not live to see its most dramatic phases. He died in 1525, one year after he had written and published his book whose originality is now clearly apparent to us. Abraham Farissol, with a sort of premonition arising straight out of two contemporary happenings of which he was eyewitness—the appearance of David Reuveni and the discovery of the New World—sensed and described, with all the incoherency but also with all the blinding intuition of a prophet, the poignant encounter between the representatives of two ideas which were the major consequences of the discovery of the New World in the Jewish consciousness: Solomon Molcho, the symbol of the Marranos, and David Reuveni, standard-bearer of the Lost Ten Tribes.

4

The myth of the Lost Ten Tribes towards the end of the sixteenth century: Azariah dei Rossi, the Maharal, David Gans

TOWARDS the year 1600, obsession with the Lost Ten Tribes had reached the trough of the wave. The shock of the events surrounding David Reuveni and Solomon Molcho in the period 1524 to 1532 had abated and had been dissipated in the general theories of Messianic dispersion elaborated in Safed in the second half of the sixteenth century: theories which can be said to have obscured the uniqueness of the destiny of the Lost Ten Tribes by ascribing their fate of 'perdition' to the Jewish people as a whole. According to these theories, it was no longer only the Ten Tribes of Joseph which had been 'lost among the nations'. The Two Tribes of Judah were also lost. If the ever-live sparks of the Ten Tribes of Joseph had smouldered ever since Shalmaneser's time beneath the embers of a kingdom beyond the River Sambatyon, there was now an awareness that the living sparks of the Tribes of Judah, Benjamin and Levi had also been 'hidden' since Titus's time, concealed beneath the embers of the empires of Edom and Ishmael. The Messianic conceptions of the School of Safed had in some way obliterated the difference between the Lost Ten Tribes, hitherto ejected from the course of history, and the other Two Tribes, active in history, by reducing their fate to the same common denominator of 'sleep' in dispersion. Judah would have to be 'awakened' in the same way as Joseph. The two separated branches of the Jewish people experienced one and the same dramatic situation, for this was a cosmic drama with roots in the drama of creation.

The Lost Ten Tribes regained their topicality only in 1648 when Menasseh ben Israel made his tremendous attempt to transpose the dream of Safed into reality. At that time, Aaron Levi Montezinos' evidence assumed a decisive importance, for now that it appeared that the Lost Ten Tribes had been 'awakened' by their discovery in America, the awakening of the other two tribes was also to be imminently expected, since they all had the same destiny. The return of the Jews to England would be a natural consequence of the discovery of the Lost Ten Tribes, for, according to the theories of Safed, before the Messiah could come, the Jews had to be 'scattered to the ends of the earth', and the redemption, expected by Cromwell as much as by the Jews, could come about only through the 'revelation' of the hitherto 'hidden' presence of the Jews—whether those descended from Joseph or from Judah—in those geographical 'ends' of the earth which was America for the entire globe, and England for the European continent.

Just as in 1532 the idea of the Lost Ten Tribes had given rise to Messianic stirrings (a process epitomized by that inseparable pair, David Reuveni and Solomon Molcho) so, in 1648, without knowing one another, Levi Montezinos and Shabbetai Ẓevi also had their encounter in history.

Halfway between 1532 and 1648, however, at the end of the sixteenth century when Azariah dei Rossi, David Gans, and the Maharal were alive, Messianism had a less dramatic character. There was neither an atmosphere of feverish expectation nor the revelation of a Messianic personality. It is hardly surprising if, in consequence, the theme of the Lost Ten Tribes was also de-dramatized and had reached, as we said, the trough of a wave. We will now study this situation more closely.

Azariah dei Rossi in 1575, David Gans in 1592, and the Maharal of Prague in 1600 each published works in which the subject of the Lost Ten Tribes was broached from the point of view we have described. For none of these writers did it represent an existential encounter, a challenge to their Jewish consciousness, compelling it to take up an immediate stand, as had been the case around 1530 and as would be the case again in 1648. The question was abstract and academic: the theme formed part of the literary baggage of the 'Jewish gentleman' of the last quarter of the sixteenth century. A historian like Rossi or Gans or a theologian like the Maharal could not speak about certain dates and certain facts without raising the question of the Lost Ten Tribes. It was more a matter of curiosity than of involvement. But if these three writers' deep motivation was essentially the same, the angle of vision and method of approach varied in each case in a way which it is worth our while to examine.

Azariah devoted nearly half of the thirteenth chapter of his *Me'or Einayim* to the problem of the Ten Tribes. I call it a 'problem', because these ten pages are a model of historical enquiry, starting with a specific question and arriving at equally specific conclusions through a process of informed and logical reasoning.

The initial question was a simple one. We should note at once (for it confirms what we have just said about the dispassionate way in which the problem of the Ten Tribes was treated at that period) that it was of a purely statistical character. The historical documents of the Second Temple period, from the last books of the Bible (Ezra and Nehemiah and Chronicles) to Josephus Flavius and the Talmud, give figures for the Jewish population (particularly in Alexandria, Jerusalem, and Bethar under the Ptolemies, Titus, and Hadrian) which are far too high to correspond with the figures for the First Temple period if one supposes that from the time of Shalmaneser the Ten Tribes were wrenched from the body of the Jewish people and that the subsequent demographic information concerned only the tribes of Judah, Benjamin, and Levi. It might seem more reasonable to suppose, like certain commentators, that after Shalmaneser, in the reign of Josiah, most of the exiles of the Northern Kingdom returned from their place of deportation, forming, together with the inhabitants of Judah, the 'Jewish people' who passed through the tribulations of the Babylonian exile, of the return under Ezra, and of the period of the Second Temple.

But, in that case, the theme of the Lost Ten Tribes would be no longer part of history. It would be only a legend, unworthy of being taken seriously by the historian.

Azariah dei Rossi, however, tried to prove the historical rather than the legendary character of the theme of the Lost Ten Tribes. As a historian who prided himself on his objectivity, he was convinced that the Ten Tribes, separated from the main body of the Jewish people, really existed even in his own time, and that their existence somewhere in the world could be proved by more valid arguments at the end of the sixteenth century than formerly.

We can quickly pass over the exegetical gymnastics in which
Azariah dei Rossi indulges like his predecessors (with the
important difference, however, that he does not rely only on the
Bible, but also, and to the same degree, on Alexandrian literature
and particularly the fourth Book of Ezra). There is nothing
especially original about it, but it does permit the solution of the
statistical problem initially raised. Thus, do not the elementary
rules of style allow a whole group to be referred to by a single
name? When speaking of Rome, do not historians often mean the
Roman empire and not just the city? Similarly, Judah, in the Bible,
is a collective term and many inhabitants of that kingdom may have
originated from other tribes and settled in the Kingdom of Judah at
certain periods specifically mentioned in the Bible (2 Chronicles
15: 9, 13: 18, 43: 9, and I Chronicles 9: 3). They shared the fate of
the Judeans who were exiled in Babylonia and then returned with
them to Jerusalem. Then, from the beginning of the Second
Temple period, the ranks of the Judean population were swollen by
proselytes (Zechariah 2: 15) in accordance with the Jewish tradition
of 'opening the gates to the masses of Gentiles' reaching back into
the distant mosaic of ancient Jewish history (Exodus 12: 38) and
forwards into the periods when the demography of Judah became
'explosive' (Esther 8: 17). But this is followed by a far more original
train of argument which is worth attention because it is modern in
form and content in the sense that it is based on premises which
would have been unknown to a writer who lived before the
sixteenth century.

First of all, there are bibliographical references to works which
had not come down from the distant past, but had been published
only in the last few years. The *Theatrum Mundi* of the non-Jewish
scholar Abraham Ortelius had appeared in Antwerp in 1570, five
years before the publication of Azariah's book. This up-to-date
cosmography claimed that there were major Jewish communities
descending from the tribes of Dan and Naphtali in India.
Moreover, he stated, the Jews in India were so numerous that there
was often a linguistic confusion between the terms *hodim* (Indians
or Hindus) and *yehudim* (Jews). Older books—particularly Sebastian
Munster's, which Azariah quotes in an ambivalent manner and
without naming it, and yet without leaving any doubt about the
work to which he is referring—claimed that a large Jewish
population was subject to the King of Ethiopia, the famous Prester

John, whose existence could no longer be in doubt since the recent discovery of the sources of the Nile. Azariah, however, did not think that these Jews were descended from the Ten Tribes deported by the Assyrians into Asia but were rather descendants of Moses—i.e., Falashas whose origin was attributed now to the Queen of Sheba, now to Moses' Ethiopian wife (Numbers 12: 1).

After referring to these books, Azariah turned to the historical facts which were certainly disputable, but he subjected them to critical scrutiny in order to separate the wheat from the chaff. The appearance in history of Eldad the Danite and, much more recently, of David Reuveni, could not be airily dismissed as mere legends or impostures. Perhaps there was some grain of truth in their claims. Azariah set about discovering this grain of truth by re-establishing some facts which had been distorted in the *Theatrum Mundi*. Ortelius had written that David Reuveni had been burnt in Mantua in 1531, but Azariah declared that this was a serious confusion, for the person who had died at Mantua had been Solomon Molcho. As for David Reuveni, it was probable, thought Azariah, that he, too, had been a victim of the Inquisition, but we do not know where or when. Charles V, whom David Reuveni had wanted to convert to Judaism (after first having attempted to convert Francis I of France) had clapped the poor fellow in irons, but nobody knew in exactly what circumstances he died. However that may be, Reuveni asserted that he belonged to the Lost Ten Tribes and claimed that he had come from Tartary where the Great Khan ruled, all of which—thought Azariah—was quite probable and confirmed the hypothesis of the existence in his own time of the Lost Ten Tribes somewhere in Central Asia.

It now only remained to reply to the inveterate sceptics whose arguments, ignoring the evidence of books and facts, were inspired solely by 'common sense'. The Lost Ten Tribes, it was asserted, were 'separated' from the Jewish people by insuperable mountains, and by the celebrated Sambatyon River, as impassable as the 'mountains of the moon'. But if these unfortunate people could not overcome these obstacles in order to return, how did they overcome them in order to get there? And if people like Eldad and Reuveni had been able to overcome these obstacles, why were the masses unable to follow?

Azariah answered that such reasoning was puerile. The examples of Eldad and Reuveni exist precisely in order to demonstrate that, from the geographical point of view, no obstacle is 'insuperable': neither mountains, nor rivers. If the masses did not follow, it was quite simply because they felt comfortable where they were and constituted an entire society with its laws, its customs and its places of worship, and they felt no particular need to 'return'. They were separatists who had deliberately chosen to sever themselves from the rest of the Jewish people. The example of the Temple of Heliopolis in Alexandrian Egypt demonstrated that this way of thinking existed among the Jewish people even at a time when Jerusalem and the Temple enjoyed their full prestige and central position. It was little to be wondered at that this separatist mentality existed at a time when the body of the Jewish people was dispersed throughout the world and possessed neither a political nor a religious centre of gravity.

Such is Azariah dei Rossi's account of the Ten Tribes. It is striking in the moderation and conciliation of its tone. This sceptical scholar, usually so quick in making judgements, who never feared to attack tradition when it seemed at variance with history, here deliberately took the side of tradition, regardless of the fact that it was immersed in a mass of inaccuracies, contradictions, and fantasies which Azariah dei Rossi would normally have relegated to the realm of legend. He was at pains to prove that the Lost Ten Tribes were not a legend, and that they were worth a historian's consideration.

But, on the other hand, this demonstration only touched the surface of the problem. It was purely statistical in character and did not touch its historical depths and, even less, its eschatological implications. Furthermore, it did not establish any link between the Lost Ten Tribes and the discovery of the 'New World'—that 'New World' with which Azariah dei Rossi was acquainted through his reading, and whose appearance on the geographical scene he had utilized in order to administer a knock-out blow to more than one traditional doctrine. Ortelius in his *Theatre of the World* suggested in places that perhaps the Ten Tribes could be found somewhere in the 'new' world revealed by the new discoveries, but in Azariah dei Rossi's 'Theatre' nothing has yet changed. No curtain has been raised; no scenery has yet shifted. The Lost Ten Tribes remain imperturbably in the place which the Bible assigned them. In the Ferrarese scholar's geographical card index, in 1575 the entry for the 'Lost Ten Tribes' needed no changing. It had only been consulted in connection with some small related problem, and now it was replaced in the file in the same form as it had possessed in the library at Alexandria in the time of the Ptolemies.

We are far from the emotional involvement, the perplexities and the timid or audacious suggestions of Abraham Farissol fifty years previously. But the fact is, as we should not forget, that in 1524 David Reuveni had entered Ferrara in person, in flesh and blood, bearing aloft the banner of the Lost Ten Tribes, whereas in that same city of Ferrara, half a century later, the 'David Reuveni' affair had joined Eldad the Danite among the archives.

THE MAHARAL: A FUNDAMENTAL ESCHATOLOGICAL PROBLEM. THE AMBIVALENCE OF THE NEW WORLD

In a masterly fashion, the Maharal raised the discussion onto a higher level. True to his method, he began by placing himself on the enemy's ground and joining argument with all those who doubted the existence of the Lost Ten Tribes and dismissed as fairy-tales the Midrashim and Aggadot which situated these Lost Tribes beyond the Sambatyon, behind the Mountains of Darkness, in Africa, and heaven knows where. Had not the decisive argument of the so-called 'modern' cosmographers been shattered by a still more modern event—that, precisely, of the discovery of America? Only a short while previously, it was believed that they had drawn up the map of all known countries with not the smallest area left out of account, that the whole of human habitation was contained in the closed orbit of the known world, but now this closed space had been broken open. A new world—an *olam ḥadash*—had been revealed, with its continents, oceans, mountains, plains, and rivers of which nobody hitherto had dreamt. Why could not other such 'new worlds' appear in the future? Why (a question implied by the Maharal in this passage, the only place in all his works in which he mentions America)—why could not the Sambatyon, the Mountains of Darkness, all these legendary names concealing the Ten Tribes from view at the present time be situated somewhere in this America, a new and hitherto unknown world, or, at least, why could they not be discovered, and, beyond them, the Lost Ten Tribes, by some expedition comparable to that of Columbus or Vespucci?

Thus, the discovery of America had made the geographical existence of the Lost Ten Tribes plausible, and made their rediscovery appear possible. Or, at least, this would certainly be the case if the location of the Lost Ten Tribes were a matter of geography, and if their fate were measurable by the power of reason. In that case, one could cherish that dream and hope for a return of the Lost Ten Tribes to the Jewish fold in consequence of some maritime discovery, today or tomorrow.

But, once again, the Maharal sets us on our guard against such pseudo-Messianic illusions. Writing at the end of the sixteenth century, and taking the opposite view from Isaac Abravanel whose calculations had given the signal for the Messianic agitation at the beginning of the century, the Maharal, here as elsewhere, discouraged any immediate expectations of deliverance. And, here as elsewhere, he reaches out towards another horizon in accordance with his familiar method of transposing onto a metaphysical plane a physical hypothesis which he had put forward only as a foil.

Is the New World, the *olam ḥadash*, the place of refuge of the Lost Ten Tribes? Yes, indeed. But how could one imagine for an instant that this New World could be America, could be one of the new worlds which were already in reach of the explorers' armadas? The *olam ḥadash* with which we are concerned here is the ultimate, meta-geographical New World; it is the *olam nivdal*, the 'separated' metaphysical world which man will never reach in his human condition, but which he is assured of in his meta-human vocation.

There is a superb play on words here which suddenly brings to light all the ambiguity of a badly stated problem, for the Ten Tribes were not, in fact, lost but separated, and the ambiguity of the Hebrew word *nivdal*, which means both 'separated' and 'meta-physical', echoes the ambivalence of *olam ḥadash* which refers both to the new-found continent and the 'end of days'. The 'separation' of the Ten Tribes is thus not a historical accident whose trace can be found on a map of the world. It is part of an all-embracing divine plan which introduced rupture, division, separation into this world (the Torah begins with *bet*, the second letter of the alphabet, not the first) in order the better to transcend it with a *hashlamah*, fulfilment, in the next world. It was prefigured by the separation of Joseph (progenitor of the Lost Ten Tribes) from his brothers, which was not a geographical but an essential, ontological separation. Could not Joseph, viceroy of Egypt, have easily rejoined his brothers who remained in Canaan? No maritime expedition, no voyage of exploration would have been needed to bring about such a reunion.

But the separation of Joseph and his brothers was something intended: it was the typological illustration of the subsequent situation of the Jewish people, a people limping like its ancestor Jacob, a people rent by an internal division like its ancestors Joseph and Judah—a limping and a tearing apart which were inevitable in a limping and rent world of which the people of Israel was the sign and symbol.

The reunion of Judah and Joseph was inevitable also, but it would take place only at the end of history, in a 'New World' whose newness would not be geographical but eschatological, and in which history would be eclipsed by meta-history.[1]

DAVID GANS: AN UNSOLVED PROBLEM

And what about David Gans? What was his position with regard to the myth of the Lost Ten Tribes? He was obviously interested in the theme as he included a note about it in *Zemaḥ David* (32b). We can infer from the tone of this note that, once more, he refused to follow the Maharal's metaphysical and theological lead: he regarded the problem as a historical and geographical one. He had read Azariah dei Rossi on the subject and saw the problem in a similar way without immediately expressing an opinion about his ideas. He had also read Farissol, but, in that case, he protested:

All this [Farissol's views, but also Azariah's] counts for little with me, and there is nothing in it which can satisfy my curiosity, especially as in the *Orḥot Olam* [of Farissol] and in what is quoted in the *Sefer Yuḥasin* [posthumous editions of Abraham Zacuto's chronicle] we find a terrible confusion, since these two books try to establish a connection between the place of exile of the Lost Ten Tribes and the Kingdom of Prester John, whereas these two places are as far apart as the East is from the West.

It was quite natural that in 1592 Gans should be shocked by the gross geographical error committed by Abraham Farissol in 1524, firstly because, like Azariah dei Rossi, he was no longer able to understand why or how the theme of the Lost Ten Tribes could fascinate a Jewish writer to such a degree as to completely obliterate the dividing-line between myth and reality in his consciousness.

But, above all, as we said previously,[2] the idea of a Kingdom of

---

[1] *Neẓaḥ Yisrael*, chs. 34, 49b. See. B. Gross, *Le messianisme juif* (Paris, 1969).
[2] See II, 3 above.

Prester John in the East, in Asia, corresponding to the 'traditional' Kingdom of Prester John in the West, in Africa—an idea which the Jews employed as a sort of counter-argument in a period of Messianic agitation—had fallen completely out of use since Farissol's period. Nobody in David Gans's circle could take it seriously. No one among the Jews, moreover, had any use for such an argument now that Messianism had become de-personalized and had taken on a purely Utopian character.

David Gans therefore postponed a consideration of the problem until later. He concluded his note in *Zemaḥ David* (32b) with the following words: 'This is not the place for me to elaborate on the subject. However, in a book [or in *the* book] I intend to write, with God's help I shall speak about it at greater length.'

God's help, alas, was not forthcoming. Did David Gans have his *Manual of Geography* in mind? Did he intend to include in it a chapter on the Lost Ten Tribes? It is quite possible, but this Manual has never come down to us, and it would appear to be irretrievably lost. Did he intend to write a separate monograph on the Lost Ten Tribes? That, again, is possible, but, in that case, one of two things must have happened: either he never wrote it, or, as in the case of his Manual, the manuscript was lost. Whatever actually did happen, when David Gans came to write his work of astronomy (*Magen David*, which was given the title of *Neḥmad ve-Na'im*) and included the geographical section we are now studying, he made no allusion to the theme of the Lost Ten Tribes. We therefore have to assume that David Gans conceived—and perhaps wrote—a text dealing with this problem, so that he did not have to go back to it in *Neḥmad ve-Na'im*, but, much like David Gans when faced with Azariah dei Rossi and Abraham Farissol, we are left in doubt by *Neḥmad ve-Na'im*, and in the present state of our knowledge of his work we cannot satisfy our curiosity concerning this precise point of his opinion about the myth of the Lost Ten Tribes.

Perhaps the key is to be found in an unanswered question raised by a second entry on the Lost Ten Tribes in *Zemaḥ David* (p. 74b). His chronicle had reached the year 1532 (5293), and David Gans felt the need to devote a substantial note to Solomon Molcho.

In this note we sense a personal involvement which makes it worth our while to transcribe it so as to acquaint ourselves with certain facts:

Rabbi Solomon Molcho was one of the Marrano proselytes of Portugal. Secretary to the king, he secretly returned to Judaism and became the companion of David Reuveni who had come from the Land of the Lost Ten Tribes via Great Tartary which is situated far beyond the [biblical] River Gozan.

This Rabbi Solomon who throughout his youth had been separated from the Torah of Moses, nevertheless became an outstanding Torah scholar. He preached in public in Italy and Turkey and wrote a work of *Kabbalah*.

I, the writer of this present book, have seen with my own eyes a copy of this work [of Molcho] in the possession of my close relative, my nephew, the Gaon Rabbi Nathan of Grodno, of blessed memory.

Rabbi Solomon, whom I have just mentioned, and his companion David the Reubenite, pleaded their cause before the King of France and before the Emperor Charles V, attempting to convert them to the Jewish faith, with the consequence that the said Rabbi Solomon Molcho was condemned to death in Mantua in the year 5293. Before he was burnt, his mouth was gagged to prevent him from speaking. As for David the Reubenite, the Emperor clapped him in irons and took him with him to Spain where, according to the information we possess, he was tortured to death.

See *Divrei ha-Yamin* by Rabbi Joseph Ha-Kohen, page 206 and *Orḥot Olam*, chapter 9.[3]

One notices that, in addition to the preceding biblical sources, Gans refers to the chronicle of Joseph Ha-Kohen who insists on the Messianic character of the Molcho–Reuveni episode.

One especially notices that there is a subjective link between David Gans and Solomon Molcho which is entirely lacking in the case of Azariah dei Rossi.

David Gans held in his hands one of the precious copies of the Kabbalistic work written by Solomon Molcho. He might have added that in 1534, one year after the martyrdom of Molcho, the Messianic agitation aroused by Molcho and David Reuveni had reached the city of Prague, where the mantlet worn by Solomon Molcho and the banner he had proudly carried in the streets of Rome were acquired by the Horowitz family. They can still be seen today in the State Jewish Museum in Prague.[4]

This Horowitz family—the possessor of extraordinary privileges —which founded the Pinkas Synagogue, a rival to the venerable Altneuschul, constituted a kind of autonomous entity within the Prague Jewish community. Its over-visible support for the Messianism

---

[3] *Zemaḥ David* 74b.   [4] See Muneles, *Prague Ghetto*, pp. 28–32.

of Molcho stirred up such trouble in Prague that Rabbi Joselmann of Rosheim had to be called in to help, but it appears that his assistance was unavailing, since it was quite probable that the dissidence of the Horowitz family underlay the expulsion of the Jews from Prague in 1541.[5]

We have already pointed out that David Gans passed over the two journeys of Joselmann of Rosheim to Prague after the expulsion, in 1542 and 1547, without mention.[6] Now he omits to mention the close connection between the Horowitzes and Molcho, and, more generally, the trouble caused by the 'Horowitz affair' previous to the expulsion of 1541, the year of David Gans's birth.

This omission is at least partly due to the fact that, like Azariah dei Rossi, David Gans, in approaching the problem of the Lost Ten Tribes, tried to be entirely objective. But that required a psychological effort, and the non-realization of his project for a Treatise on the Lost Ten Tribes (or the loss of his manuscript, if he wrote it) is possibly due to the mental paralysis of a man torn between history and legend, between reality and myth, as soon as one touched on one of the sensitive chords of his inner being—his quasi-mystical attachment to the city of Prague.

[5] See H. Horowitz, 'Die Familie Horowitz in Prag im 16, Jahrhundert', *ZGJT*, 2, pp. 89–165, 225–8; Mordechai Breuer, 'R. David Gans, Author of the Chronicle Ẓemaḥ David' (in Hebrew), *Ann. Univ. Bar Ilan*, xi (1973), pp. 97–118.

[6] See I. 3 above.

5

David Gans's map of the world

As a cosmographer, David Gans belongs wholly to his age. He gropes, loses his way, retreats, regains his pace, and finally reaches the truth, far in advance of the majority of his Jewish contemporaries and most of his non-Jewish contemporaries. The road from the scattered entries in *Zemah David* to the thirty-six chapters of the third part of *Nehmad ve-Na'im* is a sinuous progression, but one which leads from darkness to light, from confusion to precision, from the imaginary to the real.

DAVID GANS'S RESEMBLANCE TO SEBASTIAN MUNSTER

One cannot read these pages of David Gans without being struck by their inner resemblance to the work of one of his most eminent predecessors, Sebastian Munster (1487–1552). The fact that this author of one of the most popular cosmographies of the sixteenth century was Professor of Hebrew at Basle, and that he was mentioned, albeit somewhat enigmatically, by Azariah dei Rossi,[1] permits this comparison with David Gans.

The successive editions of Sebastian Munster's *Cosmography*, whether published in his lifetime or posthumously, improved by the editors, display typical sixteenth-century characteristics. The world is revealed piecemeal, as it was revealed to the navigators: the scholar at his work-table is an explorer who is subject to the same errors and makes the same discoveries as the people whose living testimony he uses.

The first German edition of Sebastian Munster's *Cosmography* dates from 1541. It mentions Christopher Columbus's voyages but is still unacquainted (thirty-five years after St Dié's map!) with the name of America. In the Latin edition of 1550 (the last to be drafted by the author himself and also the one which contains

[1] See the index to Cassel's edition of *Me'or Einayim*.

Prester John's famous letter to the Pope), there is a map of the world in which the South American continent is called Peru and the North American continent is called Florida. Florida is joined to China, as America usually is in the maps of that period.

We should also note that this map of the world is drawn according to the Ptolemaic and medieval rules. It does not utilize the principle of projection which Gerard Mercator began to use and disseminate only from 1568 onwards. The 1561 edition of Sebastian Munster's *Cosmography* also presents a map of the world on the ancient model, but one that is less advanced than that in the edition of 1550. The two American continents (here called Brasilia and Florida) are depicted as separate.

Only in the edition of 1588 does one find a 'modern' map of the world comparable to those of Mercator and Ortelius, but with still very fantastic accounts of the voyages of Columbus and Vespucci and a description of the empire of Prester John (which contradicts Sebastian Munster's account in the edition of 1550).

In 1588 the publication of David Gans's *Ẓemaḥ David* was only four years away. There is nothing surprising if we find in this Jewish writer the same hesitant progress that we have just observed in his great non-Jewish predecessor.

DAVID GANS'S TENTATIVE EFFORTS IN ẒEMAḤ DAVID

Ẓemaḥ David, written in 1592, one century after the discovery of America, is still full of confusions and even contradictions. In an entry based on Heinrich Rättel (the precise reference is given: page 257 of Rättel's book), the discovery of the *Olam Ḥadash* which the Christians call *Novo Mundi* is indeed attributed to the Genoese Columbus, but he is described as 'a great philosopher and a great scholar', his patron is said to be King Ferdinand of Naples and the year is given as 1494 (*ZD* 187b).

The entry ends with a cross-reference to the year 1533 when another figure appears on the scene: Americi 'a warrior who gathered together a band of desperadoes and, lured by the promise of riches, ventured so far into the ocean that the wind carried them to a new land to which he gave his own name of Americi, which is the name of that country to his day'.

Gans does not tell us where he obtained the (obviously incorrect) date of 1533 for Amerigo Vespucci's expedition. He merely points out that Rabbi Joseph Ha-Kohen (page 154 of the chronicle mentioned previously) gave the date as 1520, and he recalls that Rättel gives the date of the discovery of the New World by a Genoese called Columbus as 1492 (*ZD* 193a).

Unembarrassed by these contradictions, Gans continues his entry with a short account obviously taken from Joseph Ha-Kohen of the subsequent conquests of this New World, which he now calls 'America' and no longer Americi: namely, the conquest of New Spain by Charles V and of New France by the King of France. Then he pauses for a moment to take stock of the geographical facts which had come to light through these successive discoveries: 'Know that in the opinion of the cosmographers who are the experts in this science, the New World is of greater extent than the whole of the contemporary Christian kingdoms in Europe. According to their account, this whole region is situated on the opposite side of the earth's surface from ours; but this is not the place for me to elaborate upon this subject on which, God permitting, I intend to elaborate elsewhere.'

This entry ends with a reference (once again, given very exactly, *Me'or Einayim*, chapter 11) to Azariah dei Rossi's fascinating suggestion that this New World was none other than the biblical Ophir to which King Solomon sent his fleet (I Kings: 9; 2 Chronicles, chapter 8).

We know that David Gans wrote a geographical work called *Gevulot ha-Arez*, all traces of which have unfortunately been lost.[2] Gans mentions it in chapter 71 of his *Nehmad ve-Na'im*, for which it must have been used as source-material. In *Nehmad ve-Na'im*, twenty years after *Zemah David*, we have a structure in which all the facts are assembled, yet all the problems stated, with regard to both the theoretical and practical domains.

DAVID GANS'S MASTERY IN NEHMAD VE-NA'IM, THE FIRST CORRECT AND COMPLETE JEWISH DESCRIPTION OF THE NEW WORLD

First of all, let us make this last point perfectly clear: the third part of *Nehmad ve-Na'im* represents a cosmography in the fullest sense of the term. It is a manual of geography no less than a history of the stage-by-stage discovery of the world.

[2] See above I. 5.

In the centre is a *mappa mundi* (map of the world): a map drawn up by David Gans, and thus an instrument of practical geography, without which this science would remain imprisoned in theory (ch. 68).

David Gans gave this world map a contemporary form, hewn in the living instant of that turn of the century which was at the same time a turning-point in the history of cartography; and, if his map still followed Ptolemaic principles like the first maps of Sebastian Munster, in chapter 70 he explained a new and different method of drawing a map of the world. This method used by 'a few of the most recent geographers' had, he said, the enormous advantage over the first method that it enabled one to take in at a single glance the whole world, including the New World which the older method left submerged in the waters and cut off from the known part of the old world.

THE INFLUENCE OF MERCATOR AND ORTELIUS

It is not difficult to identify these 'most recent geographers' referred to by David Gans, as the long explanatory text accompanying his map of the world is sufficiently revealing. They were Gerard Mercator and, above all, Abraham Ortelius. In Azariah dei Rossi, David Gans had come across a reference to Mercator and a more explicit one to Ortelius's *Theatrum orbis terrarum*. He must have owned and used a copy of this work, which inspired the 'legend' in chapters 71 to 79 of *Neḥmad ve-Na'im*. This was a sometimes literal reproduction of the legends of Ortelius and provided a sort of explanatory text to the great map of the world with which the large folio volume of Ortelius began.[3]

Here, once more, we put our finger on one of those contradictions typical of the sixteenth century.

Unfortunately, David Gans's map of the world is no longer in existence. In the book published at Jessnitz in 1743 there is a note at the end of chapter 68: 'I have not found the maps referred to in this book. No doubt the writer's pen slipped here. Anyone who

[3] Abraham Ortelius was born in 1527 and died in 1598. David Gans therefore had access to all the editions of the *Theatrum* published in Ortelius's lifetime. It is an interesting fact that, according to his calculations, the maps of Ereẓ Israel by Gerard Mercator (1512–94) found their largest number of buyers among the Jews of Morocco. This is one more proof of the religious and Messianic attachment of the Jews to Ereẓ Israel.

wishes to see a map of the world such as the writer referred to need only consult a *Land-Karte* such as one finds everywhere today.'

In the manuscripts, however, we are not yet at the stage of the popular dissemination of 'Land-Karten' which rendered that of Gans superfluous. The Brno and Jerusalem manuscripts show a mere geometrical framework for this map of the world without any of the contents filled in.[4] The scribe of the Geneva manuscript said quite plainly: 'The map of the world referred to by Gans is not found in the book I am copying. One merely finds two circles on two pages in a symmetrical position. I am not reproducing them as they serve no purpose to the reader'.[5]

Thus, the prototype of the Geneva manuscript contained the 'two circles' which are also to be found in the Brno manuscript, but the scribe of the Geneva manuscript very intelligently pointed out the purposelessness of their reproduction. Indeed, this outline, which Gans probably did not have the time to fill in, can only draw attention to Gans's contradictory point of view in cosmography. It follows to the letter the old method described in chapter 69, despite Gans's acquaintance with the new method, and despite the exposition in chapters 71 to 79 which constitute a kind of commentary on a new map of the world.

He was *homo bifrons*, a man facing two directions. Just as Gans,

[4] In the Brno manuscript the two circles appear after the end of chapter 68, as is logical. In the Jerusalem manuscript on the other hand, the scribe placed one of the circles at the end of chapter 68 and the other at the end of chapter 69, where it has no connection with the text.
[5] This observation is significant for the history of *Neḥmad ve-Na'im* for two reasons: (1) It shows that the Geneva manuscript was not written by David Gans himself but by an unknown scribe in David Gans's lifetime who made a few slight alterations concerning which the author was probably not consulted, perhaps because he was already too ill, the manuscript being completed only a few days before his death. (2) It confirms G. Alter's idea that it was not the Brno manuscript but another one (which we have identified as the Geneva manuscript) which served as the basis for the book published at Jessnitz.
In the original, French edition of this book (1974), I mentioned in a footnote the astonishing fact that this manuscript was no longer to be found in the library of the Jewish Community in Geneva where Dr Allony had photographed it when sent there by the Jewish National and University Library about the year 1952. Nobody in Geneva knew why it had disappeared or was even aware that it had once been there. Were it not for the microfilm in Jerusalem, I would not have known that the manuscript had existed at all. My footnote, however, prompted Mr David Banon to search for the manuscript when he took up an appointment with the Jewish Community in Geneva in 1979, and he found it somewhere on their premises. I used it in the preparation of the Hebrew edition of my book.

as we shall see, remained faithful in astronomy to medieval Ptolemaic ideas while at the same time being dazzled by Copernicus and Tycho Brahe, so here he remained attached to medieval cartographical practices while using them as the basis for a modern theory.

But this theory itself precedes the practical part of David Gans's cosmography. Before the map of the world in chapter 68 come chapters 55 to 67 in which Gans attempts to prove the roundness of the world, the existence of the antipodes, and the division of the world into eight continents, all of which are concepts completely contrary to the assertions of medieval dogmatism.

This proof depends on an empirical fact, given in chapter 56, which David Gans had completely passed over in silence in *Zemah David*: namely, Magellan's round-the-world voyage. This circling of the earth, this voyage from east to west returning to the point of departure without ever diverging from a single direction, was the event which furnished the decisive proof of the sphericity of the earth and the existence of the inhabited antipodes.

In chapter 56, Gans was content to repeat Azariah dei Rossi's truncated version of this voyage round the world. The name of Magellan was not mentioned, just as it had not been mentioned by Azariah. All the credit for the voyage went to El Cana, who had the honour of disembarking at Seville displaying a banner bearing the proud inscription *ata ha-rishon sibavtani* ('As if', said Gans, 'the terrestrial globe had addressed him and said "You are the first to have encircled me"'), which had indeed been the case, since Magellan was killed in the Philippines and his second-in-command El Cana had continued the expedition and carried it through to the end.

But in chapter 77 Gans fills in the details, specifically mentions Magellan as the captain of the expedition, gives an account of his tragic death, and thus completes the story he had begun to relate in chapter 56, which ends, however, with the remark, astonishing in its accuracy, that since the Magellan–El Cana expedition in the years 1519–21, a round-the-world voyage had been accomplished for a second time in 1576, not by the Portuguese but by an English captain, Francis Drake (Francisci Drako). These two round-the-world voyages, Magellan's and Drake's, gave rise to radically changed conceptions whereby the Ptolemaic world was so transformed that now it was no longer a matter of adding on the countries recently discovered to the former ones but of restructuring the world and giving it its true shape.

These two voyages confirmed the absurdity of the ancient theory of a globe half of which was sunk into the sea (chapter 64), and the absurdity of the fable of a *torrida zona* (the Latin expression is transcribed by Gans into Hebrew), uninhabitable because of the sub-equatorial heat. For years now, the French, Spanish, and Portuguese fleets had skirted Africa, taking a route in the form of a reversed Hebrew letter *kaf* (or, in other words, like a hook encircling Africa from west to east. The journey had become so familiar that David Gans did not even take the trouble specifically to mention Vasco da Gama and his successors) (ch. 65). These round-the-world voyages enabled the exact shapes to be established of the eight continents, three of which (Europe, Africa, and Asia) were joined together as well as two others (America and Peru, or North and South America), while the remaining three (New Guinea, the boreal continent, and the austral continent) constituted separate areas of land.

Chapters 71 to 79 describe these eight continents in detail. Here one must repeat: this description is intended as an explanatory text accompanying the map of the world, unfortunately lost. However, this legend can be understood if we set it against one of Ortelius's maps of the world.

Where Europe was concerned, there was no problem. Nearly all the countries were enumerated according to a grid which ran horizontally from Lisbon to Constantinople and vertically from Sicily to Iceland. Africa was described as a huge island in the form of a triangle: only a narrow tongue of land bordering the Red Sea connected it to Asia. Asia was the biblical continent *par excellence*. India was mentioned in the Bible, and far beyond it there were innumerable empires of which David Gans was content to mention only that of the Great Khan, China, and Japan (chapter 71).

The two Americas were joined together by a narrow isthmus, but the two of them constitute an entity separate from the other continents. North America is called America because of the historical circumstances of its discovery. As for South America, David Gans, like cartographers for some time to come, called it Peru, but he makes it clear that Peru is actually only part of the continent, which includes, among 'many other countries', Brazil (chapters 73 and 74).

Gans, like Ortelius, used the term New Guinea to refer to the whole of what we now call Australia and New Guinea. And that is quite natural, as the existence of the Straits of Torres was known in Europe only in 1770, nearly two centuries after Ortelius and David Gans (chapter 77).[6]

The boreal (northern) continent was vast and inhabited. It lay around the North Pole like a skull-cap and had been sufficiently explored for geographers already to be able to discuss its precise extent (chapter 78).

The same was not true for the austral (southern) continent which constituted the replica, so long disputed by ancient and medieval geographers, of the boreal continent, but the intense cold had prevented the explorers from determining the exact contours of that vast area of land. At that point of the globe, but only there, there still remained territories which waited to be discovered in the future. Everywhere else, continents and oceans had been furrowed and trampled on by man, and it was no longer scientifically possible for a hitherto unknown continent to appear on the map of the world (chapter 79).

This up-to-date exposition enabled David Gans to draw up a table of longitudes and latitudes for the principal cities of these eight continents (chapter 88). Once again, we should not be surprised at the fact that we find in this alphabetical table only ancient names and, generally, ancient information. It is a Ptolemaic table, amended only by a few medieval touches. It is drawn up as if the world still comprised only the three classical continents: Europe, Asia, and Africa.

We ought not to be surprised, first of all because in this case, as with his geographical diagrams, David Gans was not in a position to complete his work and to give it the finishing touches. In both the published book and the manuscripts, at least half the spaces for cities remained empty.

But, above all, here, once again, we come upon David Gans's fundamental concern: to take a courageous look at the revolution brought about by the maritime discoveries at the same time as remaining faithful to the tradition of the Ancients.

In a characteristic and sometimes moving chapter (80), Gans explained that the revolution did not take place all at once: there

---

[6] The existence of the straits discovered by L. Vaez de Torres in 1606 remained a secret until 1762, and was fully confirmed only by Cook in 1770.

had been a continuous chain of patient, persistent activity which had led from the scholars of Antiquity whose reputation was established—Archimedes, Hipparchus, Ptolemy—to the modern geographers and astronomers. If the moderns had extended the field of human knowledge to its limits, it was because of the assistance provided, on the one hand, by the courageous enterprises of the explorers, and, on the other hand, by the discovery of more and more perfected instruments, among which the astrolabe and compass were of decisive importance. In chapter 87, entitled 'The Magnetic Stone', Gans gave a detailed description of the compass, invented three centuries earlier. It was the compass, he said, which enabled the longitudes to be determined without the calculation being connected to the lunar eclipses. And David Gans concluded this discussion on the continuity of progress with a blessing which forms the end of chapter 80: 'Blessed be the Lord who has favoured us with his benefits and has permitted us to witness all these wonders.'

There was a price to be paid for these 'wonders', however, for they raised certain problems from which David Gans did not turn aside. He was prepared to pay the necessary price and to play his own part in the search for truth.

We have an idea of these problems: they recur constantly in his exposition. It was not only a matter of reconciling the existence of the New World with Ptolemy, but with the Bible and Talmud and with Jewish tradition in general. What was one to do with the biblical, and, especially, rabbinical texts which seem to state categorically that the antipodes are inconceivable and that the earth rests on the waters or, contrarily, that the waters rest on the earth? In short, what was one to do with the whole Ptolemaic-medieval system on which David Gans had based his book from its first chapter and which was now crumbling before one's eyes? Was not Jewish tradition bound up with this ancient and now superseded system?

Two groups of chapters (63–5 and 89–90) are devoted to an elucidation of these burning questions of method and of the general conception of the relationship between revealed truth and scientific truth. We shall leave until later an examination of chapters 63–5 which deal with the repercussions of the new geography on astronomy,[7] but we shall now look at the problem

[7] See below, III. 2.

discussed in chapters 89–90, which is of a purely geographical nature. It concerns the important question of the central position of Jerusalem and the Holy Land in medieval maps, a position which was now mightily contested by the discovery of the New World.

AN IMPORTANT RELATED PROBLEM:

Is Jerusalem the centre of the world?
Is Erez Israel the foremost among all countries?

It was inevitable that David Gans should confront these two questions, and that he should insist on the question mark with which he had necessarily to provide them.

The very fact that in his table of longitudes and latitudes (chapter 88 of *Neḥmad ve-Na'im*) Gans remained faithful to Ptolemy's figures and gave Jerusalem a longitude of 66°20 and a latitude of 32°15 (notwithstanding the observation to which he devoted chapter 91, that since the time of Ptolemy the prime meridian had been shifted some ten degrees to the west)—this very fidelity to Ptolemy would have been sufficient in itself to place Gans in opposition to the texts which gave Jerusalem the central position in the globe. But, in addition, the cosmological revolution resulting from the recent maritime discoveries which he had just described in the preceding chapters represented a very real challenge for him. The new map of the world would not allow a centre: the roundness of the earth had been demonstrated by experimental means in as decisive a manner as it had been shown that the very idea of a 'centre of the earth' was unfounded. Any individual in any part of the globe had a perfect right to regard himself as being in the centre. It was a purely conventional question, and this relativization of the concept of a 'centre of the world' made nonsense of the absoluteness of the proud assertion in the sacred texts that Jerusalem was that 'centre', placing Jerusalem in the centre of the world on medieval maps and on most maps right into the sixteenth century.

David Gans, for his part, devoted two chapters, the eighty-ninth and ninetieth (intermediate chapters between the table of Ptolemaic longitudes and his observation concerning the need for corrections necessitated by the choice of a new zero meridian), to a search for a solution to this problem. The problem touched too deep a chord in the Jewish soul to be lightly dismissed. One had to find an answer, and David Gans proposed one, taking his cue from an unexpected authority, Azariah dei Rossi, the gist of whose arguments he was content to reproduce.

Was David Gans unaware that on this very point Azariah dei Rossi was the object of a severe and almost insulting criticism on the part of his Teacher, the Maharal? He could not possibly have been unaware of it, since on two occasions (in *Ẓemah David* and in the epilogue of *Neḥmad ve-Na'im*) he acknowledges having read the Maharal's *Be'er ha-Golah* (Well of Exile), whose sixth chapter ends with a complete demolition of Azariah dei Rossi's book—a book Gans mentions specifically in the two chapters to which we have referred, adopting its conclusions as his own, whereas in these two chapters he makes no mention of the Maharal, his book, and his refutation of the *Me'or Einayim* of Azariah dei Rossi.

It is one more proof of David Gans's freedom of thought—something which he had learnt with his first Teacher, the Rema, but also with the Maharal. He is not afraid, here, to distance himself from the Maharal and to place himself deliberately on the side of Azariah dei Rossi, and we can only be glad about this, as it allows us to draw from this triangular confrontation two conclusions of equal importance.

We pointed out in *Puits de l'Exil* (p. 111) that the disagreement between the Maharal and Azariah over the problem of the centrality of Jerusalem and the Holy Land was a matter of approach and not of content. David Gans had only to disregard the question of their approach in order to discover in the Maharal conclusions similar to those of Azariah. The only difference was that in Azariah these conclusions were simply expressed and limited to the subject in hand, whereas with the Maharal they form part of an imposing dialectical edifice before which David Gans modestly recoils, preferring to turn away from such an unapproachable spectacle. Once again, he remains at the foot of the mountain with Azariah, whose language is accessible to him.

In his treatment of this problem, the Maharal uses the terminology of his dialectical system. The centre of the earth, the *emẓa*, is the equilibrating force between two extremes. The Holy Land, situated between Being and Nothingness, is the centre, the Land of Life, the crux of contradictions transcended at the highest metaphysical level.

Azariah dei Rossi divested this terminology of its metaphysical implications, but the idea is similar. Azariah argued that despite the sudden increase in the number of known inhabited countries, the Holy Land retains a specially privileged position in that it is situated in the centre of the most populated, temperate, and civilized area of the globe.

David Gans appropriates this idea at the same time as taking from Azariah a number of other interpretations of the same kind. Thus, the expression *olam* ought not to be understood in its strict meaning of 'universe'. First of all, in the Bible it generally has the meaning of 'eternity'. Then, in many biblical and rabbinical texts, *olam* refers only to a part of the world and not to the whole world. Similarly, the term *aliyah*, ascent, applied to the Holy Land, Jerusalem, and the Temple (this concept underlies the proposition that the Holy Land is above all countries) does not only mean a physical ascent but a spiritual excellence. And who would deny that Erez Israel, Jerusalem, and the Temple have an elevation, dignity, and glory which is possessed by no other country, no other city, no other building in the world?

It is curious that David Gans adopts these arguments of Azariah dei Rossi, yet fails to mention another argument which is unconnected with the somewhat over-simplistic allegory which Azariah supposes to be implicit also in the non-Jewish writers who affirm the centrality of Jerusalem (except, he claims, in the case of Dante, whom Azariah believed to have accepted the centrality of Jerusalem for geographical reasons).

This argument, ignored by David Gans (and also, surprisingly, by the Maharal) was put forward by Azariah dei Rossi in a rather moving way. This was the astronomical argument expounded at length by Judah Halevi in his *Al-Kuzari*. Thus, is not the Land of Israel the criterion used for the calculation of the times of the Sabbaths and festivals of the Jewish calendar? Whether Erez Israel is the centre of the earth or not, one thing is certain, and that is that the timing of the Sabbaths and festivals, regardless of the influence of the complex mechanism of the celestial orbs in the rest of the world, is linked to Erez Israel. The Holy Land constitutes a kind of axis for the celebration of the religious holidays, just as, in a more general way, it constitutes an axis for the observation of the corpus of the divine commandments of the Torah. In this way, one may speak of the centrality of Jerusalem in a sense which Azariah dei

Rossi claims is entirely rational, so that 'reason bears it with love into its choicest chambers'.

Let us agree that this language is not lacking in nobility. Let us do justice to Azariah dei Rossi whom the Maharal undoubtedly treated too harshly, and regret that David Gans did not deem it necessary to offer this typically Jewish argument of Judah Halevi. We finally see from all this that David Gans, like the Maharal and Azariah, transcended the letter of the concept of the centrality of Jerusalem and thus took up a basically different position from the mainly non-Jewish champions of a literal interpretation of this theme.

THE PARALLEL BETWEEN DAVID GANS AND HEINRICH BUENTING: THE RATIONALISM OF GANS

Nothing could illustrate this fact in a more striking manner than a comparison between David Gans and one of his most famous sixteenth-century Christian contemporaries: one who has been forgotten since, but whom an unexpected circumstance has given an amusing celebrity in our twentieth century.

A reputable Jerusalem firm, Universitas Booksellers, has printed tens of thousands of copies, elegantly and attractively presented, of a sixteenth-century map showing Jerusalem in the centre of a trefoil whose three leaves represent Europe, Asia, and Africa. Jerusalem is not only the centre of the Old World on this map, for on the left of the map, floating in the ocean, America, so to speak, displays the tip of its ear, and to the north appear a few islands of the 'Septentrion'. A model of piety, artistic elegance, and scientific error, this map is signed Henry Buenting, and few are the tourists and pilgrims in Israel today who can resist the temptation to spend a few shekels to acquire this 'souvenir' with a slip attached informing them that its original was engraved by its author at Helmstedt in 1581. In this way a merchant who knew how to combine good taste with the fascination of ancient things was able to score a success in the geographical market.

Henry—or rather, Heinrich—Buenting was not only a contemporary of David Gans, but he was, so to speak, his spiritual replica. David Gans, a learned Jewish rabbi, lived in Central Europe from 1541 to 1613, and Heinrich Buenting, a no less learned Protestant pastor, was born in Hanover in 1545 and died there in 1606.

To within a few years, the two men were complete contemporaries, and there was also a contemporaneity in their writings. Apart from Buenting's last book (*The Harmony of the Evangelists* (1589)) which deals with a purely Christian subject, his three other great works, like those of David Gans, dealt with history, geography, cosmography, and astronomy—in fact, all the subjects which the sixteenth-century humanists had in common.

Heinrich Buenting's first work was his *Itinerarium Biblicum Sacrae Scripturae*, written in 1581. As its title suggests, it was a kind of historical atlas of the Holy Land, based on the information provided in the Old and New Testaments. It proved to be Buenting's best-seller. The first edition appeared at Wittenberg where Buenting made his theological studies, a second (which is the one sold to tourists in Israel) followed immediately at Helmstedt, and there was a large number of others, including one in Latin in 1597, translated by the author himself. By 1646, forty years after Buenting's death, it had run into thirty-one editions! It was a record for the period. Moreover, a magnificent re-edition with learned notes appeared in 1718 at the beginning of the eighteenth century under the auspices of Johann Georg Leukfeld, who was the first person to correct Buenting's monumental errors, and particularly the dogmatic assertion at the head of the third chapter, so naïvely illustrated by the trefoil map:

Die wunderschöne Stadt Jerusalem hat mitten in der Welt gelegen.
'The wonderful city of Jerusalem is situated in the centre of the world.'

Buenting, however, did not use the trefoil device only for the 'wonderful city of Jerusalem'. We can find a similar map in his second work, *Braunschweigische Lüneburgische Chronicon*, which appeared in Magdeburg in 1586. Hanover, Buenting's home town, was the main subject of the description and also the centre of a trefoil map representing the provinces which were especially dear to him. Even here, one thinks of Gans's praise of his native Westphalia and his adoptive Bohemia as constituting a parallel between the geographical approach of Buenting and that of Gans.

But the parallel becomes amazing in its exactitude with Heinrich Buenting's third work. This book appeared in 1591, that is to say exactly one year before David Gans's *Zemah David*, of which it constituted a real Christian counterpart, even down to the astronomical sequel promised in the preface to *Zemaḥ David* and which took shape a short time afterwards as *Magen David* and *Neḥmad ve-Naʾim*. The title of the work was *Chronologica omnium temporum et Annorum series ex Sacris Bibliis, aliisque fide dignis scriptoribus, ab initio mundi ad nostra usque tempora fideliter collecta et calculo Astronomico exactissime demonstrata et confirmata*. Alas, the ultra-exact demonstrations and confirmations of this *Chronology* of Buenting's were hardly any more accurate than those of the *Chronology* of David Gans.

It is by no means surprising to find Buenting mentioned several times by David Gans in *Zemaḥ David*. This is one more proof, if any were needed, of Gans's erudition, his intellectual curiosity, and his wish to be up to date and to possess the most modern works in his library.[8]

But the remarkable thing is that if Gans, in the twenty years which still remained to him, totally revised his scientific conclusions, Buenting in his remaining fifteen years continued to stick to the medieval clichés of a strictly conservative theology. And this despite—or perhaps because of—the tragic circumstance that the cultured and educated Buenting, like Johannes Kepler at the end of his life, was the object of a witch-hunt.

Buenting's pastoral career had begun very respectably (too respectably, as we shall see in a moment) in Calenberg in 1571; then he became pastor at Grunow and, in 1591, the year his *Chronology* appeared, he was appointed to the desirable position of superintendent at Goslar. In 1599 he had to resign his appointment after a bitter trial for heresy by his ecclesiastical superiors comparable to Kepler's trial, thirty years later, by a group of pastors. If Kepler, however, had the strength to withstand the test of excommunication and to appeal to the judgement of posterity against the narrow and ephemeral representatives of the Church, Buenting appears to have been broken by the struggle. After his dismissal, one loses sight of him. It is not until 1718 that Leukfeld, in his moving biography, informs us of Buenting's innocence and states that after 1599 Buenting retired to his native city of Hanover where he died and was buried in 1606.

Here we see one aspect of the careers of David Gans and

[8] See Sedinova, I, 11.

Heinrich Buenting where the parallel between them suddenly changes into a violent contrast. A Jewish rabbi, placed before the fearful choice between theological dogma and the centrality of Jerusalem on the one hand and the scientific accuracy of the new maps on the other, opted courageously for the latter. Forced to choose between maps like that of Buenting (which continued to be current until well into the eighteenth century) and the world maps of Mercator and Ortelius, David Gans abandoned Jerusalem to a profane destiny and decided to follow Ortelius, yet this daring decision neither brought an accusation of heresy nor aroused a polemic, nor, even less, involved an excommunication from the synagogue. On the contrary, the leading rabbinical figures of the Prague Jewish community sang his praises when he published his *Magen David* in 1612, although his point of view was already expressed there in a clear and unequivocal manner.

As against this, a Protestant pastor, doggedly attached to the dogma of the geographical pre-eminence of Jerusalem, was attacked for other theological reasons, divested of his ecclesiastical functions, and excommunicated from his Church! What a contrast, and what an instructive contribution to the historical problem of tolerance in the sixteenth century! We shall find that this same problem recurs in connection with the astronomical revolution.

We should add, however, that if the Buenting–Gans parallel is instructive on this level, it is nevertheless hard to accept, in that circumstances have added an ingredient which people will find either cynical or ironical, according to taste. No doubt both adjectives can be used to describe an incident which makes the celebrity of Buenting's map in Israel appear to be a reversal of history. We are thinking of the episode, briefly alluded to previously, which took place at the beginning of Heinrich Buenting's pastoral career in Calenberg in 1571. If it is placed in the context of its time (the sixteenth century of the humanists and the Renaissance, unfortunately), it will appear to be only one casual example among thousands of Jewish–Christian 'friendship' as it was practised not only by the Catholics, as in the Middle Ages, but also by the Protestants.

In pages 77 to 79 of the Magdeburg edition of the third part of his *Braunschweigische und Lüneburgische Chronica* (1584), this incident is related by Heinrich Buenting with such naïvety and assurance, such sadism and cynical delight, that we cannot resist the temptation to publish it one day in its entirety. For the present, we shall limit ourselves to a brief note.[9]

We shall end our description of David Gans's map of the world with an impressive observation: one concerning chapter 58, one of the first chapters of the cosmographical part of this book. Gans speaks there about the smallness of the earth in the light of the nautical discoveries. He does so objectively, in a measured tone, putting forward fantastic figures, yet without ever giving way to the sentiment of terror which, fifty years later, overcame Blaise Pascal before these openings into the infinite. But he does so, and it is doubtless not just a matter of chance that the title of this chapter 58 of David Gans's *Neḥmad ve-Na'im*—*She kaddur ha-areẓ la-rov katnuto ein lo erekh o shi'ur murgash le-marot einenu neged otsmerhav galgal ha-mazalot*—is like a variation of *De immensitate coeli ad magnitudem terrae*, the title of the sixth chapter of book I of *De Revolutionibus Orbium Coelestium* by a certain Nicholas Copernicus. Copernicus is struck by the contrast between the vastness of the earth and the immensity of the skies. David Gans takes this audacity further: he contrasts the immensity of the skies with the

---

[9] It concerned the unhappy story of two Jews who had confessed under torture to having murdered their Christian innkeeper. Heinrich Buenting was given the task of converting these two Jews before they were put to death. The elder, Manoah, resisted to the end and died in his diabolical stubbornness reciting the Shema, but the younger, Simon—persuaded by the catechism which the worthy pastor Heinrich Buenting had taught him (in prison, on his stool of punishment, and, again, on the cart which carried him to the scaffold and under the strokes of the red-hot irons of his torturer!)—asked for baptism. This created a serious dilemma which Buenting was unable to solve without consulting about a score of eminent colleagues and pious people assembled for the occasion. The law of the Reformed Church required that a Jew condemned to death who asks for baptism should be baptized ... by drowning, but Simon had been condemned to die by being broken on the wheel! They decided to make exception in his case. He was baptized, without being drowned, and then broken on the wheel, disembowelled, and flayed; but, as he could no longer speak, when asked whether he believed in the Trinity, he indicated an affirmative answer with a nod of the head. This Christian head was now cut off and set on a pole, next to the head of the 'stubborn' Jew Manoah. In order to demonstrate the difference between Simon, now become Adam by his baptism, and Manoah, they hung the carcass of a dog next to Manoah's head, which they omitted to do in the case of Adam ex-Simon. The most—what shall I say?—unspeakable passage in this narrative is the one relating how, when Adam–Simon, his limbs broken on the wheel, his body flayed, his guts disembowelled, gave his nod of the head: 'Da wir das sahen, fingen wir alle an zu singen: Nu bitten wir den heiligen Geist. . .'. I prefer not to translate this passage, thus sparing the reader ignorant of German the sense of nausea which is also aroused, to a slightly lesser degree, by the conclusion of this edifying narrative: 'I have related all the details of this story so that one may recognise the great Grace and Divine Mercy which the Lord manifested in connection with this poor sinner, converted in so wonderful a manner.'

smallness of the earth. The cosmographical revolution has driven Gans to embrace the astronomical revolution in all its vertiginous amplitude. The opening up of the earth has resulted in the opening up of the entire cosmos. The relationship of the earth and the heavens has to be modified; Jacob's ladder and Euclid's scales are extended into infinity.

PART THREE

DAVID GANS, ASTRONOMER

I

The Genesis of the Infinite: the sixteenth-century astronomical revolution

'THE Exodus towards Infinity' is the definition we gave of the discovery of America as experienced by the man of the sixteenth century. If we wished, in a parallel formula, to attempt to describe the significance, for that same sixteenth-century man, of the astronomical revolution whose stages were marked by the names of Nicholas Copernicus (1473–1543), Tycho Brahe (1546–1601), Johannes Kepler (1571–1630), and Galileo Galilei (1564–1642), none better could probably be found than that of 'the Genesis of the Infinite'—the sixteenth century being the one in which astronomy opened to the Infinite a universe which, more than a thousand years earlier, human reason had enclosed within the rigid framework of the Finite.

In that case, also, the development which took place could be called a Renaissance, in the true sense of the word (i.e., rebirth), for there had once been a time when conceptions of the universe had been full of the idea of the Infinite; but that time had vanished into the distance and human memory had blotted it out, just as America had once existed for a moment and then disappeared from human sight; just as—to a lesser degree—the canons of ancient art had irradiated Athens, Rome, and Alexandria and then been hidden among the ruins. Thus, in effect, for sixteenth-century man, the passage to the Infinite in the domain of astronomy was not the rediscovery of an ancient idea but the genesis of something new.

The discovery of this new world of the heavens, however, like the discovery of the terrestrial New World, was not the work of reason alone. It was the joint product of reason and mystical insight, and it, too, was an adventure in which the transcendence of reason by a meta-reason and an intimate interconnection of reality and myth were from all viewpoints significant and important.

THE NEW ATTITUDE OF HOMO ASTRONOMICUS

From the Closed World to the Infinite Universe, The Sleepwalkers: these
titles of two books, one by Alexandre Koyré, the other by Arthur
Koestler,[1] are sufficient in themselves, in their strikingly complementary character, to describe the spirit of the sixteenth-century
astronomical adventure which these writers have narrated with
such erudition, feeling, and inspiration.

    In the whole history of mankind there have been very few
adventures which have revealed such a consistent pattern, on the
one hand, in its revolutionary development, and have been as
phantasmagoric on the other in the wild romanticism of its
progenitors.

    There was a geometrical progression underlying it, leading from
Nicholas Copernicus (whose only but all-important work, whose
title included the word 'revolution', appeared in the year of the
author's death, 1543), through Tycho Brahe and Johannes Kepler
to Galileo, who was born in 1564 and died in 1642, the very year
when Isaac Newton was born. For exactly a century, from 1543 to
1642, there was an apparently linear development, a slow but
persistent erosion of the Ptolemaic system which, for more than a
century, had enclosed the world within itself and placed the
immobile earth in the centre of a sort of giant clockwork constituted
by the circular orbits of the planets rotating around it with a
complex and intangible regularity.

    We said apparently linear, for nothing is more mistaken than the
common belief in an evolution given an initial 'push' by Copernicus
and spread by his successors to the whole of mankind.

    We must remember, first, that in substituting a sun-centred
system for Ptolemy's earth-centred system, Copernicus was only
putting out a purely mathematical hypothesis. It had not been based
on any concrete observation, quite simply because astronomy had
not yet taken the giant step of passing from the abstract to the
concrete. The first observatories only came into existence at the
end of the sixteenth century, fifty years after Copernicus. The best-
equipped among them was that of Tycho Brahe in the island of
Sveen in Denmark and later at Benatek near Prague where Kepler
also worked, but neither Brahe nor Kepler was able to prove the

---

[1] A. Koyré, *From the Closed World to the Infinite Universe* (London, 1962); *La révolution
astronomique* (Paris, 1961); A. Koestler, *The Sleepwalkers* (London, 1958).

correctness of Copernicus's hypothesis by practical observation. Only the telescope, developed by Galileo in 1609, was able to furnish material proof in an area in which pure mathematics had hitherto reigned supreme. Basically, Copernicus was still a captive of the Ptolemaic universe, and everything took place as if the fall of the Bastille had not happened through an assault from outside but had been dreamed up by a prisoner in one of its cells. One of the dominant characteristics of the evolution from 1543 to 1642 was not the general adoption of the Copernican hypothesis in astronomy, but the increasingly important place given in that science to observation rather than to mathematical calculations. Instead of continuing to pore over tables and, literally, over his work-table, *homo astronomicus* now lifted his eyes up to the heavens. This is the first aspect of this breakthrough from the 'closed' world of Ptolemy to the infinite universe opened up by Copernicus.

THE SENSE OF THE VERTIGINOUS

The second aspect of this breakthrough follows logically from the first. In lifting up his eyes, man was overtaken by the physiological, psychological, and moral derangement attendant upon the purely physical sensation of the loss of balance which we call vertigo or dizziness.

This feeling of the vertiginous was already known to the architects and builders of the Gothic cathedrals of the Middle Ages. One sees signs of it in architects' drawings, breaking and contorting the regular circular shapes of the Romanesque period and giving rise to ogives, leaping arches, towers, spires—so many Tower of Babel-like reversals of the established horizontal order in order to mount higher, always higher, as if they wished to tear the earth away from its foundations and offer it up to the heavens. One senses this vertiginousness in the tireless daily labours of the masons, sculptors, workers, risking everything—their security, their lives, their comfort—to translate the architects' dreams into the reality of stone... A whole people giving themselves up to a revolution which was to devour whole generations, and which often, after all these centuries of backbreaking work, would remain unfinished like Strasburg cathedral, with its single tower like a stark finger admonishing mankind that human dreams have impassable limits, or like that of Cologne, a stricken monster whose carcass would remain until the nineteenth century a sort of modern Tower of Babel, riveted to its site by the very divinity it was intended to honour.

But at least this vertiginous audacity of the cathedral-builders of the Middle Ages was circumscribed by the very institution in whose service it leapt and effervesced—the Roman, the Catholic Church, with its authority, its grandeur, its serene patience, its unshakeable certainties. It was a storm in a teacup, and even if this teacup had the dimensions of the cosmos, it was nevertheless true that its boundaries were clearly defined and proof against all testing. The vertiginous rapture of the cathedrals took place in an airtight chamber. It was a vertiginousness that was softened and attenuated by the sense of security provided by the grandiose inertia of the Church.

It was the collapse of one of the principal elements of this inertia which provoked the astronomical revolution of the sixteenth century. The Church based its conception of the cosmos on that of Ptolemy, feeling all the more reassured by the Ptolemaic system in that it was shared by most of the peoples of medieval Europe, and especially by the Jews and Arabs, from whom it had reached the Church. Nothing, indeed, offered the human soul a greater sense of security than the Ptolemaic system, heir to the Aristotelian system and, to a lesser extent, to that of Plato. Even if it was adapted to certain biblical models, closer to monotheistic thinking than the Greek models, that made little difference. Whether it was conceived in terms of the Tabernacle in the Book of Exodus or as Augustine's City of God, or whether, more rationally, it was imagined according to the Aristotelian pattern as a number of spheres turning like wheels, or, according to the Platonic pattern, as the graduated rungs of a ladder, the universe of Ptolemy—and that of Avicenna, Maimonides, and St. Thomas Aquinas—remained static and closed in upon itself.

In the centre stood the earth: flat or round, no matter. The main point was that it was *at rest*—the first element of reassuring stability for its inhabitant, man—and also that it was *in the centre*—a second element of stability, since the only thing which could develop around this centre was the ideal geometrical figure which the centre required: namely, the circle. The circular movement of the stars and the immobility of the earth at the centre were the factors of inertia which in the sixteenth century *homo astronomicus*, through visual observation, was to destroy, not all at once but in a spasmodic manner which gave rise to a feeling of dizziness which could be allayed neither by the safety devices of the Church, nor by those of philosophical reason, also the faithful servant of the Ptolemaic system.

Whether it was a matter of Copernicus's spectacular 'push', tearing the earth from its repose and thrusting it into space, or of Kepler's more modest action (without which Copernicus's would have had no consequence) of moving from a circle to an oval and from an oval to an ellipse, it was enough to intoxicate the observers, and especially those who were actually taking part.

Yes, the fact must be admitted: Copernicus, Tycho Brahe, Kepler, and Galileo were 'sleepwalkers'—an expression which has nothing pejorative about it but perfectly describes the hybrid character of their genius.

A fearful revolutionary: Copernicus

No doubt Koyré was right to reproach Koestler for his almost caricature of a portrait of the 'fearful canon' of Frauenburg, working in his lost province at the edge of the Baltic in a jumble of instruments and in a solitude so distrustful of everyone, and, first of all, of his own discoveries, that, to this very day, the historian may ask himself if the *Book of Revolutions of Heavenly Spheres* was not a hoax worthy of the century of Rabelais. 'It is very difficult in our days', writes Koyré, 'to understand and to appreciate in their true grandeur the intellectual effort, audacity, and courage represented by Copernicus's work'.[2]

That is undoubtedly so, but this difficulty is due to certain characteristics not of the work but of the man, exaggerated, no doubt, by Koestler, but unquestionable in their mysterious simplicity. Here was a man who had studied in Cracow, Bologna, Padua, and Ferrara, where he became Doctor of Canon Law; a man who was in Rome in the jubilee year 1500—that is to say, at a time and place where all the scholars, humanists, artists, and patrons of Europe were gathered together, as enlightened as they were avid for new light on all subjects—a man who, in this climate where the radical changes were being prepared which were to transform the Middle Ages into the modern world, rediscovered

[2] A. Koyré, *La révolution astronomique*, p. 15.

Aristarchus and his sun-centred universe, and who, dazzled by this reversal of the Ptolemaic system, from 1507 onwards began to commit to paper the fundamental propositions of his own sun-centred re-interpretation of the universe. This man hid his notes, his calculations, his manuscript in the secret drawers in his Nordic tower of Frauenburg and took thirty-six years—yes, four times nine years—to give them a form which he regarded as worthy of being submitted to the publisher! When the finished book was sent from the Nuremberg publishers to Copernicus, he was already dying in his fortress of Frauenburg. He died on 24 May 1543, carrying at least two unsolved riddles to the grave. One was his dedication to Pope Paul III written in June 1542 in which he publicly thanked those who finally made him decide to publish the book, but completely forgot to mention his faithful, his only, disciple Rheticus, without whose persistent efforts the *Book of Revolutions* would never have been brought to press. The other riddle was the preface, probably written by Osiander, which Copernicus had approved, and the proofs of which he could still have corrected. Now, this preface informed the reader in the best Rabelaisian style that everything that he was about to read was only a series of hypotheses, full of absurdities but, still, no less worthy of being put forward than the absurd hypotheses of the Ancients. These ideas, which were intended for mathematicians alone and not for astronomers, philosophers, and theologians should above all not be accepted as true 'lest one should leave this work more foolish than one entered it'.

What was Copernicus afraid of? It would be wrong to imagine that he feared the wrath of the Church, the Inquisition, the stake. At that period, they were still far from that distrust of which Galileo was a victim nearly a century afterwards, following vigorous action by the counter-Reformation. Moreover, whatever of his theories came out in his lifetime was criticized much more by the Protestants—Luther and Melanchthon—than by the Catholics, and, from a purely political point of view, Copernicus and his colleagues in their distant province of Ermland were sheltered from the fratricidal struggles which were beginning to shake the Church. One of Copernicus's few close friends, the Canon Tiedemann Giese who later became Bishop of Ermland (and who was mentioned in the preface dedicated to Pope Paul III) was able in 1525 to publish a plea for tolerance and reconciliation whose letter-preface mentioned the name of Copernicus and contained the famous declaration: 'I refuse the battle'.

But if Copernicus, like Giese, was in a position to refuse to do battle with the opponents of his 'revolution', there was another battle which he was unable to avoid. Who was Copernicus afraid of? We should like to know, and we think it was of himself, of his calculations, vertiginous sallies into a universe in which one could not go forward without asking oneself, like Erasmus: what was behind these explorations, reason or folly? To a certain degree, Koyré and Koestler were agreed in their protrait of Copernicus. They both realized that the *Book of Revolutions*, so far from being a joke, reflected a tragedy, only that tragedy was played out in such intimate areas of Copernicus's soul that, seen from the outside, it looks like a farce. The indecisiveness, the conjuring-tricks, the masquerades—these were the psychological defence-mechanisms of someone desperately trying to convince himself of his own sanity. They were also so many grotesque masks assumed by somebody who is unable to express his anguish. Copernicus was the Rigoletto of one of the most dramatic phases of the sixteenth century, in which the proud spirit of man amused itself in murdering the children of its most intimate friend: Reason.

A 'grand seigneur': Tycho Brahe

Compared to Copernicus, Tycho Brahe was a 'grand seigneur'. He was the *condottiere* of the astronomical revolution, just as his disciple and immediate successor, Johannes Kepler, was its magician. Tycho Brahe's project was an ambitious, yet simple one: to achieve a compromise between Ptolemy and Copernicus by envisaging a universe in which the earth would be static and have a central position, and in which the other main planets apart from the earth would turn around the sun. However, there was only one way to arrive at such a compromise: observation—ceaseless, exact, meticulous observation of the heavens. Brahe's 'career'—if it is possible so to describe such a short and turbulent existence, but one which nevertheless represented a rapid rise in the social hierarchy, transforming a Danish squire into the undisputed prince of the starry realm—Brahe's 'career' began with his observation of the new star of 1572 which we mentioned earlier,[3] and it was to

---

[3] See above I. 5.

continue in this same direction of unceasing, unremitting exploration of vaster and vaster areas of the heavens.

But in order to be able to set out upon this path of observation, Tycho Brahe needed complicated and expensive instruments, collaborators who had to be well paid, and unlimited leisure such as science requires when it is a matter of patience—gilded leisure, relieving the researcher of all material cares. Tycho Brahe obtained all this in superabundance, and he knew how to make excellent use of it. Copernicus lived a mean existence all alone in his tower, unknown to anybody, but Tycho Brahe twice held a royal and then imperial court in which there were masses of objects, people, and research grants (as one would say nowadays) such as no scholar had ever known before him. The splendour of his observatory, Uraniborg, the castle of Urania—the first worthy of the name in the history of astronomy—which he constructed according to his own plans, irradiated the age of the Renaissance like the Sistine Chapel.

It was an observatory made up of completely detachable parts, and Tycho was thus able to set it up in two different places, one after the other, whose names, thanks to Uraniborg, were among the most brilliant of the Renaissance: first the Island of Sveen, also known as the 'Isle of Venus' between Copenhagen and Elsinore, and then the castle of Benatek, also called the 'Bohemian Venice', ten leagues (thirty-five kilometres) to the north-east of Prague.

Uraniborg functioned on the Isle of Venus for twenty years, from 1576 to 1596, thanks to the enthusiastic support and the generosity of King Frederick II of Denmark. In the Bohemian Venice, Tycho Brahe reigned for only two years, from June 1599 to the twenty-fourth of October 1601, the date of his premature death, as mathematician to His Imperial Majesty Rudolph II of Hapsburg, but Uraniborg continued to exist at Benatek, for on the sixth of November 1601 Tycho Brahe's disciple Johannes Kepler was appointed imperial mathematician in his place, retaining that position until the death of Rudolph II in 1612. That was the end of Tycho Brahe's dream, not only because Kepler, while remaining the mathematician to Rudolph's successor, the Emperor Matthias, had to leave Benatek and retire to Linz, but also and above all because Kepler, while sincerely protesting his fidelity to Brahe, had completely demolished his master's system since his death and created a new astronomy based on a form of physics which had been unknown to Tycho Brahe. It was the end of a dream. We said that, in order to realize his dream, Tycho Brahe needed patrons, time, money: he found these, both in Denmark and Bohemia, to a degree unknown to any scholar before him, and to a degree unknown to any of his contemporaries. He also needed technical assistants, devoted collaborators, each one of whom would be engaged in the investigation of some precise field of observation and capable, through his observations and calculations, of adding a new fixed star to the great bronze globe enthroned in the library at Uraniborg.

Tycho Brahe had found these patrons and assistants in Denmark: he was to find them again in Prague. The chief of these patrons was Emperor Rudolph II of Habsburg himself. The bait had been cast by Tycho Brahe according to the best methods of modern publicity.

In 1598 he published *Tychonis Brahe Instauratae Mechanica* (Wandesburgi, 1598): a magnificent folio volume with illustrations, poems, notes, and digressions, containing a most attractive description of Uraniborg and the instruments which Brahe had set up there. It is through this volume that we know the date and the contents of Galileo's inaugural lecture at the University of Padua in 1592 which, as we said earlier, contained eulogistic references to Copernicus and Brahe.[4]

Tycho Brahe had the ingenious idea of dedicating this volume to the Emperor Rudolph.[5] The Emperor, who regarded himself as

[4] See above I. 2. Among the eulogies in prose and verse included by Tycho Brahe in his volume, he published a letter from Padua 'in order to fill half a page left blank by the printer'. In this letter, an anonymous friend described how the physician Giovanni Vincento Pinelli, one of the most celebrated patrons in Padua, had accorded his patronage to Galileo's inaugural lecture given on 7 December 1592 in an amphitheatre full to bursting-point. Before an enthusiastic audience, Galileo expounded the theories of Copernicus and praised Tycho Brahe's contribution to instrumental observation in astronomy. According to Emil Wohlwill, *Galilei und sein Kampf für die Copernicianische Lehre* (Wiesbaden, 1969), (2), i, 119, Tycho Brahe's book is the only historical source describing this inaugural lecture of Galileo. We should observe in passing that in his two large volumes Wohlwill fails to mention Joseph Solomon Delmedigo among Galileo's listeners or the presence of Jewish students in the University of Padua, referring to its open and cosmopolitan character but 'forgetting' the Jews in his list of foreigners and non-Catholics registered at Padua for their higher education. And yet, between 1517 and 1619, nearly eighty Jewish students obtained medical diplomas at the University of Padua (Alter, p. 8), which is a not inconsiderable number.

[5] On Tycho Brahe's *Astronomiae Instauratae Mechanica*, Dreyer writes (*TB*, p. 200, n. 2): 'This original edition now only exists in a few great libraries. In the Royal Library in Copenhagen are two copies with all pictures beautifully illuminated and gilt, the one presented to the Grand Duke Ferdinand de Medici, the other to the Bohemian

something of an astronomical/astrological expert, was flattered by this dedication and hastened to take over from the Danish sovereign, making Tycho Brahe his imperial mathematician. Tycho Brahe's entry into Prague in June 1599 was a princely cavalcade, and soon Uraniborg was set up in the castle of Benatek near the capital, enabling Brahe to participate in the social and intellectual life of the Prague aristocracy, for, apart from the Emperor himself, one must count among Tycho Brahe's patrons in Prague the imperial physician Hagecius, Martin Buchazek, the Rector of Prague University, Baron Johann von Hasenburg, and Baron Peter Wok Ursinus von Rosenberg with whom Tycho Brahe ate his last supper on 13 October 1601.[6]

Among the assistants, there was Longomontanus (Christen Sövensen Longberg), who was one of those who had been with him on the Island of Sveen and who had since acquired a well-deserved reputation in the astronomical world; a newcomer, Johannes Kepler, who had been originally only the research assistant responsible for observation of the most difficult of the planets, Mars, and the drawing up of new astronomical tables, but who was soon to eclipse all the others; two professors of mathematics from the University of Wittenberg, Melchior Joestelius and Ambrosius Rhodius; more modest collaborators—Johannes Eriksen, Simon Marius, Mathias Seiffart, Poul Jensen Coloing, and our David Gans;[7] and, finally, the mathematician of the Elector of Brandenburg,

nobleman "Peter Vok Ursinus, Dominus a Rosenberg". In the Trahöfer Stiftsbibliothek in Prague is one presented to Baron Hasenburg; in the British Museum is a copy presented to Hagecius, etc . . .'.
We can explain Dreyer's 'etc.' by the discovery we have made of one of these very rare, beautifully illuminated copies in a perfect state of preservation in the Schocken Library in Jerusalem. Tycho Brahe dedicated it to Fugger.

[6] Kepler gave a restrained but moving account of Brahe's sickness at this dinner on the thirteenth of October which resulted in his death on the twenty-fourth of October. In his delirium, he several times spoke the words '*Ne frustra vixisse videar*' ('Let me not seem to have lived in vain'), expressing his dissatisfaction at the incompletion of his project (Dreyer, pp. 386–7).

[7] Like Kepler, David Gans must have been a 'research assistant' at the observatory of Benatek, where he had the task, among others, of translating astronomical tables from Hebrew to German for Tycho Brahe, who acted as his 'patron'. Were these tables the 'Alphonsine Tables' as described by David Gans (*NN* 9a)? This point is worth investigating.
David Gans twice mentioned the history of the Alphonsine Tables in *Ẓemaḥ David*: in the Jewish section, in relation to Ibn Sid (see III, 2) and in the general section under the date 1251 (*ZD* 70b and 170b).

Johannes Muller. Of the entire team at Benatek, Muller was the only person apart from Tycho Brahe and Johannes Kepler to be mentioned by David Gans in *Neḥmad ve-Na'im.*

A Tychonides who exceeded himself: Kepler

Tycho Brahe's dream was far-reaching. Just as Nietzsche later claimed to be the last of the philosophers, having ended a development which Pythagoras had begun, so Tycho Brahe believed he was the last of the astronomers, also ending a development which had begun in Greece. An enormous wall-painting covered one side of his study at Uraniborg. It represented the eight great astronomers of history from Timocharis to Tycho Brahe himself, followed, however, by the last of the last who had not been born yet, but who was already baptized. His name was Tychonides: he was the follower who was to synthesize the work of the Master and provide it with the seal of the absolute. Tycho

When he treated this subject in *Neḥmad ve-Na'im* (9a), he gave less importance to the historical aspect, and the date given, 1225, was obviously an error which ought to be corrected to 1252 which corresponds, to within a year, to the date given in *Zemaḥ David.* The main point of importance in this entry is a biographical one: 'I, the writer of this book, have seen a copy of these Tables translated, on the orders of King Alfonso, from the Spanish language into the holy tongue by Rabbi Jacob Alquarsi in 5020 (1260), and I have translated this work from the Hebrew language to the German language for the great scholar Tycho Brahe.'

The fact that Tycho Brahe several times mentioned the Alphonsine Tables and the fact that these Tables had been superseded by the *Tabulae Prutenicae* published by Erasmus Reinhold in 1542, which themselves had become obsolete to the point that one of the main tasks given to Kepler by Tycho Brahe was that of drawing up up-to-date Tables (these were the Rodolphine Tables, published by Kepler in 1627, more than a quarter of a century after Tycho's death and dedicated to his memory)—all this raises the question of the usefulness for Tycho of David Gans's translation from Hebrew into German of the Alphonsine Tables, which he already had in Latin.

According to Steinschneider (*Die Hebraïschen Übersetzungen des Mittelalters* (Berlin, 1893, p. 638)), David Gans did not translate the Alphonsine Tables but the Tables of Pedro IV, drawn up about 1367, about a century after those of Alfonso X. A translation of these tables from Spanish to Hebrew is to be found in an eighteenth-century bibliographical Catalogue (Jacob Leenwarden (Amsterdam, 1797)) under the title 'Alphonsine Tables translated from the Spanish by Jacob al-Carsi'. It would be reasonable enough to suppose that in the sixteenth century also the Tables of Pedro were commonly known as the Alphonsine Tables. Thus David Gans, when translating the Tables of Pedro, thought he was translating the Alphonsine Tables, and it may be that Tycho Brahe did not possess a copy of the Tables of Pedro, the original of which was in Paris.

We may also, like Freedman (Introduction, p. 31) entertain the possibility that Tycho Brahe heard from Gans that there was a Hebrew translation of the Alphonsine Tables in existence and wished to know in which respects this translation varied from the familiar, classical text.

Brahe thought he had found Tychonides in Kepler, and, indeed, Kepler would never have been Kepler had he not been acquainted with Tycho Brahe and his work, but when, after Tycho's death, Kepler ought logically to have become Tychonides, he did in fact affix the seal of the absolute to Tycho Brahe's system, but this seal bore the mark of such an original genius that Tycho would not have recognized himself in this system which honoured his own by pulverizing it. Tychonides emerged stillborn, and from his ashes arose Johannes Kepler in the form in which he is known to posterity.

Tycho Brahe's charisma, his feudal authority, his royal style were such that, after his premature death, Kepler could not have been anything except a follower and a faithful disciple of the Master, but Kepler's hands and eyes were fired with such a magnetism, his thought was so bursting with genius that his 'completion' of Tycho Brahe's system was in reality a radical transformation of the aims and conclusions of that system. Whatever he touched, he impressed with the mark of originality. To whatever he continued, he gave a new, unexpected direction, although leaving the work unfinished so that others, Galileo and, above all, Newton would have the task of clearly defining the laws which had already wholly replaced those of Ptolemy, but were still expressed in the hybrid form which was characteristic of the sixteenth century: a mixture of certitude and uneasiness, of strict logic and wild lyricism, of physics and metaphysics, of reason and mysticism, of lucidity and superstition, of mathematics and hallucinations which gave rise to the most contradictory reactions.

THE REACTIONS TO THE REVOLUTION

How did the man of the second half of the sixteenth century and the beginning of the seventeenth century react to this astronomical revolution? In many different ways, obviously, but ways which we must examine carefully so that we can place the Jewish reactions and in this area, as in that of the discovery of the New World, disprove clichés, re-establish the facts, and attempt to provide an accurate image of Jewish humanism. This is all the more important in that the Rema, the Maharal, David Gans, and Azariah dei Rossi were not, as in the case of America, late reapers where earlier men had sown but immediate contemporaries, living in the same places—Cracow, Prague, and Italy—as Copernicus, Tycho Brahe,

Kepler, and Galileo. They witnessed the effect of the astronomical revolution on the circles of the great astronomers. It is for us to ascertain to what degree they too were affected.

The most common idea of the reception which the theories of Copernicus and his successors met with is that these new systems aroused the fierce opposition of the Church. The decree of the Inquisition condemning Copernicus's book in 1616 and Galileo's trial in 1632 and his condemnation the following year are regarded as the serious consequences of this long and violent struggle between science and religion.

There was indeed a struggle; intolerance and fanaticism did join forces against the scientific revolution, but it should be clear that, from the very beginning, another reaction was far more in evidence than this ideological combat: laughter, uproarious, Rabelaisian laughter which can be much more injurious than criticism—the hissing of the spectator which drives the actor from the stage, the lampoon which covers a writer with a ridicule which he may never get rid of. We know that Copernicus lived in a perpetual fear of sarcasm, and this psychosis, only too well justified by the number of quips made at his expense and that of his theory, was passed on to those who took up that theory on their own account—less to Tycho Brahe, no doubt, who himself had a splendid faculty of laughing at everything and could reply to a nasty remark with an even nastier one, than to Kepler, anxiety-ridden, eager to salvage his intellectual dignity in the midst of a too often beggarly and threadbare existence, and, above all, to Galileo, living in perpetual fear of being covered with ridicule like Copernicus and his book.

Laughter: Martin Luther

In this concert of laughter, the dominant note was given by Martin Luther, and we know what an effect one word from Luther, expressed in the rude, vulgar language of which he was a master and which he knew how to put to clever diplomatic use, had on the mentality of the period. One explosive word from Luther could change the course of history. His terrible diatribe against the 'Jewish pestilence' held up the emancipation of the Jews for two centuries and kept them in the social and political Middle Ages until the French Revolution.[8] It was a word of this kind, aimed

[8] Renée Neher-Bernheim, *Histoire juive de la Renaissance à nos jours* (Strasbourg–Paris, 1971), i, 47.

against Copernicus in 1539, even before the publication of his book, which created an enormous obstacle to the emancipation of astronomy, which also had to wait two centuries, until the time of Newton, in order to be finally liberated from the curse of laughter to which it had been subjected by Luther's remarks which we reproduce here:

Es ward gedacht eines neuen Astrologi, der wollte beweisen dass die Erde bewegt wurde und umginge, nicht der Himmel oder das Firmament, Sonne und Monde; gleich als wenn einer auf einem Wagen oder in einem Schiffe sitz und bewegt wird, meinete er sässe still und ruhete, das Erdreich aber und die Baüme gehen um und bewegen sich. Aber es gehet itzt also: wer da will klug sein, der soll ihm nichts lassen gefallen, was Andere machen, er muss ihm etwas Eigens machen, das muss das Allerbeste seyn wie ers machet. Der Narr will die ganze Kunst Astronomiae umkehren, aber wie die heilige Schrift anzeiget, so heiss Josua die Sonne still stehen und nicht das Erdreich.[9] [There is talk of a new astrologer who wants to prove that the earth moves and goes round instead of the sky, the sun, and moon, just as if somebody moving in a carriage or ship might hold that he was sitting still and at rest while the earth and the trees walked and moved. But that is how things are nowadays: when a man wishes to be clever he must needs invent something special, and the way he does it must needs be the best! The fool wants to turn the whole art of astronomy upside-down. However, as Holy Scripture tells us, so did Joshua bid the sun to stand still and not the earth.]

(Luther's *Tischreden*, i. 419)

In Luther's diatribe, one should first of all notice the insulting term 'Narr' which since the time of Erasmus and Sebastian Brandt had described all those who were implicated by the terrible promiscuous condition which haunted the man of the sixteenth century no less than it fascinated him: the ambiguous condition of genius and buffoonery. Now, we say 'buffoonery' and not madness, because we know that a madman is sick, and in the sixteenth century he was thought to be incurable. But a 'fool' or buffoon was at that time a hybrid creature who could allow himself to say anything, the noblest truth or the most absolute nonsense, and nobody would pay any attention to his perpetual ramblings since, picking up the crumbs under the sovereigns' tables, the only, very limited function of the fool was to make people laugh. Tycho Brahe

[9] Despite the reservations of Klaus Scholder (*Ursprünge und Probleme der Bibelkritik im 17. Jahrhundert* (Munich, 1966), p. 57), we have followed Koyré's excellent elucidations of Luther's text (Koyré, p. 77).

had such a fool, the dwarf Jeep, in his royal domain at Uraniborg, and, hearing him chattering on, one could gather from his lips the most arrant stupidities but also mathematical data, figures, and equations of real astronomical value. But what Tycho Brahe, because he had made astronomy his kingdom, could allow himself, like a king gathering scraps of political or moral science from his fool, Copernicus, Kepler, or Galileo could not take without being hurt by it, and without their discoveries being hurt by it. To confront them with a 'fool' who aped their image was to touch them at their weakest point. For more than two centuries, anti-Copernicanism was largely based on this suggestion of buffoonery. Earlier we pointed out how Andreas Osiander, in Copernicus's own lifetime, helped through his preface, read and approved by the writer himself, to cast this terrible suspicion of buffoonery on Copernicus's book. This Osiander was one of Martin Luther's associates from the very beginning of the Reformation.[10] Whatever the case, to a greater or lesser degree, this heavy guffaw accompanied the astronomical adventure until the time of Newton.

The authority of the Holy Scriptures: Melanchthon and the Inquisition

Luther's burst of laughter ended with an appeal to the authority of the Holy Scriptures, and particularly to that passage in the Book of Joshua which was to be fatal to the Copernican theory, leading to its explicit condemnation in 1616 and its implicit condemnation through the trial of Galileo in 1632. This was the second obstacle to the astronomical revolution: next to laughter, the Inquisition. And this raises the whole problem of intolerance.

But again there are different aspects of the question which allow a thousand different interpretations according to the viewpoint of the historian. The Catholic historian, eager to defend the honour of the Church, will rightly insist on the fact that Copernicus's book was placed on the Index only three-quarters of a century after its publication[11] and that, during his lifetime, Copernicus had found supporters and even admirers among the high dignitaries of the Church, that Pope Paul III had accepted the dedication of the *Revolution of the Celestial Orbs*, and that, finally, Galileo's trial had been tactfully handled, with a proper concern for fair treatment, and did not create a scandal.

[10] He also followed Luther in his theological anti-Judaism.
[11] Copernicus's book was struck off the Index only in 1835.

It is nevertheless true, however, that Copernicus's book and consequently his ideas were condemned on behalf of the Church by the Inquisition, that Galileo was forced to make a solemn recantation under threat of torture, and that, from the beginning of the seventeenth century at least, the Catholic Church displayed an attitude of single-minded, dogmatic intolerance towards the Copernican theory. It was the Church which, until the beginning of the nineteenth century, mounted the campaign of scriptural authority versus science.

But the Catholic historian is certainly not wrong in reproaching the Protestant historian for presenting the astronomical revolution as something which had grown out of the Reformation, as if it were one of its finest fruits which had sprung up quite naturally in the climate of liberty which the Reformation had introduced into the Church. We have just noted that Luther used a scriptural argument against the new astronomy. Melanchthon, however, went further Like Luther, he used the argument of absurdity against Copernicus and appealed to the authority of Scripture, but he added that harsh measures would have to be taken against this impious doctrine.[12]

What kind of measures? There was a constant, unremitting Protestant anti-Copernican pressure during the second half of the sixteenth century, so that Kepler who, for his part, was a Protestant, had to defend himself against both the left and the right with this courageous statement in his introduction to *Astronomia Nova* (1609):

So much for the authority of Holy Scripture. Now as regards the opinions of the saints about these matters of nature, I answer in one word, that in theology the weight of Authority, but in philosophy the weight of Reason, alone is valid. Therefore a saint was Lactantius, who denied the earth's rotundity; a saint was Augustine, who admitted the rotundity, but denied that antipodes exist. Sacred is the Holy Office of our day, which admits the smallness of the earth but denies its motion: but to me more sacred than all these is Truth, when I, with all respect for the doctors of the Church, demonstrate from philosophy that the earth is round, circumhabited by antipodes, of a most insignificant smallness, and a swift wanderer among the stars.

These few lines of Kepler's are a cry, like Galileo's thirty years later—a cry of alarm which was no more heeded by the Protestant Church than was Galileo's by the Catholic Church, for we know

[12] P. Melanchthon, *Initiae doctrinae physicae* (Wittenberg, 1549), pp. 60 ff., 99 ff.

that when the Thirty Years War broke out and the fateful moment came when one had to opt for one side or the other, Kepler was suspected and persecuted, and his mother accused of witchcraft and finally even deprived of the sacraments on her deathbed, excommunicated in so far as that term applied to the Lutheran Church, just as Galileo was to a degree excommunicated from the Catholic Church.

The authority of reason: the Cartesian rearguard action

But let us now beware of falling into the complacent traps of the lay historian, of the enlightened philosopher who delights to contrast the 'tolerance' of reasonable men with the 'intolerance' of the Church. He could use as evidence this cry uttered by Kepler: Kepler, who so judiciously opposed reason to Scripture.

In reality, however, Kepler, and Copernicus and Brahe before him, had to suffer from Reason no less than from the Church, for in the sixteenth century the authority of Aristotle remained at least as great as that of the Church. The Ptolemaic system, shaped, moulded, and rounded off by Averroës, Maimonides and St. Thomas Aquinas successively, was an integral part of the impressive but artificial, unassailable yet imaginary, work of art in which Aristotle's daughter Reason had imprisoned the medieval universe. It was even one of its main elements, for it was within these stout, solid walls that Reason and the Bible had concluded their reassuring pact of agreement. The physical and the meta-physical came together, constituting a whole which no anxiety troubled. The most perplexing problem of metaphysics, that of the origin and nature of Evil, had been solved, since Evil had been relegated entirely to the sublunary part of the world. And the most difficult problem of physics, that of the forces underlying the movements of planets and stars, had also been solved by the supposition of a Divine Will operating the world like an astronomical clock.

Medieval Reason had undoubtedly experienced some dangerous threats. An important metaphysical position had been assigned to Evil, sometimes even making it a part of God, thus upsetting the Aristotelian hierarchy and at the same time giving rise to intuitions of various elements of the pre-Aristotelian Greek universe which Copernicus, shortly preceded by Nicholas of Cusa, was to take up on his own account and pass on to his successors. But these jolts came from the side of mysticism: when it was Jewish, it was contemptuously called *Kabbalah* and judged unworthy of the attention of any reasonable person, and when it was Christian it was quickly throttled, banished from the Schools and universities, and relegated to the cloisters, when it was not simply declared heretical and condemned to the flames. Within Judaism, as we saw, the *Kabbalah* had to remain clandestine and did not dare to reveal itself and confront philosophy on equal terms until the second half of the sixteenth century, the very period when the astronomical revolution took place.

Thus, throughout the sixteenth century, the authority of Aristotle, no less than that of the Bible and perhaps even more so, continued to be invoked against a sun-centred system of the universe. The discovery of the New World, the redivision of a supposedly flat earth made no difference: we have seen that the consequences of the maritime Exodus towards Infinity only began to affect the human spirit at the very end of the sixteenth century. The Reformation made no difference either: Melanchthon, as we have also seen, founded his strictly anti-Copernican arguments on the authority of Aristotelian physics together with that of the Holy Scriptures. The Sorbonne was not the only university to have remained medieval right into the age of the Renaissance. In Italy, in Germany, in England, the scholars, men of learning, and professors all swore unanimously by Reason and Aristotle as against the absurdities of the new astronomy.

The tone was given in a sort of flashback, right in the seventeenth century, by Descartes, mathematician and physicist of genius, but also a philosopher, the apostle of that 'common sense' which Melanchthon had also invoked a hundred years earlier. Descartes's criticism of Kepler and Galileo was undoubtedly the most violent and symptomatic rearguard action of the tenacious struggle of Reason against the truth.

From the terror of Pascal to the wonder of David Gans

And, together with Descartes, Pascal—also a mathematician, physicist, and philosopher—followed suit. Not because he had any confidence in that Reason with which his mystical soul could never agree, but because, with a lucidity which the Jewish Kabbalistic Masters had already possessed, he glimpsed the extent to which the new vision of the universe upset the position of man. Man, already so small when compared with God's infinity, had now become smaller still, a mere atom within the infinity of the cosmos. Once the earth had entered into the affair, the dweller upon the earth, half-giant, half-grasshopper, was engaged in a perpetual wavering between infinities. If Descartes had been content with the smug celebration of 'common sense', Pascal was afraid for man's destiny: 'the silence of these infinite spaces terrifies me', he cried, and this terror of Pascal has to be placed next to the obstacles of Reason and Theology and the laughter of Luther as one of the reactions with which, for more than a century, modern, cultivated man received the astronomical revolution.

But there was also one other possible reaction—simple, moving, direct: that of wonder.[13] Let us say at once, by way of an introduction to what is about to follow, that such a warm reception of the astronomical revolution, an acceptance of it as a new and marvellous revelation, confirming that at Sinai, was to be found among the Jews.

[13] The theologian Abraham J. Heschel, applying the key-notion of his theology, the idea of wonder, to science, specifically cites Kepler as an example of a scholar who was 'wonderstruck' at the laws of nature (Abraham J. Heschel, *God in Search of Man*, (Philadelphia, 1958), p. 107).

2

Praeparatio astronomica: *David Gans on the threshold of the revolution*

How did the Jews react to the astronomical revolution? That is the question we shall now attempt to answer. After all I have said about David Gans, do I need to state that it is in him, in his book *Neḥmad ve-Na'im*, that we shall find the reaction of wonder at its most varied, and in its most developed form?

Among the Jews of the end of the sixteenth century, he was the only one to have had the privilege of close personal contact with Tycho Brahe and Johannes Kepler. It is true that at that same period Joseph Delmedigo was attending Galileo's lectures at Padua, and that his book *Elim* in which he cited his 'master Galileo''s opinion in his account of Jewish astronomy was published in Amsterdam in 1629, even before Galileo's trial, when the 'revolution' was still in its pristine freshness, whereas a whole century had to pass before David Gans's book was published, a little old-fashioned and out of date at the time of its publication which was after the storming of the astronomical Bastille by Sir Isaac Newton.

The circumstances of his book's publication, however, is no reason for us to class David Gans among the representatives of the 'ancien régime'. He wrote a work vibrant with the shock produced in a Jewish soul by a meeting with Tycho Brahe and Johannes Kepler a good thirty years before Delmedigo set pen to paper. In 1612, one year before his death, he had the honour of publishing the first, eulogistic Jewish reference to Copernicus in his *Magen David*. David Gans was undoubtedly the Jewish pioneer of the astronomical revolution.

It should be pointed out that even if David Gans had never personally known Tycho Brahe or Johannes Kepler, he would nevertheless have been intellectually equipped to cope with their ideas. The particular training he underwent, his taste for research, the time he had spent in the academies of the Rema and the Maharal—all this provided him with three important qualities which equipped him to become, if not a follower, at any rate an attentive observer of the new astronomy: namely, a positive attitude to science, a freedom of thought, and a fidelity to tradition. These three qualities, if taken together, imply a great danger of inner conflicts and contradictions, but we can never stress sufficiently that the astronomical revolution made its way across an enormous accumulation of paradoxes. David Gans, similarly, set out on this path with that characteristic mixture of naïvety and courage which we find at every stage of his career.

THE EPILOGUE OF NEḤMAD VE-NA'IM

In the epilogue to *Neḥmad ve-Na'im*, the qualities we have just enumerated are clearly expressed. The positive attitude to science enabled David Gans to reactivate his talents as a historian and to give a lively account of the history of astronomy from its origins until 1600. Freedom of thought was demanded by David Gans in a conclusion, at once apologetic and polemical, in which one senses the direct influence of both his Jewish Masters, the Rema and the Maharal.

Fidelity to tradition, finally, must be understood in its widest sense—that sense in which it can lead to a clash with liberty, creating a conflict which runs through the human adventure in the sixteenth century from end to end. David Gans did not shrink from the danger of being inwardly torn apart, and in his epilogue he gave a typically Jewish account of that adventure, enabling us to see, within the general context of the sixteenth century, the specifically Jewish aspect of the spiritual drama of which nearly all the great geniuses of the time were more than spectators, being its actors and, frequently, its victims.

David Gans, historian of astronomy

The history of astronomy takes up two-thirds of the epilogue of Neḥmad ve-Na'im. It also contains an apologetical element, or, rather, the purely historical account is continually accompanied by a strain of apologetics which in no way detracts from the interest of these pages, steeped as they are (as one definitely feels) in the atmosphere of David Gans's life at the time of writing. It is less a display of erudition than the projection in a book of an existential experience.

We should not forget, first of all, that Gans was a historian by temperament. More than his predecessors, a number of whom had made historical outlines of Jewish astronomy, he knew how to enliven his account with original details, and, above all, he broadened the scope of the subject and in his historical survey gave a comprehensive view of it, embracing both Jewish and non-Jewish astronomy. And this horizontal universalism is paralleled by a vertical universalism. David Gans took the history of astronomy back to Adam, the very first man, and he took it forward to Copernicus and Tycho Brahe and his team, of which David Gans himself was a member.

What were the principal stages of this evolution of five millennia plus three and a half centuries? Here, as in his chronicle *Zemah David*, Gans dealt first with the Jewish aspect, and then with the non-Jewish aspect of the question.

The history of Jewish astronomy

According to David Gans, Jewish astronomy began with the patriarch Abraham followed by the 'scholars' of the biblical period: David, the tribe of Issachar, and, above all, Solomon, whose works extended beyond the canonical Bible and overlapped into apocryphal literature. In order to demonstrate the authenticity and the importance of the *'Wisdom of Solomon'*, Gans referred to the opinion expressed by Nachmanides in the introduction to his commentary on Genesis. He could also have referred to the opinions of his contemporary Azariah dei Rossi, whose book *Me'or Einayim* contained a rehabilitation of the Jewish Alexandrian literature as a whole.

The biblical figures are followed by numerous Talmudic and Midrashic scholars: true astronomers, fully deserving that title through their erudition and their vast knowledge of the related sciences—mathematics, geography, geology, astronomy. The list could have been a long one, but Gans limited himself to a few outstanding names: Rabbi Eliezer ben Hyrcanus, the author of the *Pirkei de Rabbi Eliezer*, which are full of astrological and astronomical observations; Rabban Gamaliel, known for his arithmetical and geometrical tables which enabled him to set empirical observations against mathematical reckonings; Rabbi Eliezer ben Ḥisda and

Rabbi Yohanan ben Gudgada, encyclopaedic talents who were conversant with a wide variety of sciences; Mar Samuel, who boasted of the fact that the paths of the heavens were as familiar to him as the streets of Nehardea, where he directed the Academy (he has come down in history as Samuel-the-moonstruck); and, finally, Rav Adda, whose calculations and computations formed the permanent basis of the Jewish calendar, which had been admired by scholars the world over from ancient times (as Hipparchus bears witness) up to the time of Gans, when it was praised by contemporary astronomers. We should remember that Gans wrote his book scarcely fifteen years after the Gregorian reform of the calendar, whereas the Jewish calendar had not needed any change whatsoever, nor had it been taxed with the slightest error since it had been fixed by the master-astronomers of the Talmud, to whom Gans gives a brief accolade.

Then come the Jewish astronomers of the Middle Ages and David Gans's contemporaries, who were his own teachers. This part of the account interrupts the quiet flow of the narrative, for these names are provided in connection with the painful problem of the flagrant contradiction between Talmudic astronomy and the Aristotelian astronomy universally accepted in the Middle Ages, as much by the Jews as by the Gentiles.

We shall be returning to this problem, with which all the Jewish scholars who are mentioned on this page—which should be regarded as a sort of 'methodological parenthesis'—had to contend. We shall see later the exact circumstances in which Gans himself encountered the full force of this controversy, but, for the moment, we shall restrict ourselves to repeating the list of astronomers mentioned by Gans in this section, who, from the Talmudic period onwards, had enriched astronomy with their knowledge: first, the great Maimonides, whose chapter on the rules for fixing the calendar in his *Mishneh Torah* is full of astronomical information; Rabbi Abraham Ibn Ezra, the celebrated exegete and poet of the Spanish golden age, although Gans admits to not having read his works on astronomy; Rabbi Abraham bar Ḥiyya, a great astronomer and astrologer, and also a distinguished geographer; Joseph Albo and Isaac Arama, who were philosophers like Maimonides, and, like him, competent astronomers; Rabbi Isaac Israeli, the celebrated author of the great works *Yesod Olam* and *Sha'ar ha-Shamayim* (the first of these two books is the 'classic' work of Jewish astronomy in the Middle Ages); and Zerahia Gerondi, whose *Sefer ha-Ma'or* is a classic of the same quality as *Yesod Olam*. Then, there was the great Gersonides (in Jewish tradition known as the Ralbag), concerning whom David Gans made a revealing observation:

The Ralbag distinguished himself in astronomy in the first chapter of the fifth part of his *Wars of the Lord*. Unfortunately, the publisher omitted this chapter on the grounds that it constituted a separate book. I must confess that until now I have not come across this work, and there are no doubt many other Jewish writers with whose writings I am unacquainted, and whom I have not mentioned here.[1]

---

[1] David Gans's observation is perfectly correct. Gersonides' *Wars of the Lord* were first published in Riva di Trento in 1560. The publisher, Jacob Mercarra, stated in the preface that he had kept aside for a later edition the first chapter of the fifth part which constituted an astronomical treatise in itself, and had no immediate connection with the two following chapters in which Gersonides returned to the original subject of his book: theology and religious philosophy.

Renan-Neubauer, working from the manuscripts, gave (in *Les écrivains juifs français du XIVᵉ siècle*, xxi (Paris, 1893), pp. 586 ff.) a detailed description of the hundred and thirty-six chapters of this section omitted by the publisher (cf. also Joseph Carlebach, *Levi ben Gerson als Mathematiker* (Berlin, 1910)), and stated that the famous Latin translation of extracts from the *Wars of the Lord* made in Gersonides' lifetime in 1342 at the request of Pope Clement VI was really 'a little work taken from the fifth book' (p. 621). This 'little work' contained a detailed description of Jacob's Staff and of the *camera obscura* invented by Gersonides, and it is this 'little work' which must be taken into account, together with the published book, in Tycho Brahe's frequent references to Levi ben Gerson (*Opera Omnia* ed. Dreyer 1929, i, ix, xxiv, v, 320, 322) and in Kepler's references to Rabbi Levi (*Optica*, 214, 215). In the frequently mentioned correspondence between Johann Remus Quietanus of Ruffach and Kepler, however, (*Gesammelte Werke*, ed. Caspar, vol. 18, *Briefe* nos. 1095 and 1103, letters written in December 1628 and March 1629 respectively), what the two friends were looking for was precisely the purely astronomical (and not optical) parts omitted by the editor in 1560.

It would therefore be wrong to say, as has often been done, that Kepler tried in vain to procure Gersonides' works. Kepler had a very good knowledge of the works of Gersonides that were available at the time, and he was also aware of the existence of a fragment which he supposed was known from manuscripts in Basle, in Tübingen, or in Jewish circles.

But this has not been the only error which has been made with regard to Gersonides. This Jewish philosopher who was born in Bagnols in 1288 and lived in Avignon and Orange until 1344, suspected of having converted to Christianity because of the Pope's interest in his work, and confused, because of the Latin transcription of his name Levi into Leo, with Judah Messer Leon or with Leo Hebraeus in the sixteenth century, and because of his father's name Gerson with the Christian philosopher Jean Gerson (1363–1429), has had the authorship of his optical discoveries challenged (see above, II. 2). Here are two quotations from recent writers whose scientific authority is too well established for it to be anything other than a repetition of stereotyped formulas, handed down from generation to generation:

And finally, there come two figures already known to us as David Gans's own Teachers: the Rema of Cracow and the Maharal of Prague.[2] It is an incomplete list, and one would have to add the names which appear in the other parts of David Gans's book: particularly that of Judah Halevi. The writer did not deem it necessary to include them in his historical account, which he now continues in passing from the Jewish realm to the provinces of the Gentiles.

The history of non-Jewish astronomy

These terms 'realm' and 'province' which we use here were not employed by David Gans, but they seem to us to be an accurate

'The sailors of the fifteenth century used the arbalest or Jacob's Staff, an instrument invented in the previous century by Leon the Jew who lived in Provence. This invention was later wrongly attributed to Regiomontanus.' (E. Doublet, 'L'astronomie nautique et les grandes découvertes maritimes du XV⁰ du XVI⁰ siècles', in *Scientia* (Milan, October 1935), p. 216). This information is perfectly correct, but in which encyclopaedia will one find this 'Leon the Jew who lived in Provence' and who is supposed here to be anonymous, whereas in reality he was Levi ben Gerson to whom Renan-Neubauer devoted at least twenty pages?

And this is the second quotation:

As for the astrolabe, its invention has been attributed to the Greek astronomer Hipparchus who lived in the second century B.C. It was replaced by the quadrant which was an improvement but lacked precision because the plumbline which acted as its lubber's point wavered with the movements of the ship. In order to counter this defect, navigators adopted the marine arbalest, also known as the balestrille or Jacob's Staff, which is said to have been perfected by the German astronomer John of Koenigsberg, better known in scholarly circles as Regiomontanus, about 1531.

(Jean Babelon, *L'Amérique des Conquistadores* (Paris, 1947), pp. 68–9.) I hope the date 1531 given for Regiomontanus is a misprint (see below III. 4), but why should one name the German astronomer who is said to have perfected Jacob's Staff and overlook the Jewish astronomer who undoubtedly invented it?

It is also difficult to understand why Pierre Duhem (in *Le système du monde* (Paris, 1913), v, 201–3 and ix. 325 ff.) insisted on trying to show that Gersonides' intuitions concerning the rotation of the earth were influenced by the teachings of the University of Paris, when these 'intuitions' already existed in the *Zohar* (see above, II. 2), or why Duhem, again, described Nicholas d'Oresme as the 'French precursor of Copernicus', without suggesting for a moment that this French Christian (1320–81) could have been influenced in turn by the French Jew Gersonides (1288–1344).

Finally, Baruch Raphael Goldstein (in 'Al trumato shel ha-Ralbag le-astronomia', *Divrei ha-Accademia ha-leumit ha-Israelit le-mada' im* iv. (Jerusalem, 1971), pp. 174–85) stated that he searched vainly among the manuscripts for Gersonides' one hundred and thirty-six chapters on astronomy whose omission from the printed edition was noted by David Gans, and which Kepler tried to obtain. See, however, Goldstein's recent bibliography in *Les Juifs au regard de l'histoire*, *Mélanges Bernhard Blumenkranz*, Paris, 1985, p. 245–6.

[2] See above I. 4..

reflection of the relationship between Jewish and non-Jewish astronomy in *Neḥmad ve-Na'im*. The latter is regarded as only a province of the former.

To be sure, the origins of Jewish astronomy cannot be traced back further than Abraham, father of the Jewish people, while non-Jewish astronomy goes back all the way to Adam, the ancestor of all humanity. But if Adam was an eminent astronomer before the Jews existed, he passed on his accumulated knowledge, not to humanity as a whole, but to Abraham the first Jew, and it was from Abraham that a series of regular historical contacts carried astronomy from the Jewish realm to the non-Jewish provinces which inherited the science: first, Egypt, then the Greeks, the Chaldeans, the Arabs, and finally, the Moderns.

It is here, in his list of names of non-Jewish astronomers, that Gans introduces the theme of the Jewish origins of universal astronomy. For clarity's sake, let us first examine the list, and then go back to the Adamic and Abrahamic sources in order to examine Gans's account of their repercussions throughout history.

The first place goes to the Egyptians, for three reasons, the first being the interconnection of Jewish history with that of Egypt. But there were also other reasons why Egypt was an autonomous and especially distinguished province of astronomy. First of all, there was the physical circumstance of the regular flooding of the Nile: this, to some degree, was the economic cause of the invention by the Egyptians of geometry, land-surveying, and the redistribution of land, discoveries which had to be used after each bout of flooding. From land-measurement, the Egyptians passed to measurement of the sky, so that even in Gans's day astronomy was metaphorically called 'geometry' (measurement of the earth)—a proof, if ever there was one, of the derivation of the measurement of the sky, of the planets, of the zodiac, from the measurement of the earth.

But does not the Bible attribute to Egypt the privilege of being a land without rain and consequently without clouds (Deuteronomy 11: 10)? It is in no way surprising, then, if it was in that country with perpetually clear skies that the first methodical observations were made, leading to astronomical science, one of the most remarkable contributions of Egypt to universal wisdom.

From Egypt, astronomy moved to Greece first and then Chaldea. In writing about developments in these two regions of the earth,

Gans adopted a different method. He did not give a chronological list of names, as for Egypt, but divided the astronomers into two groups: those whose works have been lost, and those whose precious books or manuscripts we still possess. The theories of the former group have come down to us only by means of the latter.

The Chaldeans all belong to the first group. Only two names, in fact, were mentioned by Gans: Timocharis and Aristyllos, famous as the pioneers of the study of the fixed stars, but they are only known to us through Hipparchus and Ptolemy. As for the Greeks, Gans classes among the astronomers whose works are lost the pre-Athenians Kidon, contemporary of the Trojan War, Siron, contemporary of the prophet Daniel (whom Alter was right in seeing as a corruption of Hesiod), and Thales of Miletus. And then there come the mighty representatives of the glorious Athenian school: Solon, Pythagoras, and (a doubtful reading) Empedocles.

There follows a list of those Greek writers whose works still today form the basic texts of the astronomical library. It is given in chronological order with certain digressions, also in chronological order, which provide David Gans with the opportunity of referring to Jewish historical works such as Abraham Zacuto's *Sefer Yuḥasin* and Azariah dei Rossi's *Me'or Einayim*. This list, however, is also given in a hierarchical order, and constitutes an interesting outline, in three columns, of the evolution of astronomical ideas in ancient Greece. Euclid was positioned at the base of the hierarchy, and Ptolemy at the summit.

Although it was not, strictly speaking, astronomical, Gans claimed that Euclid's geometry laid the foundations of astronomy. It was 'the ladder linking the earth to the heavens. Without that ladder resting on the earth, we could not have gone up to the heavens.' We earlier quoted Gans's encomium of Euclid, and related how his discovery of Euclid's book as an adolescent was a matter of love at first sight.[3]

Where Euclid was pure reasoning, Archimedes contributed the element of empirical observation. In Syracuse, he constructed a model of the heavenly sphere in transparent glass, large enough for him to be able to install himself within it and use this miniature reproduction of the heavens for making his own computations.

Aristarchus put forward the idea of the movement of the earth.

[3] See above I. 3.

The genius of Hipparchus eclipsed that of all his predecessors, and his calculations of a hitherto unequalled precision served as the basis for the system of Ptolemy, who recognized him as his teacher. In Gans's account, there is also an allusion to Kallipos and Sosigenus, whose work enabled Julius Caesar to establish the calendar which bears his name, and which remained in use until the Gregorian reform in Gans's own lifetime. And, finally, we come to Ptolemy. To this genius who succeeded in synthesizing all that had been thought and discovered by his Egyptian, Chaldean, Greek and, already, Christian predecessors (he lived in Alexandria in about AD 140); to this star performer to whom we owe the masterwork of universal astronomy, *The Almagest*, David Gans devoted not only a careful chronological study (from which we learn in passing that Gans wrote this in 1611) but a veritable panegyric, particularly significant in view of the fact that Gans said that it was taken 'from the eminent scholar, Sire Tycho Brahe'. Thus, he said that the Romans had conquered Alexandria but their empire crumbled, while the Alexandrian Claudius Ptolemy made an everlasting conquest of the empire of the heavens and the earth, and his double empire was still in existence.

Passing to the Middle Ages, the astronomical harvest was a poor one compared to that of the ancient world. Gans mentions only two names: Albitini (Al-Battani) to whom Maimonides acknowledged himself to be greatly indebted, and King Alfonso of Spain and Sicily (Alfonso X), a famous astronomer in his own right, who gathered together a group presided over by a Jewish Rabbi, Isaac Ibn Sid, which produced the celebrated Alphonsine Tables which David Gans, precisely, had translated from Hebrew to German for Sire Tycho Brahe.[4]

The Middle Ages had not much to show for themselves, but, in effect, who could still 'discover' anything in astronomy, who could take this science any further after Ptolemy?

The first mention of Copernicus in a Hebrew work

And now, suddenly, there is a reference to a sixteenth-century astronomer, Nicholas Copernicus. Why him, precisely? Because, in the unanimous opinion of the astronomers contemporary with David Gans, at the end of the sixteenth century, nobody, from the

---

[4] See above, I. 3.

time of Ptolemy, had equalled the Alexandrian genius except the Prussian, Nicholas Copernicus.

This is what David Gans has to say:

Nicholas Copernicus, a Prussian, is the most celebrated and remarkable astronomer among our contemporaries. The scholars of our period are unanimous in acclaiming his genius and the depth of his astronomical knowledge. It is said that he is unequalled since Ptolemy. With his wide knowledge and keen intelligence, he attempted to prove that the earth is in continual rotation. It should be pointed out that this idea is not a new one: it had already occurred to men who lived two thousand years ago. I myself have discovered in the second chapter of the fourth part of the book entitled 'Of the Heavens and the Earth' that such was the opinion of the celebrated scholar Pythagoras and his pupils.[5]

On this idea, Copernicus wrote an admirable, systematic, and extremely profound book, completing his book in the year 1500 of the non-Jewish era which corresponds to the year 5098 of the Jewish era.[6]

This scholar died in his native province, Prussia, in the year 1543 which corresponds to the year 5303 of our era.

Did Gans think that the history of astronomy had ended with Copernicus? Apparently so, since the epilogue now suddenly made a sharp about-turn and passed from history to apologetics. Gans devoted a couple of pages to a defence of astronomy against its detractors in the synagogue: we shall look at these later on.[7]

However, there still is, as we said, right at the end of the epilogue, the titbit of the 'conclusion of conclusions'—that final touch with which David Gans terminates both the epilogue and *Nehmad ve-Na'im* as a whole. Now, this conclusion, as we also said, with its evocation of the hours he spent with Tycho Brahe in the observatory of Benatek and its description of his system, was the most moving and inspiring tribute which David Gans could have paid to the figure he undoubtedly regarded as the supreme genius of astronomy, the only one who had not only equalled Ptolemy as Nicholas Copernicus had done, but had surpassed him. David Gans considered his system the culmination of the whole history of astronomy from Adam until the beginning of the seventeenth

[5] Aristotle's reference to the Pythagoreans (*Treatise of the Heavens*, ii. 9) was accepted by Copernicus himself, who never mentioned Aristarchus, his real 'precursor' among the ancients.

[6] Here there is a confusion between the date when Copernicus began his researches in Rome and Padua (1500) and the date of the completion of his book (1543).

[7] See below III. 2.

century—until the years 1611–13 when he completed the manuscript of *Neḥmad ve-Na'im*.

The Jewish influence on non-Jewish astronomy

However, as we have pointed out, there was one more link in this chain which led from Adam to Tycho Brahe: the Jewish impact on non-Jewish astronomy. Here apologetics truly comes into its own. It begins with Adam who, according to Gans, passed on his universal knowledge to Abraham, the first Jew, and we find it at each important stage in the universal history of astronomy. Egypt, for example—from where could it have gained its astronomical pre-eminence if the Jewish people had not lived there for centuries? Climatic considerations alone were not enough to explain the importance of astronomy in that country. No: it was the children of Abraham, Isaac, and Jacob, during their sojourn in Egypt, who had flooded the country with this knowledge they had received from the Patriarchs. And, as for the Chaldeans, did not the Jews maintain a permanent contact with Chaldea, and did they not spend a second exile there, after their first exile in Egypt? And what of the Greeks, the Athenians? Were they not the first to acknowledge (read Pythagoras and Hipparchus on the question) how much they owed to the Jews? As for the great Ptolemy, how could he have culled his knowledge in the great library at Alexandria if it had not been built up and brought to its culmination by the Alexandrian Jews?[8]

Could one say then like Maimonides, that since Ptolemy's time astronomy had changed sides, and that the tribulations of exile made the Jewish people forget the true astronomy which then became the prerogative of the Gentiles?

If David Gans put this question, it was only in order to respond with a resounding 'no' to Maimonides' defeatist attitude re-adopted by the Rema. Emphatically and with great conviction, David Gans insisted that not only the non-Jewish astronomers of the Middle Ages, but above all his contemporaries, the universal geniuses of the sixteenth century, the Copernicuses and the Tycho Brahes, like Ptolemy and Pythagoras before them, had acquired their knowledge from the Jews.

---

[8] All these ideas were taken from Josephus, and also from Tycho Brahe, who frequently referred to Josephus as a source for the history of astronomy in antiquity (see Tycho Brahe, *Op. Om.*, index).

This, however, was not a conviction which David Gans had arrived at through theorizing or as a result of merely abstract considerations. Excited, enthusiastic, triumphant, he had retrieved it from the close encounters which he had the extraordinary privilege of experiencing with these giants; he had gained it in the course of his overwhelming experience in the castle of Benatek, in Tycho Brahe's observatory, which he made, for reasons whose full significance we now understand, the 'conclusion of conclusions' of his book.

Before reaching this conclusion, however, he had to deal with the difficult problem treated in what we have called the 'methodological parenthesis' of the epilogue—a parenthesis which Gans could not have done otherwise than develop at length, because, as we said at the beginning of this chapter, he inherited from his Jewish Teachers, together with the taste for history and science, two other characteristics which Gans could scarcely have avoided, contradictory though at first sight they may seem: freedom of thought and fidelity to tradition.

DAVID GANS'S FREEDOM OF THOUGHT

Freedom of thought: in the sixteenth century, as in the Middle Ages, these three words did not denote the spiritual climate in which the overwhelming majority of humanity lived. On the contrary, it remained the prerogative of only a few brave individuals, some of whom went to the stake for it, with the difference from the Middle Ages that now they were persecuted not only by the Catholic Church but also by the Reformed Church, as we see from the martyrdom in Geneva of Michael Servetus, whom Calvin had ordered to be burnt alive in 1553, just as Étienne Dolet had been burnt in Paris under Francis I in 1546, and as Giordano Bruno had been burnt by the Pope in the year of grace 1600.

Neither the Renaissance, nor the advent of humanism, nor the Reformation had succeeded in changing the attitudes of the vast majority of people, who remained a prey to narrow-minded fanaticism, obscurantism, dogmatism, and witch-hunting. As we have just pointed out, one of the most tragic phases of Johannes Kepler's miserable last years was the frightful trial of Kepler's mother for witchcraft by the Lutheran Church. A few years later, the Catholic Inquisition threatened Galileo with torture.

It is therefore all the more remarkable that Jewish society displayed such a different attitude. Although intolerance among the Jews had never reached the point where people were tortured or put to death for their opinions, Jacob Katz has demonstrated that the Jewish community as a whole had always waged a desperate struggle against a fanatical minority.[9] There were undoubtedly obscurantists among the Jews in the sixteenth century, but the Jews as a whole, led by their great scholars, exposed themselves to the light—to the new brilliance of the light—with the passionate desire to be penetrated by it to the core.

GANS'S DEFENCE OF ASTRONOMY

Where the study of the secular sciences, and, more particularly, of astronomy was concerned, David Gans had only to follow a line of reasoning put forward by the great Jewish scholars of the past and present. He too heard the grumblings and grouses of certain rabbis who fulminated against the 'time lost' in occupying oneself with 'these futilities', when a Jew's real task was the study of the infinitely complex Talmudic casuistry which alone could dictate his duties and regulate his conduct. In the same way as Maimonides, however, or (closer to him) his immediate Teachers, the Rema and the Maharal, Gans knew that these rabbis were powerless dwarfs who utilized the *halakhah* as an easy and practical way of gaining oneself a comfortable position in the world to come. Hats off to *halakhah*! Without it, there would be no Judaism, no Jews, but one has to be disinterested in its study and observance. A Jew ought not to live with one eye on his reward, but he should carry out his duty simply because it *is* his duty.

But is not a knowledge of astronomy a fundamental duty, a *mitzvah*, in the absence of which no Jew could fix the calendar of his religious life? You say that this calendar has already been definitely fixed for centuries, and one only needs a little portable table in order to find one's way about the Jewish year, and there is no need to waste one's time studying astronomy? But that, said David Gans (as Isaac Israeli and Maimonides had said before him), is to overlook the very meaning of the Jewish calendar, whose fixed form ought not to blind us to its complex and vital implications, a knowledge of which is essential to the performance of whole groups of *mitzvot*. When the Talmudic sages spoke about the 'mystery' of the Jewish calendar, it was not only a manner of speaking. This mystery, precisely, is its astronomical content which remains eternally valid, and which cannot be reached without the 'ladder' (to use the image employed by Mordecai Jaffe and the Maharal) of mathematics, geography, and geometry.

In this Jewish defence of astronomy there was another point to which Gans liked to draw attention whenever he had the opportunity. This was that even if astronomy were not one of the foundation-stones of *halakhah*, one should nevertheless devote oneself wholeheartedly to its study, for it is through astronomy that the grandeur of God's works is revealed. Recalling David Kimhi's and Joseph Albo's commentaries on Psalm 19, David Gans, in a stylistic flight worthy of Kepler and Pascal—and also Maimonides and the Maharal—placed his reader before the heavens which proclaim the glory of God and the works of His hands. Where else, he asked, can man find the silent echo of the voice of the creator if not in the contemplation of the stars and their wonderful motions?

Is this a mystical flight of fancy? Undoubtedly, but it is also conducive to rational understanding, for these wonderful motions are so contradictory that in their very contradictions, their mysterious antagonisms, they point to the need for a creator. Astronomy is thus instrumental to faith. And then, with a sense of literary irony which once again demonstrates his freedom of approach, Gans, just when the theme of contradiction ought to make him turn to the authority of the Maharal, seeks support from the Maharal's antagonist *par excellence*, Rabbi Eliezer Ashkenazi, whose 'admirable commentary' on 'Thou shalt know the Lord thy God' in *Ma'asei ha-Shem* (chapter 21) he repeats in full. He claims that since the Torah does not say 'Thou shalt believe the Lord thy God', but 'Thou shalt know the Lord thy God', one must conclude that genuine faith can only be based on knowledge—an idea which had already been fully expounded by Maimonides, but which Gans takes here from Eliezer Ashkenazi, as if he had wished to honour at one and the same time the passionate mysticism of his Teacher the Maharal and the strict rationalism of Eliezer Ashkenazi: two scholars who in their lifetimes conducted a bitter polemic with each other which Gans wanted to transcend with his synthesis. A well-justified little lesson given by a disciple to his master![10]

Finally, one last argument was put forward in favour of Jews studying astronomy: non-Jewish opinion. Here we are confronted with the moment in time experienced by David Gans himself. He can no longer be regarded simply as a representative of tradition, but he was a man who, living in Prague in the year 1600, realized that he bore a *responsibility* in the most literal and immediate sense of the term (i.e., liability to answer): he had to be prepared to answer the questions put to him, especially on the Jewish calendar, by the non-Jewish astronomers who had asked him to work with them at the castle of Benatek. Not to reply, to assume this responsibility here and now, to remain silent before this volley of questions—would that be honouring us as Jews, would that be honouring Him who, creating all of us, conferred upon us Jews the special honour of a Torah which is 'our wisdom and our intelligence in the eyes of the *goyim* [nations]'?

THE METHODOLOGICAL PARENTHESIS IN *NEḤMAD VE-NA'IM*: THE PROBLEM IS NOT THAT OF THE AUTHORITY OF THE BIBLE, BUT THAT OF THE AUTHORITY OF THE TALMUD

The idea of fidelity is understood here as meaning fidelity to religious tradition and belief in God in the widest and most poetic sense of these terms, as we often find it in Brahe and even more often in Kepler, but it also has the more restricted sense which we also often find in Brahe, Kepler, and Galileo, of fidelity to biblical tradition. For David Gans, however, because he was Jewish, fidelity to rabbinical tradition had to be added to this fidelity to biblical tradition and was even more important. This point, which exceeds in importance the particular case of David Gans, illuminates a major difference, too often overlooked, between the Jewish and Christian approaches to the astronomical revolution of the sixteenth and seventeenth centuries. We should note this difference, and bear it in mind throughout this book: namely, that the offence caused by Copernicus which finally brought first his book onto the Index, and

---

[10] We have already pointed out (see I. 4) that David Gans could have found the idea that the contradictions in the motions of the stars indicate the necessity for a Divine Creative Will in Mordecai Jaffe's *Levush*.

then Kepler (on the Protestant side) and Galileo (on the Catholic side) to excommunication and recantation, was produced by the clash between the new astronomy and the Scriptures, whether, as was usually the case, it was the Old Testament (Genesis, Joshua, the Psalms, Job) or the New Testament (St. John's Gospel and the Book of Revelation). The Jews, on the other hand, in so far as they were offended by Copernicus (but this term is too strong: one should reduce it to its true proportions and say, rather, in so far as they were surprised and astonished by Copernicus) rarely reacted by a reference to scriptural authority.[11]

True, one does find in Jewish writers lists of contradictions between the Bible and astronomy, and David Gans devoted a rather lengthy passage in chapter 64 of *Nehmad ve-Na'im* to an attempt to demonstrate that certain verses in Genesis and the Psalms were in agreement with the new and, to his mind, unquestionable concept of the existence of the antipodes. These verses had been used in the Middle Ages by Abraham Ibn Ezra and David Kimhi, as well as by astronomers as competent as Maimonides, Abraham bar Hiyya, and Isaac Israeli, and even 'enlightened' contemporaries like Azariah dei Rossi, to justify the old Ptolemaic hypothesis of an earth whose lower half sank into the waters. In the following chapter (65), Gans dealt with the greater and more complicated problem of the 'upper waters' and the 'lower waters' with which the account of the creation of the earth in the Book of Genesis begins. But Gans maintained that these contradictions were only apparent, as Jewish biblical exegesis was sufficiently many-sided and flexible to allow these verses to be interpreted as being in perfect agreement with the new ideas, which experience had shown to be irrefutable. Thus, the 'oceans' upon which God founded the earth (Psalm: 24:2) were not the cosmic waters, but quite simply, as we read at the end of the verse, the seas and rivers. And, as for the 'vault' referred to on the second day of the creation (Genesis 1: 6), it refers first of all to the waters on the earth's interior rather than to the cosmic waters of the universe. Here we must point out that, once again, David Gans had recourse to a commentary of Eliezer Ashkenazi, the anti-Maharalist *par excellence*.

But all this is quite secondary, and basically is only an exegetical problem within Judaism. Chapter 65 concludes with the modest

---

[11] See the appendix.

assertion that the writer is prepared to uphold his exegetical hypothesis only as long as he has not received better ones from the scholars, and that, in any case, Gans is profoundly convinced that the Bible provides no obstacle to the new astronomy. He never foresaw the day feared by Kepler when one might be forced to choose between the truth and the Scriptures.[12]

On the other hand, what he did fear was the necessity of having to choose between the truth and the Talmud, for the Talmud, which constituted a sort of oral Bible for the Jews, is full of passages which were so much at variance with the new astronomy that it was obviously there that the Jew would find the obstacle that would have to be faced if he did not wish to be unfaithful to the very life and breath of the Jewish tradition.

It was the Talmud which reigned supreme in the synagogue. It was in the light of the Talmud and in no other that the Bible was read and interpreted by the Jews of the Middle Ages and the sixteenth century, natural and spiritual heirs of the Pharisees.

The contradiction between what one might call Talmudic and Copernican astronomy, however (and it is there, if at all, that one could speak of an 'offence' in Jewish eyes, but it was one which never led to any kind of excommunication or Index) was by no means a new phenomenon, for a similar contradiction had been observed by the Jewish scholars of the Middle Ages, particularly the great Maimonides, between Talmudic astronomy and the Ptolemaic system. The 'offence', then, of a contradiction between Jewish and non-Jewish astronomical systems had already existed for centuries, and, in so far as 'non-Jewish' astronomy was accepted as 'true' on the combined authority of Ptolemy, Aristotle, and the power of reason, the problem was to discover a method which would vindicate, if not the 'truth' of Jewish astronomy, then, at least, its honour.

Such was the problem. In chapter 64 David Gans declared that he would deal with it in a 'little note'—the little note we have decided to call a 'methodological parenthesis', since this note is concerned with a method of remaining faithful to tradition.

[12] Kepler's thinking underwent an evolution, a long development. The wonderful exclamation we quoted earlier, reaching out towards the truth, was preceded by attempts at compromise similar to those of David Gans. Kepler attempted a reinterpretation of Joshua and the Psalms before he reached the point where he declared himself ready to jettison the whole of Scripture if scientific truth required it (see Klaus Scholder, *Ursprünge und Probleme der Bibelkritik im 17. Jahrhundert* (Munich, 1966), p. 68).

We shall now study this 'methodological parenthesis' within the context of a great controversy which had engaged Jewish thinkers for centuries, and which David Gans now had to face in one of its most intense forms. In his brief account of this controversy, David Gans recalled that in Jewish tradition there were two extreme positions in this matter, between which some moderates had attempted to construct a bridge of compromise and conciliation.

David Gans between the rationalism of Maimonides and the meta-astronomy of the Maharal

One of these extreme positions was that of Moses Maimonides, re-expressed a century later by Isaac Arama. Maimonides placed himself squarely on the side of science and boldly asserted that, in the Talmudic period, the Jewish scholars had possessed neither the broad overall view nor the knowledge of details which could have brought their thinking into line with that of the contemporary non-Jewish astronomers. In astronomy as in medicine and the other exact sciences, the Talmudic sages had never claimed to represent a revealed truth, a tradition, going back to Sinai. They expressed opinions in accordance with their own subjective points of view which varied with the time and place in which they lived, their personality, and their environment, and their 'teaching' on the subject lacked the 'heteronomous' (subject to external law) character connected with everything in the Talmud which is concerned with the commandments revealed at Sinai and infallibly transmitted from generation to generation. Besides—added Isaac Arama—why should the rabbis have wasted their time considering the purely scientific aspects of astronomy? What interested and concerned them was precisely the revealed commandments, the *mitzvot* of the Torah, and astronomy for them was only a tool, an adjunct, which enabled them to fix the religious calendar.

Paradoxically, this position also found substantial support in the Talmud itself. In the Tractate *Pesahim* (94b), the Jewish sages admitted, in connection with a major astrological problem, that their theory was mistaken and that of the non-Jewish astronomers was right. This candid and significant admission by one of the greatest authorities of the Talmudic period, Rabbi Judah ha-Nasi, to whom Judaism owes the Mishnah, was sufficient in itself to provide a foundation for this 'enlightened' opinion.[13]

[13] 'One should not be surprised at finding that Aristotle's opinion here is in

206 Jewish Thought and Scientific Revolution

At the other extreme from this opinion, there was the position adopted by the Maharal, which was also 'enlightened', but through the *Kabbalah* rather than through reason. The Maharal believed it was wrong to regard the Talmudic sages as scholars in the Aristotelian sense of the word. They undoubtedly knew a great deal about medicine and astronomy, but none of them was either a physician or an astronomer. They undoubtedly said a great deal about medicine and astronomy, but neither their language nor their intentions was medical or astronomical. Behind the phenomena they aimed, successfully, at discovering the essence, and it was this essence which they were concerned with, not appearances. Thus, if there appeared to be a contradiction between Talmudic and Ptolemaic astronomy, this was due neither to the ignorance of the rabbis in astronomical matters nor to a contemptuous attitude towards this respected science. The contradiction was much deeper: it sprang from the inevitable opposition between philosophical thinkers who spoke of phenomena and mystical thinkers who were concerned with essences. Rabbi Judah's 'admission' in the Tractate *Pesaḥim* was neither an admission of failure nor an admission of ignorance, but reflected the irreconcilable difference between people who saw the world as it appears to the senses, and people who, while readily acknowledging that, on the physical level, their colleagues were right, claimed that the truth was nevertheless on their side because, on the metaphysical level, the image of the world was drastically reversed. *Olam hafukh*—the world upside down: this favourite concept of the Maharal's, so important for an understanding of his thought, has an application to this problem of astronomy and is always present in his way of seeing, close to Philonic and neo-Platonic allegory, steeped in *Kabbalah*, but no less tolerant towards others than the 'enlightened' viewpoint of Maimonides.

If David Gans had followed Maimonides, at the period when he was writing, the end of the sixteenth century—a period when

opposition to that of the Jewish Sages, for this opinion that the stars make sounds only follows the belief "that the spheres are fixed and the stars turn". But one knows that in these astronomical matters they regarded the opinion of the Sages of the Nations as more competent than their own. Thus, they said clearly: "And the Sages of the Nations of the world won". And that is true, for all those who have spoken of these speculative matters have only reached their conclusions by means of speculation, and for that reason one must believe what has been established through demonstration.' (Maimonides, *Guide*, ii. 8.)

enlightenment easily turned into scepticism, or even a dogmatism of doubt—he would probably have adopted the position of his contemporary, Azariah dei Rossi. Like him, he would have strongly insisted on the importance of the conditions in space and time in which the Talmudic rabbis worked, ignorant as they were of the scientific developments which had taken place in more than a millennium. Like him, he would no doubt have suddenly exposed the historical and scientific errors handed down by Jewish tradition, applying a critical method to the biblical and Talmudic texts which, in the case of Azariah at least, fails to be entirely convincing owing to the absence of the element of soul-searching. Azariah dei Rossi never gives the impression of passing through an inner struggle. He has skirmishes, or engages in polemics with writers or their works, but he is never torn asunder by the deep-rooted passion that one senses in David Gans.

Azariah's approach never touched on real astronomical problems such as aroused the passionate curiosity of David Gans. Azariah failed to mention any of the 'new' astronomers whom, chronologically speaking, he could already have known. In his book, which is full of names of contemporary writers, one finds neither that of Copernicus nor that of Tycho Brahe. No doubt that was because nothing could be 'revolutionary' for Azariah dei Rossi, who regarded everything as being in a state of permanent evolution, constituting a kind of kaleidoscope of perpetual microscopic changes. Astronomy, for Azariah, was the observation of a display jar at an apothecary's, whereas for David Gans, as for his Teachers, it was an exploration of God's universe. A hypothesis such as that of Copernicus might have led to the momentary displacement of some object on Azariah dei Rossi's work-table or made him readjust his spectacles, whereas it touched David Gans at the very core of his being and led to an agonizing reappraisal of his condition as a creature *vis-à-vis* the creator.

It was precisely the method by which this agonizing reappraisal could be carried out that David Gans could have learnt from the Maharal of Prague, but—how many times need I repeat it?—the Maharal was like some isolated peak, and his disciples could only stand below and admire the vertiginous upward thrust of his thought without ever being able to follow. The idea that the truth could only emerge from the very depths of contradiction, that certitude could only result from a laceration, that the void of the middle, the *emza*, the sanctified space separating the finger of God from that of man were essential to the existence of God as God and the existence of man as man—these were concepts whose full challenge only Michelangelos, Maharals, Isaac Lurias, and Jacob Boehmes were able to face. Kepler also had an intuition of this challenge, and a study of his theology, which still has to be made, revealing the surprising and wonderful importance of the place given to mysticism at the heart of his astronomical system, might suggest that David Gans's fascination with Kepler was of the same kind as his fascination with the Maharal: an admiration for a genius who resolved the paradoxical mystery of the liberty of man, who is nevertheless the creature of God.

We shall see at the conclusion of this study that Gans also made an attempt to express this mystery, so linking up with the Maharal's grandiose astronomical scheme in his *Be'er ha-Golah*. For the moment, however, we have not yet reached the conclusion. It is the choice of a method with which we are now concerned. We see that just as David Gans decided against the 'enlightened' solutions of Maimonides and Azariah dei Rossi, so he refused to adopt the methodological system of the Maharal.

Yet, nevertheless, he might well have been tempted to follow his Teacher, seeing that (to the best of my knowledge, at least) the Maharal was the first Jewish writer to refer to Copernicus. Following an old rule of discretion observed by most Jewish writers of the Middle Ages and the Renaissance, the Maharal did not refer to Copernicus by name, but the reference (*Netivot Olam, Netiv ha-Torah* 25c) is too obvious to be missed.

This reference, however, forms part of the argument of the Maharal's criteriological system, whose main features we shall now describe. He was speaking of the difference between science (*hokhmah*) and the Torah, one of those dialectical pairs on which the Maharal establishes the unstable equilibrium of the truth.

According to the Maharal, the domain of the Torah is vertical, while that of *hokhmah* is horizontal. This is a basic idea without which the interrelationship of these forms of knowledge cannot be understood. Everything with which the Torah is concerned is *meta*physical, and the manner in which it is treated is also metaphysical. Everything that *hokhmah* is concerned with, on the other hand, is physical, and the manner in which it is treated is also physical. *Hokhmah* only deals with phenomena, whereas the Torah deals with the essence of things, the *noumena*.

The contradictions which Maimonides or Azariah dei Rossi perceive between biblical or Talmudic texts on the one hand and scientific facts on the other are thus inherent in these two different dialectical aspects of one and the same truth. To attempt to overcome these contradictions through conciliatory interpretations is therefore to overlook the very nature of this contradiction which is necessary, part of the natural order; and to be contemptuous of science and to make the Torah into an infallible scientific authority is to display a childish obscurantism. Science is true, but the Torah is not a science. But, conversely, to reject the assertions of the Torah like Azariah on the grounds that they are incompatible with science is to display ignorance of the true character of the Torah which is not a competitor with science, but a source of knowledge of another kind.[14]

What can be said about medicine, so highly esteemed by Maimonides, and rightly so, thought the Maharal, can also be applied to astronomy. Medicine is a science worthy of great respect, and so is astronomy, but they are only concerned with the physical causes of phenomena, causes which are real but only partial. The Jewish sages, the representatives of the Torah, were well aware of this physical causality but they did not speak about it. They left the investigation of it to the representatives of *hokhmah*, the sages among the Nations. What the Jewish sages were concerned with were the metaphysical causes, the divine causality overlapping with the physical causality.

Thus justice is done both to Jewish astronomy and to non-Jewish astronomy. Does not the Law require the Jew to make a blessing celebrating the wisdom of the creator on seeing a non-Jewish scholar no less than when he sees a Jewish one? But, in the case of a representative of *hokhmah*, the Jew thanks God for granting man wisdom, and on seeing a representative of the Torah, he thanks God for binding certain men to Himself in order to make them His own. It is this divine element within or beyond the human element which is investigated by the Jewish astronomy.

---

[14] We should note the remarkable resemblance of the Maharal's viewpoint to that of Galileo in his celebrated letter to Christine of Lorraine (*Opere di Galileo Galilei*. Edizione nazionale, v (1890), pp. 207, 248). This letter dates from 1615 (Copernicus's book was condemned by the Inquisition the following year). Galileo attempted to justify his Copernicanism by making a distinction between the metaphysical character of the Scriptures and the purely physical character of astronomy. The Maharal's text is from his *Netivot Olam* of 1595.

The Maharal discussed this point in the sixth 'well' of the *Be'er ha-Golah*. The so-called 'concessions' made by the Jewish sages to the sages of the nations, he said, were by no means admissions of ignorance or incapacity. On the contrary, they delimit the boundaries of the horizontal sphere, the 'lower world', to use the expression taken by the Maharal from the *Kabbalah*—a sphere in which man is sovereign, central, situated in the middle, subject to the effects of physical causality and finality. While acknowledging the existence of this sphere, the Jews left it to man's enterprising spirit to explore it. Within this sphere, which is peculiar to itself, the human spirit evolves and changes and makes discoveries: a cycle of creativity which never ends.

Now, it was precisely at this point in his argument that the Maharal of Prague (who, we should remember, was the first Jewish writer to do so) referred to Nicholas Copernicus (*NO* 24c), placing him within the context of this permanent relativity of astronomical science—thus giving due recognition to the 'revolution' effected by this genius while calmly awaiting a further 'revolution' (Kepler, Newton, Einstein!!) which would replace his:

In which way, then, are the Jews specially privileged in the sphere of astronomy? In this: that it is perfectly true that the Gentiles are most enthusiastic about this science and have attained a very high level of knowledge, which sometimes, as everyone knows, appears to be an absolute and complete understanding of the subject. And yet there constantly arise amongst them new scholars who demolish the magnificent achievements attained with such trouble. For instance, quite recently a scholar appeared who is called the inventor of the 'new' astronomy. His system was entirely new, in so far as he revolutionized all his predecessors' findings with regard to the orbits of the stars and the movements of the planets and the other heavenly bodies, giving a completely new scientific picture. He admitted, however, that he was unable to provide a system which would explain everything.

This total explanation, this key to the absolute, only the Jewish sages, according to the Maharal, possessed; but this key did not open up the world of phenomena but the immutable, numinous world.

Thus, in the final analysis, the so-called 'Jewish astronomy', according to the Maharal, is in reality a meta-astronomy, an understanding of metaphysical first causes and not a science of secondary, physical causes. The Maharal attributed this purely 'scientific' character to non-Jewish astronomy alone, with the important modification, however, of a hint of relativity which made a dent in the heavy Ptolemaic dogmatism, although not sufficiently to reveal the truth which David Gans was seeking—not the transcendent metaphysical truth, but the physical truth of the world of essences and appearances which he was able to apprehend by raising his eyes to the heavens and peering into the infinite, not as a mystical dream but through the complex yet concrete and tangible instruments of an observatory.[15]

David Gans and the Rema's conciliatory option

Between these extreme opinions of Maimonides and the Maharal, there was a third alternative—the way of compromise, ready to defer to the sages of the Talmud where it could be shown that their scientific assertions were *revealed* in the same way as their opinions of the Torah.

This was the point of view expressed by the Rema in his *Torat ha-Olah* which appeared in 1570. David Gans was then 29 years of age. He was already in Prague when the work came out, two years before the author's death. Let us visualize for a moment this young student, leafing through the thick volume in which his beloved Teacher, who had raised him like a son, had recorded the outcome of his astronomical researches. These researches were concerned with a methodological problem within Judaism—the problem, which was also to trouble David Gans, of the contradiction between certain statements of the Aggadic and Talmudic Masters and the facts revealed by non-Jewish science: contradictions which were particularly numerous, as the Rema pointed out, in the domain of astronomy.

Earlier in this book we noticed the Rema's strong taste for reconciling conflicting tendencies, and we saw how he expressed this principle in the conflict between philosophy and the *Kabbalah*.[16] We shall not be surprised, then, to find that in the second chapter of the first part of his book he made a number of attempts to show

---

[15] Like Kleinberger and Kariv, we have claimed in our *Puits de l'Exil* (p. 121) that the Maharal's relativistic system 'possesses a singularly Einsteinian aspect'. His attitude towards Copernicus resembles that which physicists have been obliged to adopt after Einstein (see, for example, M. Born, who wrote in *Die Relativitätstheorie Einsteins* (1922): 'Von Einsteins hoher Warte gesehen, haben Ptolemäus und Kopernikus gleiches Recht: beide Standpunkte liefern dieselben Naturgesetze. Welchen Standpunkt man wahlt, ist nicht aus Prinzipien entschiedbar, sondern Sache der Bequemlichkeit').

[16] See above I. 4.

that the rabbis and the non-Jewish astronomers were basically in agreement, and that neither side was in error. One quite often finds this sort of thing among the rabbis—balancing-tricks, sometimes somewhat artificial and contrived, but it might nevertheless have convinced David Gans if the Rema had not, in his summary and conclusion (folio 8a and b), suddenly put everything in doubt.

David Gans learnt that, at that time, there were three great doctrines in astronomy, each opposed to the other. The first was the familiar doctrine of Ptolemy's *Almagest*, on which the non-Jewish scholars had built up the monumental system which they still possessed at the time of writing. It was this system which the Talmud usually called 'the astronomical doctrine of the sages among the nations'. It was based on the fundamental principle 'of the movement of the spheres and the fixity of the stars'.

The second was the doctrine of the 'sages of Israel' based on the opposite principle 'of the movement of the stars and the fixity of the spheres'—a principle, however, which the Talmud itself states that the Jewish sages did not retain, 'saying that the sages among the nations were right'. But this did not mean, the Rema hastened to add, that the Talmud is suggesting that the Jews were admitting they were wrong. What happened was that the vicissitudes of exile made the Jewish scholars forget their own astronomical principle and forced them to adopt Ptolemy's principle, like the others. But this was only a question of approach. The Jewish principle, opposite to that of Ptolemy, still retains its hallmark of truth, and, as was formerly the case, it could again serve as the basis for an astronomy different from that of Ptolemy which could be called Jewish, as against the non-Jewish astronomy of the *Almagest* to which, for better or worse, the Jewish scholars had been forced to defer by a sort of accident of history.

The third doctrine was that of the talented thinker whom the Rema, like Isaac Israeli, Gersonides, Isaac Arama, and many others called *Ish ha-Ra'ash*, the man who created a storm in astronomy. This was Al-Bitrogi, otherwise known as Alpetragius.[17] In his system, the spheres career through the heavens at terrifying but unequal speeds like horses in an arena, and this fantastic vision seemed to a writer as serious as Isaac Arama to be quite likely to be correct. What Al-Bitrogi lacked, said Arama, was the ability to

---

[17] See the recent edition by Bernard R. Goldstein (Yale University Press, 1971).

synthesize or the time to develop his system. 'If he had completed his system', he said, 'the scholars, without exception, would have adopted it.'

So David Gans was faced with three systems. Is it unreasonable to suppose that the young man would have liked his Teacher to have indicated some preference between them? No doubt David Gans did not know anything about Copernicus in 1570, any more than did the Rema himself. But if, among these three great systems, one was described as belonging to Jewish tradition, ought he not to have tipped the scales in its favour? No doubt this specifically Jewish system was lost today, as it had been for a very long time, but why should one suppose that it should remain so for ever? Why should not this system contain the truth, which one day would once more be fully revealed, blinding like the Messiah, concealed today, as he had been for a very long time, but who one day would be certainly known? Why should one not add to the certainty of the Messianic coming the certainty of what might be called an astronomical Second Coming, especially as the question had been raised in a work devoted to the Messianic restoration of the Temple and its sacrifices?

But, now, instead of leading his disciple into a state of certitude, the Teacher only brought him into a condition of dreadful perplexity. Not only did the Rema not hazard an opinion concerning the respective merits of each of these three contradictory systems, not only did he avoid choosing one rather than another, but, most ironic of all, he supported his attitude with a rabbinical text, a passage from the *Midrash Bereshit Rabba* (6: 13) in which one of the most venerated Jewish thinkers, Rabbi Simeon bar Yoḥai, revered as the writer of the *Zohar*, declared: 'We do not know if the spheres fly freely through the air, if they brush against the heavenly vault, or if they proceed according to natural laws of their own. The problem is a very serious one and people cannot find a clear basis for resolving it.'

This is indeed a second-century admission of perplexity, which Rabbi Moses Isserles, writing in the sixteenth century, interpreted in the following manner:

Rabbi Simeon bar Yoḥai's three hypotheses refer to the three great astronomical systems which have just been described. 'Flying freely through the air' is Al-Bitrogi's system; 'brushing against the heavenly vault' is the system of the Jewish sages, and 'proceeding according to natural laws' is the Ptolemaic system; and it was in connection with these three systems that Rabbi Simeon bar Yoḥai stated that since each one of them could serve as the basis for a complete system of astronomy, the problem of deciding which of the three systems is right becomes particularly important. But, as for finding the truth, the absolute reality, one cannot count on anything to lead to its discovery.

Three ways, then, opened up for David Gans: that of submission to the authority of the Gentiles and acceptance of the Ptolemaic system, whose chief Jewish representative was the great Moses Maimonides; that of the Maharal, who also recognized the scientific supremacy of Gentile astronomy, but placed above it a purely Jewish astronomy which, however, is not scientific and is the only one to possess the absolute truth. And, lastly, there was that of the Rema which, with his very vague and generalized approach of a simultaneous respect for Jewish tradition and the Ptolemaic system, ended in a state of painful perplexity.

These were three ways which David Gans honestly expounded in the epilogue to his book, as if to excuse the undeniable fact that, at first sight, his astronomical treatise was based on the only proposition on which these three different systems were agreed—namely, that the scientific truth of astronomy, in the scholastic and sometimes pedestrian sense of the term, lay with Ptolemy.

But David Gans superseded these three options in a surge of enthusiasm which one feels passing right through his book with a marvellous consistency, and which one sees was produced by his unexpected meeting with a man whom, together with the Rema, who had filled him with perplexity, Providence had placed in his path: Tycho Brahe, the leading astronomer of the period. Now Brahe was troubled with perplexities as much as the Rema or even more so.

How, indeed, could people living in about 1570, at the crucial turning-point of developments avoid such a sense of perplexity? Copernicus's ideas had begun to be seriously discussed in the universities. In 1572 Tycho Brahe discovered the new star: a discovery which had made him aware of the breach which had appeared in the Ptolemaic system. In 1570 the Rema had published (in Prague) one of his main works, the *Torat ha-Olah* which he had written in Cracow where he taught rabbinical subjects and where formerly Copernicus had begun his studies. Both men, the Danish astronomer and the Polish rabbi, were looking for a way out, a solution. Both of them thought they had found it, but in fact they both only arrived at a shaky, unsteady compromise.

Tycho Brahe, as we said, had created a system which attempted to combine both Ptolemy and Copernicus, but the difficulties were so serious, the points of obscurity so many, and the points of connection so weak that he could only hope for a Tychonides who would resolve the difficulties, bring light to bear on everything, and transform clashing discords into sublime harmonies. Assailed with insoluble problems, encumbered rather than helped by the variety and complexity of his instruments, ensnared in his masses of calculations and observations, he was in danger of giving way to a psychosis of perplexity, had he not, rousing himself in an act of nobility and courage, quixotic though it might seem, swept aside this psychosis with a lordly gesture, laughing at life and its problems, prophetically confident of the truth of his vision, if not for today—well, in that case, for tomorrow. In the gallery of the giants of astronomy, he had placed his own statue. If he had been preceded by geniuses, no doubt he would be followed by others. At least he could invoke God as a witness to the stone which he had placed in the edifice of eternity.

But if Kepler was indeed to confirm Tycho's system by passing beyond it, not without struggles and temporary setbacks, but nevertheless attaining ultimate victory through the irresistible power of his genius, how were Tycho's humble assistants, his technical aides to react—they who, full of goodwill as they were, had timid or feeble wings? How was David Gans to react, whose character did not belie the slow and timid quality of the feathered creature whose name he bore? Would not a goose spreading its wings for an eagle's flight run the risk of being ridiculous?

Under Tycho Brahe's guidance, David Gans did, in fact, spread his wings for an eagle's flight, and he, too, came upon the stage as a Master. To be sure, he never attained the genius of a Kepler, but he alone among the Jewish astronomers of the end of the sixteenth century was able to confront the new discoveries and the new problems and appraise them at the highest level. He alone was able to assign Jewish astronomy a place—its proper place—within the general astronomical revolution, situated, as he was, at the very storm-centre of that revolution.

3

The turning-point: David Gans meets Tycho Brahe and Kepler

IN every spiritual experience, there is a sudden jolt which sets everything in motion, an instant of illumination which makes Archimedes leap out of his bath and run through the streets crying 'Eureka!' It is not difficult to trace David Gans's Eureka-moment: he recorded it in chapter 25 of the first part of his book. In this short chapter, he described a crucial meeting with Tycho Brahe which overshadowed in importance all that he had learnt and taught till then and all that he was to learn and teach from that time onwards.

The title of this chapter was 'Concerning the problem of ascertaining whether the stars are stationary [and the spheres move] or whether, on the contrary, the spheres are stationary and the stars move'.[1] In this chapter we read that this had been the subject of the famous astronomical debate between the sages of Alexandria and Jerusalem in which, according to the Talmud (Tractate *Pesaḥim* 94b), the sages of Jerusalem acknowledged their defeat and submitted to those of Alexandria—an act of submission which enabled the medieval Jewish astronomers to embrace the system of Ptolemy.[2]

---

[1] This is the wording of the chapter-heading in the manuscripts and in the table of contents of the book as published. The words in brackets are omitted in the chapter-heading as given in the book.

[2] Salomon Munk (notes to *Le Guide des Égarés* (Guide to the Perplexed) ii, 8, pp. 78–9) noted perspicaciously that the Jewish sages' submission to the Gentile sages (Tractate *Pesaḥim* 94b) refers in our edition of the Talmud to a different problem from that of the movement of the stars and spheres discussed by Tycho Brahe and David Gans: i.e., to that of the nocturnal course of the sun. Either Maimonides was using a variant of the Talmudic text, or else his extreme point of view (cf. above III. 2) led him to believe that this acknowledgement of defeat applied to all the problems referred to in that page of *Pesaḥim*. Whatever the case, we share Munk's opinion that in David Gans's time it was not the Talmud that was used as the source but Maimonides' classic commentary on it in his *Guide to the Perplexed*. It should be pointed out, however, that the Maharal correctly related the sages' act of submission to the subject referred to in the Talmud and not to the one referred to by Tycho and Gans (*BH* 1070, 109a).

David Gans begins the chapter by referring to this astronomical debate and recalling the strange act of submission by the Jewish sages to the wisdom of the Gentiles. If the manuscript of *Neḥmad ve-Na'im* had gone astray like other manuscripts of David Gans such as the *Prozdor* whose loss he mentioned, this little chapter, had it survived, would have been sufficient to provide us with a clear and comprehensive idea of the writer, his approach, and his doctrines. This chapter is a turning-point in the development of David Gans's astronomical system, and it is also a turning-point in the Jewish approach to the history of astronomy.

TYCHO BRAHE TELLS GANS: THE JEWS WERE RIGHT

At the heart of this change there was, first of all, this sudden jolt, this moment of awakening. Two contemporary non-Jewish astronomers entered the fray and took up a position in the ancient controversy of Alexandria versus Jerusalem. They, the non-Jews, turned the balance in favour of Jerusalem, reproaching the sages of Israel for having laid down their arms before the non-Jewish sages of antiquity.

Thus, the little word *rov* with which the chapter begins may be regarded as more than merely a trick of style: '*Most* ancient and modern authorities . . . including the Jewish sages, according to the Talmud, claim repeatedly that the stars themselves are motionless and only the spheres carry them in their motions. . . '. *Most . . .* there is a controversy; opinion is not unanimous. Somewhere, once, there were scholars who claimed the opposite, just as the Jews did before they surrendered: ancient scholars whom Gans is about to mention. But before relating this historical episode— important, no doubt, but belonging to the past—Gans recalls the far more vital fact, vibrant with actuality, experienced here and now by David Gans himself, that in Prague in the year 1600 two non-Jewish scholars broke the ranks of apparent unanimity and took up a position in favour of the doctrine once favoured by other non-Jewish scholars and, before them, by the Jews.

These two non-Jewish scholars, moreover, were not modest and insignificant occupants of chairs in some minor contemporary university. One was the unique Tycho Brahe, the leading figure in the team of eminent scientists gathered together by the Emperor Rudolph in Prague, and the other was his immediate disciple and collaborator Johannes Kepler, whose reputation already equalled his master's. The master and disciple were both agreed in taking the opposite view from the sages of Alexandria, and, most remarkable of all, the Jew David Gans was addressed by the non-Jew Tycho Brahe as follows: 'Your sages were wrong to submit to the non-Jewish scholars. They assented to a lie, for the truth lay with the Jewish sages.'

These words had not been transmitted to David Gans by a third party or transcribed by him from a written document: he received them from the mouth of Tycho Brahe himself to whom he had probably pointed out the relevant passage in the Talmud.[3] The similar opinion of Kepler, his colleague at the observatory at Benatek, he also received by word of mouth.

Nor had these words been spoken casually or off the cuff. David Gans was careful to point out that the opinion of Tycho Brahe and Johannes Kepler was founded on two criteria which the former had expounded in one of his books. The first criterion was the classical one of deduction, of logical and mathematical proof, of the 'philosophy' of astronomy. The second, entirely new, was that of observation—by probing the heavens with wonderful instruments whose accuracy was undeniable.

So it was not only a matter of pure reason; empirical observation had also played a part in the controversy which, owing to this new direction in astronomy, had now taken a turn favourable to Jewish tradition. We have just said that this chapter constituted a turning-point. It was so in two respects. The truth returned to the Jewish side, but this had happened only because the astronomer, since Tycho Brahe, had become an observer rather than a reckoner. In this chapter David Gans appears before us as one of those men of the sixteenth century who, instead of keeping their eyes fixed to the work-table crammed with books, figures, and equations, lifted their eyes to the heavens, scanning them with the instruments of a new vision. And by this action of turning to above from below, from the earth to the heavens, the Jewish truth, stifled by the *Almagest's* heavy pages, was retrieved in the stars.

---

[3] David Gans had already mentioned Tycho Brahe's opinion in chapter 16, but in a more impersonal way. This, according to David Gans, was Tycho Brahe's 'first law' as described in the 'conclusion of conclusions' of *Neḥmad ve-Naʿim* (see below III. 5). Chapter 25, however, describes Tycho Brahe's transmission of this law to David Gans in a personal conversation.

CONTRARY TO JEWISH TRADITION

Here we must make a necessary digression. The logical process supported by observation, mathematics corrected by experience—this development, so necessary for the revolution in astronomy, thanks to which David Gans was able to retrieve the original Jewish truth, went contrary to the direction taken by Jewish science since the Middle Ages, contrary to a principle which Maimonides in the thirteenth century had made into a law and which the Rema had reasserted in the last third of the sixteenth century.

In the third chapter of the third section of *Torat ha-Olah* by his master the Rema, Gans could have come upon the following passage based on Maimonides (*Guide to the Perplexed*, part 2, second chapter): 'Everyone knows that this is the method of the astronomers. They rely entirely on hypotheses deriving from reason alone, basing on these hypotheses the theory of the movement of the stars, although it is possible that what really takes place in the heavens is quite different.'

Thus, reason and reality were split in 'classical' Jewish astronomy as they were in astronomy as a whole until the advent of Tycho Brahe, whose admirable instruments of observation permitted calculation to be matched with experiment, reason with reality, and principles with truth. And one of the most remarkable consequences of this betrothal (which Galileo's development of the telescope was soon to turn into a marriage) was to demonstrate that the Jewish sages had been right: yes, those very sages who had denied their own truth, those sages amongst whom David Gans felt himself bound to include, with amazement and with even a touch of hidden shame, his revered Master, Moses Isserles!

Shock and embarrassment are the dominant feelings betrayed by the continuation of this key chapter. In Gans's reaction, to be sure, there must have been a certain element of inner jubilation, a sense of compensation for the too frequent medieval controversies between Jews and Gentiles, in which the latter always emerged victorious, if not through argument, then at least by means of force. And now, like some magnificent fireworks display concluding the counter-action of the Renaissance in which so many Gentile scholars had lent an attentive ear to the rabbis, two non-Jewish geniuses threw to the flames not the Jewish truth but their own doctrine vanquished by that of the Jews. But even stronger than this feeling of triumph must have been David Gans's acute sense of anguish at the price he had to pay for it—a loss of confidence in his Jewish teachers. How he must have suffered from the fact that it was a non-Jewish scholar who had saved the honour of Jewish science! A respect for his Jewish teachers was too deeply implanted in him for him to have reacted as Azariah dei Rossi would certainly have done in similar circumstances and thrown scornfully onto the rubbish-heap those Jewish scholars who had followed the Jewish sages of old and submitted to the 'sages of the nations'.

THE ATTEMPT TO SAVE THE HONOUR OF THE JEWISH TRADITION: THE APPEAL TO ABRAVANEL'S AUTHORITY

David Gans now attempted to save the honour of Jewish science by seeking support from within the Jewish tradition. The support of Tycho Brahe and Johannes Kepler was undoubtedly significant, and yet it was not enough to satisfy the Rema's disciple whose perplexity about the subject had now been removed, except in so far as he was disturbed by the fact that such feelings had also troubled his master.

David Gans therefore sought to justify the Jewish truth by seeking the support of some Jewish authority, and he found one in Isaac Abravanel. The manner in which he approached him, however, deserves careful examination.

The extract from Abravanel's commentary on Genesis 1:17 ('God set the lights in the firmament of the heaven to give light upon the earth') quoted by Gans in the second part of the chapter in support of Brahe's and Kepler's assertions, hardly amounts to conclusive evidence. It ends, moreover, with the very *Midrash* (*Bereshit Rabba* 6:13) with which the Rema had concluded his astronomical reflections, and which can serve as a kind of basic text for the theme of perplexity (Rabbi Simeon bar Yoḥai said: 'We do not know if . . . or if . . . or if . . . and the truth is inaccessible'). And furthermore Gans, in quoting Abravanel, omits a little phrase which the former adopted as his motto: 'In order to avoid uncertainty, I shall continue to follow Aristotle.'

However, Abravanel had previously quoted two ancient authorities, also non-Jews, who had opposed Aristotle and Ptolemy and claimed, like the Jewish sages, that the spheres were immobile and the stars moved. These two authorities were Pliny and Plotinus.

Each of their testimonies deserves our attention so that we may gain a deeper insight into the critical experience through which David Gans was passing.

With regard to Pliny, Gans quoted only the following lines of Abravanel's commentary: 'Ancient philosophers such as Pliny and his school wrote in their book *Natural History*—a book highly regarded by the non-Jewish sages—that the seven planets move in the midst of the heavenly spaces. He repeats this assertion three times.'

In fact, Abravanel's reference to Pliny is longer, since his statement about the free movement of the seven planets is completed by the following words: 'As for the sun, it is in the midst of the planets. It is, as it were, the soul of the world, which it rules like a divinity.' This is a close paraphrase of a famous sentence on the basis of which historians of astronomy regard Pliny, together with Aristarchus and Plutarch, as one of the precursors of Copernicus among the ancients: 'The sun is carried around in the midst of the planets, directing not only the calendar and the earth but also the stars themselves and the sky.'

As for Plotinus, Abravanel says no more than is quoted by David Gans: 'One of Aristotle's disciples, the greatest of the great amongst them, Plotinus, who wrote books concerning all aspects of philosophy, also wrote, in complete agreement [with Pliny], that the luminaries are not fragments of spheres, that they are not fixed to them, but that the planets move in the air between the heavens and the earth while the spheres are fixed and immobile.'[4] One would look in vain for this quotation in Plotinus, but one can find such an idea unsystematically expressed in various passages scattered liberally throughout the writings of the great Neoplatonic and Neoplotinian movement which was at work beneath the surface from the fourteenth century onwards, and which rose to the surface towards the end of the fifteenth century, particularly in Italy, having a marked effect on the intellectual avant-garde which already constituted the first generation of the Renaissance. Isaac Abravanel belonged to this generation of Leonardo da Vinci and shared its flexibility of mind, its openness to vibrations, its interest in all the

[4] The manuscripts of *Neḥmad ve-Na'im* and the book itself refer to Plotinus twice, but it is clear from the context that two different ancient authors are in question. As this passage is a quotation from Abravanel, there can be no room for doubt: in Abravanel's text, the first author is called Plinio and the second Plotino.

fields which the Renaissance had opened up to the curiosity and admiration of sixteenth-century man. 'Textual criticism' had not yet been invented, and ideas continued to be attributed to Aristotle, Plato, and Plotinus which really belonged to other ancient thinkers, and which in fact had been reinvented by the minds of the fourteenth and fifteenth centuries after a lapse of more than a millennium.

Thus, in referring to Pliny, Abravanel resurrected Aristarchus, and in speaking of Plotinus, he revived the Pythagoreans.

Now, in David Gans's view, Pythagoras was the true ancestor of Copernicus.[5] He said this explicitly in the epilogue to *Neḥmad ve-Na'im*, in a magnificent paragraph devoted to this 'genius unique in his time, this new Ptolemy', and, in hiding behind the Jewish authority of Isaac Abravanel who championed Pliny and Plotinus, David Gans was clearly playing with fire. His key chapter, had it been consistent with the logic we have indicated, could and should have culminated in the following revolutionary assertion: 'Although the Jewish sages were prepared, for reasons which they alone knew and which they were unwilling to reveal, to adopt the non-Jewish astronomical system of Ptolemy provisionally, as a mere working hypothesis, in reality they were the custodians of the opposite astronomical system to which many ancient non-Jewish scholars remained attached, and whose illustrious renown Nicholas Copernicus has restored in recent years. To Ptolemy's erroneous earth-centred vision, Judaism opposes the sun-centred vision of Copernicus. That is what Tycho Brahe and Johannes Kepler confided to me.' That is how David Gans might and could have concluded the twenty-fifth chapter of the first part of his book, but, if that had been the case, the other eleven parts of *Neḥmad ve-Na'im* would have taken a very different turn.

At this turning-point we see, once again, that something was afoot. But this time David Gans appeared to be retreating from the new truths which he now knew to be identical with the Jewish truth. For, without stating the fact explicitly, David Gans finally concluded in the same way as Isaac Abravanel, his Jewish authority. He, too, constructed his book, like Abravanel's commentary, on Ptolemy's system. Discussing, in the very first chapter, the system of Copernicus (on whom he lavished magnificent praise in the epilogue), he disclaimed competence and committed himself to Ptolemy on the grounds that most authorities—and particularly the most recent ones—did not accept the Copernican system. David Gans thus returned to the ranks after having seemed to place himself among the revolutionaries.

THE GENERAL CONTEXT OF TYCHO'S AND KEPLER'S STATEMENTS TO GANS

Can this be regarded as a paradox? As a contradiction? As a confusion? To be sure, all these terms apply to David Gans's situation, but there is nothing pejorative about them. Their use here is quite natural and almost necessary. This illogic is inherent in the very logic of the general context of this key chapter, written in the few months of 1599–1600 when David Gans was in contact with Tycho Brahe who was still living ('Tycho Brahe told me') and with Kepler who was assisting him in his research.

What point had Tycho Brahe and Johannes Kepler reached in their scientific development? To be quite exact, they had reached a point beyond which the former was never to go, and which the latter was to pass beyond only much later—a point exemplifying all the sense of paradox, contradiction, and confusion which we have noticed in their modest but attentive collaborator David Gans.

Gans noted, as we saw, that Tycho Brahe's statement to him had been arrived at both as a result of logical deduction and of the observations he had made with the wonderful instruments which no one had at their disposal before him. The conclusion to which these many careful observations had brought Tycho Brahe was that the motions of the planets contain an unpredictable element which causes them to appear sometimes within the solar orbit and sometimes outside it. The planets thus possess an intrinsic mobility. They are not bound to the spheres; they are not fixed to them as though with nails. They are autonomous.

But nothing in the work of Tycho Brahe, nothing in his empirical researches, nothing in the statements he occasionally confided to his assistants (we have an example in this chapter of Gans)—nothing explained this mobility. No law defined it, gave it substance. It was an observation, bewildering to those who believed in Ptolemy, instructive for those who followed Copernicus, but a mere observation without any theory to back it up. It was a puzzling phenomenon.

The same was true in the case of Kepler. He too assured Gans that observation of the planets had shown that their orbit was irregular and was sometimes distended to such a degree as to take the shape of the Hebrew letter *kaf*.[6] If this piece of information had been given a few years later, it would probably have been expressed as follows: the planetary orbits are not circular as Ptolemy and also Copernicus had taught, but oval (today we should say elliptical, but Kepler always skirted around this term ellipse and never used it!). But at that point we are still far from the *Astronomia Nova* which did not appear until 1609, and in which the law of the ellipse, Kepler's famous first law, was swamped in a mass of material impenetrable to anyone except the author himself, who was to clarify matters only much later, long after the death of David Gans in 1613. Around 1600, however, Kepler was still steeped in the atmosphere of his *Mysterium Cosmographicum*, published in 1596, in which theology was as important as astronomy, if not more so. But in the field of astronomy, Kepler at that date had already made the remarkable observation that the circle is not the perfect cosmic figure, and that the cosmic mystery is to be found elsewhere, in a variety of figures, any of which can be the geometrical expression of the planetary orbits. Thus, the spell of the circle was broken, but one did not yet know what other magic would take its place. And this is precisely what Kepler told Gans. It was bewildering, because it did not constitute a new system replacing that of Ptolemy, yet it represented a breach of the Ptolemaic system at one of its most sensitive points.

'We should always continue to rely on Ptolemy', Kepler told Gans a little later, and Gans carefully noted the remark in chapter 218 of his book. Kepler was talking about the revolutionary theories of Al-Bitrogi, discussed at such length by Gersonides and, more recently, by the Rema who had included them in his eclectic survey of the astronomical theories current in 1570. Al-Bitrogi claimed that there are no orbital eccentricities or epicycles. A fig for Ptolemy, Hipparchus, and Al-Battani! There is only an absolute

---

[6] Kepler knew Hebrew, which he had studied at Tübingen under Georg Weigenmaier. In his last work, the *Somnium*, (a dream about a journey to the moon), he gave the moon its Hebrew name of *Lebana* or *Levana*, on the grounds that this term was preferable to the Greek *Selentis* because Hebrew words, less familiar to the ears, inspire a greater sense of awe and are used in the occult arts. See Kepler's *Somnium*, transl. with a commentary by Edward Rosen (London, 1967), p. 53.

liberty in the cosmos in which the planets run their courses like horses in the hippodrome! These theories, thought Kepler, were absurd: gross errors, worthy of boors who brutishly scan the heavens without suspecting that there are laws contained within them. In reality, said Kepler, all these opponents of Ptolemy were the followers of ancient astronomers, each of whom proposed abstruse theories like that of Al-Bitrogi. But these 'revolutionaries' overlooked the fact that, in his *Almagest*, Ptolemy had long ago refuted these ancient astronomers, by that very act disposing also of the fantasies of the 'moderns'. Copernicus himself had based both his calculations and his theory on the Ptolemaic system.

Thus the *Almagest* remained the Bible of Tycho Brahe and Kepler, as well as that of Galileo, and yet . . . and yet!

PTOLEMY WAS RIGHT . . . AND YET . . .

And yet, something was afoot. Galileo, for instance, knew it and even hurled his conviction at his judges, the inquisitors, at the very moment of his solemn recantation.[7]

David Gans, within the modest scope of his researches, also knew that something was going on. In that key chapter 25 where he tells us how he was personally informed by Tycho Brahe and Kepler that something in Ptolemy's system had 'shifted', and how he learnt at the same time that the secret underlying this development lay with the Jewish sages who had always possessed it, he made ingenious use of a stylistic idiom in order to express the meaning of this discovery.

We may recall that the Talmudic metaphor of the 'bird flying in the air' had been applied by the Rema to Al-Bitrogi's system. David Gans now applied it to the various orbital eccentricities mentioned by Tycho and Kepler. But he also exploited—and we think that the

---

[7] It is interesting to note that about the year 1600, at the time when David Gans talked to Tycho Brahe and Kepler, Galileo, in Padua, was writing (but had not yet published!) his *System of the World*. Basing himself on Aristotle (see above III. 2 n.5), he gave a very exact account in this work of the problem of the movement of the stars which was treated in chapter 25 of Gans's *Neḥmad ve-Na'im*, and, having stated the problem, he too decided in favour of the Ptolemaic belief that the stars were fixed and the spheres move! E. Wohlwill (p. 209) called attention to the underlying irony of these lines written by Galileo, who had long since sided with Copernicus. I do not feel that here it is a matter of irony, but a symptom of that same condition of indecision, perplexity, and inability to detach oneself from the old system that one finds simultaneously, at that date, in Tycho Brahe, Kepler, and Galileo. How could it be otherwise with the humble David Gans?

play on words is deliberate—the ambiguity of this metaphor, for in the Talmud and rabbinical writings, the 'bird flying in the air' denotes an unsupported assertion, an unproven theory, and, above all, a rabbinical doctrine unconfirmed by the biblical text from which it claims to be derived.

Thus, by his choice of this winged metaphor, David Gans associated the astronomical opinion of the Jewish sages with that exact point in evolution where general astronomy had reached a peak of imprecision. With Tycho Brahe and Kepler, it had now reached a point where it was an unsupported assertion, an unproven theory, a doctrine claiming to be drawn from the Bible and the *Almagest* without being substantiated by the Bible. The astronomical truth lay with the Jews: it had now been revealed to some non-Jewish geniuses, but it was still covered over with a veil of paradox and contradiction. You seem to have it in your hands, but then it flies away like a bird, turning this way and that like the wayward path of the planets which jealously persist in guarding their secret.

So it was on Ptolemy's *Almagest* that David Gans based his book. As we have already pointed out, he informs us of this fact in the very first chapter. He also based his book on empirical observation, as he duly reminds us in the third chapter, whose title evokes the spiritual atmosphere we have described: 'Concerning the inutility of searching for a cause or factor which can explain why the terrestrial globe is suspended in the midst of the cosmos in a void.' Yes, the cause, the wherefore, the explanation—in short, the *laws*, and, amongst them, the Law *par excellence*, that of gravity, which Newton was to discover only over a century later—we do not have them yet. We know that the earth is round and that it is situated in the midst of the planetary system, and that this raises a host of problems: notably that of the stability of this ball thrown into the void and that of the existence of the people of the antipodes who walk with their heads on the ground. But to try, like Aristotle, to explain the stability of the earth by the influence of invisible celestial forces is as absurd as to refuse to believe in the existence of these men of the antipodes on the grounds that they would fall into the void. We have reached a point, said David Gans, where we should realize that the purpose of astronomy is not to explain but to ascertain; to observe facts but not to search for their causes.

Already, in the Middle Ages, Isaac Israeli had warned astronomers against the temptation of seeking to know the 'wherefore'.[8] Does even the most skilled worker in metals seek to know the origin, nature, and composition of the materials with which he is working? Thus, the astronomer would be stupid to waste his time looking for causes: the celestial laws undoubtedly exist, but they remain a secret with God, who has not seen fit to deliver the key into the hands of mortals. Man can observe the most infinitesimal and marvellous details of the cosmic creation, but he does not possess the means to discover or comprehend its laws.

Thus, these laws can be regarded as, in a sense, miraculous. The waters of the Red Sea divided, like those of the Jordan, and the sun 'stood still' upon Gibeon in the time of Joshua. Who would doubt it? But who would be insane enough to think that these were due to natural phenomena? Similarly, like these miracles, the laws of the cosmos transcend nature and lie beyond the power of reason to comprehend. It is enough for us to be permitted to explore the cosmos and admire its wonders which the progress of science, the ever-increasing perfection of instruments such as those invented by the genius of Tycho Brahe have made more accessible than ever before.

Such was David Gans's approach. It was identical with that of Tycho Brahe or Kepler, whose 'laws', for the one who discovers them, are merely observations and descriptions, or to that of Galileo, whose telescope was only intended to enlarge the field of vision. For all these contemporary astronomers, the explanation still remained a divine prerogative,[9] and mere mortals did not feel frustrated at being only granted the power to probe ever more deeply into the divine creation without ever being able to understand its causes. There was no trace of the Promethean about these giants who felt mighty before God for the sole but sufficient reason that the creator allowed them to embrace the cosmos with a single sweeping glance of godlike dimensions. One would have to await Isaac Newton to obtain, encapsulated into a narrow mathematical formula, the explanation of this gigantic panorama which with Kepler still vibrates with musical harmonies. It is only then that the observations of Kepler and Galileo could be also understood as being explanations, laws. But in 1600 Kepler and Galileo would have countersigned the profession of faith placed by

[8] *Yesod Olam*, ii. 1.
[9] Cf. Scholder, p. 62. This was Osiander's claim in his preface to Copernicus's book.

Gans as a kind of caution in the very first chapter of his book.

But if David Gans's astronomical edifice was built upon the foundations laid by this preliminary caution, he was also fully aware that the structure was unstable, and he was not afraid to indicate the difficulties, the incoherencies, the points of instability. He raised problems, asked questions and was prepared from the beginning to run the risk of receiving an answer which went contrary to the *Almagest*, or, more frequently, to meet with a demurrer ('Your question is correct, but for the moment there is no answer.')

This courageously fought battle constitutes the living and original element of David Gans's book. He drew into the struggle the team of astronomers in the castle of Benatek of which he was a member and placed it with its back to the wall. Tycho Brahe, Johannes Kepler, Johannes Muller, and all the other eminent scholars engaged in the service of the Emperor Rudolph were consulted by David Gans, who carefully noted their answers. Thus, the dryness of a purely theoretical narrative is enlivened by elements of a continuous dialogue whose fascinating development we shall now examine.

4

The dialogues and the Colloquy of Prague: David Gans at the heart of the astronomical revolution

WE should note, first of all, the sense of satisfaction with which David Gans recorded the successive occasions on which his non-Jewish teachers expressed their approval of Jewish astronomy. After expressing their general approval, as described in chapter 25, they recognized the mathematical erudition of the Talmudic rabbis with regard to the length of the solar year (chapter 164), and then, on another occasion, with regard to that of the lunar year (chapter 203). We know the importance of these two factors in the fixing of the Jewish calendar since, unlike the Christian calendar based exclusively on the solar year and the Muslim calendar based exclusively on the lunar year, Judaism is the only one among the monotheistic religions to create a synthesis which was originally empirical, but which the patriarch Hillel II in the fourth century BCE set on clear mathematical foundations. Adda bar Ahava, the rabbi-mathematician whose tables and calculations Hillel II had used, had lived a century earlier, at the time when Ptolemy published his own calculations in the *Almagest*.

Here David Gans took the opportunity of providing a brief preliminary survey of the general history of astronomy, of which he gave a more detailed account in the epilogue of his book. In it, he drew attention to the difficult mathematical problems raised by the exact definition of these data indispensable to the astronomer, and insisted on the fact that none of the ancients had reached conclusions as precise and acceptable as those of Ptolemy. Rav Adda, basing his conclusions on his own calculations, came quite close to Ptolemy, but there was still some distance between them.

However, when David Gans consulted Tycho Brahe and Kepler on this point, they proposed their own solutions which, both for the solar year and for the lunar year, were closer to those of Rav Adda (only six minutes' difference) than to those to Ptolemy. In the case of the lunar year, this information was especially important in that it implied Rav Adda's recognition that the moon moved in epicycles —an idea which had been discounted in Ptolemy's time, but which Kepler strongly confirmed in his conversations with Gans (chapter 200). Thus, there could be no doubt at all about the fact that we have already learned in Kepler's key chapter: namely, that ancient Jewish astronomy (or its 'secret', to use the Talmudic term), was based on data that the new astronomy of the sixteenth century had finally brought to light again after the long eclipse of the Middle Ages.

Consequently, David Gans now felt that he was able to speak on terms of equality (as he did in chapter 213) with the giants of medieval Jewish astronomy such as Maimonides and Isaac Israeli. If these, befuddled by the Ptolemaic system, had been unable to identify themselves with the views expressed in the Talmud which contradicted those of Ptolemy, it was because they were ignorant of the great truth which David Gans was the first Jew to hear from the contemporary giants of astronomy, which was that Ptolemy was wrong on many points, and that it was the Talmud—in some of its apparently erroneous assertions, but also in some of its deliberate silences—that was the depository of the 'secret' of astronomical truth, retrieved in his time by Copernicus, Tycho Brahe and Kepler.

Quite apart from any apologetic intentions, however, *Neḥmad ve-Na'im* contains a number of disinterested questions put by David Gans to his masters and collaborators out of pure curiosity, in the hope of obtaining elucidation on particular points. Where books of the past—whether the *Almagest* or Jewish astronomical treatises— left him unsatisfied, why should he not refer to the books which had been published or which were now being written by the men whom he met so often in the castle of Benatek or in Prague, why should he not avail himself of the opportunity for a private discussion with Tycho Brahe, Kepler, or Muller with the intention of solving a problem, or, at any rate, of stating it correctly?

The value of these discussions depended on the importance of the subjects concerned. Some were only of passing importance, but others were of interest for the general history of astronomy, so that it seems all the more regrettable that David Gans's *Neḥmad ve-Na'im* should have been so totally neglected by the historians of the sixteenth-century astronomical revolution. Here we relate these discussions in the order in which they are given in Gans's book, leaving the specialists to decide on their scientific value.

In the first chapter (1–20) of the first part of his book, David Gans broaches the subject of the movement of the spheres in the Ptolemaic system. Set one within the other like the layers of an onion, the eight spheres carrying the seven planets and the fixed stars move, according to this system, in a regular manner—although complicated by epicycles—from west to east. Encircling all of them, the ninth sphere, which has no epicycles, has the contrary characteristic of describing a regular circular movement in the opposite direction from the eight other spheres. It moves from east to west drawing the whole celestial system into its rotation, and this is the only explanation of the existence of the twenty-four-hour day, the *dies naturalis*, to use the Latin expression which David Gans introduced into his Hebrew description (chapter 17). Without this hypothetical diurnal sphere, the same would apply in the whole earth as at the poles (as David Gans pointed out in the so very modern cosmographical sections of his book): i.e., day and night would both last for six months.

Neither Ptolemy nor any of his successors, however, were able to give a satisfactory explanation of this diurnal movement. Writers with theological inclinations (among the Jews, Gans quotes Joseph Albo: *Sefer ha-Ikkarim*, iv. 3) liked to distinguish between the movement of the eight spheres which was physically determined, and the movement of the ninth, dependent only on the unfathomable will of the creator.

David Gans wondered, on rational grounds, how it was physically possible for a single sphere to pull the entire cosmic system in a contrary direction merely by its rotation, and, more generally, how two contrary movements could coexist in the same system. To his first question he received an answer from Kepler (chapter 14). Kepler explained that the problem applied to all the spheres. It was not only the ninth sphere which moved all the others, but each sphere moved simultaneously through its own power and through that of the neighbouring spheres. He illustrated this theory with an amusing example. Imagine, he said, a ship sailing from west to east, and on this ship a man walking, also from west to east, and in his hair a fly crawling, also from west to east. By means of the combined effect of their three movements, all three will finally go from their western point of departure to their eastern point of arrival. Kepler is known for these sallies. Flies and fleas play an important part in the examples with which he illustrated his ideas.

David Gans must have been less caustically-minded than Kepler, for when returning to Kepler's interpretation in chapter 16, he illustrated it with a more serious example: that of a pregnant woman going from east to west and carrying the foetus of her baby in that direction, while at the same time the foetus independently makes a movement in the opposite direction, from west to east, within its mother's body.

But it was from Tycho Brahe himself that David Gans received ᷉ the answer to the second question, which rendered the first superfluous, as we learn in that same chapter 16. Gans asked Brahe whether the coexistence of these two contrary movements—the one predetermined and the other free—seemed to him impossible. It was undoubtedly so, he was told, according to the logic of Aristotle and Ptolemy, but we now know (and this was the secret which Tycho Brahe revealed to Gans in that crucial twenty-fifth chapter of his book with which we began our account, and to which Gans refers us here in chapter 16)—we now know that these contrary movements do not only exist in the opposition between the ninth sphere and the eight others, but each sphere carries these contradictory movements within itself. 'The spheres are stationary but the stars move'—this piece of ancient Jewish wisdom requires a fundamental revision of the Ptolemaic system, and, as a first result, renders the idea of a ninth sphere quite unnecessary. The planetary orbits are governed by complex and contradictory forces which explain the arbitrary nature of a dual movement which gives every planet its orbit and the earth its *dies naturalis*. If there is an arbitrary element (whether divinely inspired or of a purely natural origin), it applies to the system as a whole and, once again, renders the hypothesis of the ninth sphere superfluous.

Let us say once again that it is for the specialist to assess the scientific value of these few pages of *Neḥmad ve-Na'im*, but even for one like myself who claims no special competence in astronomy, their historical interest is clear. George Alter has pointed this out before me. Firstly, we feel in this section how much Tycho Brahe and Kepler were still groping, in ignorance of the laws of gravitation which Newton was to discover only a century and a quarter later. But, above all, we see that when Gans put his question to these two masters, Kepler's ideas were still far more rigid and Ptolemaic than those of Tycho Brahe, which were already quite flexible. If Tycho Brahe's premature death prevented him from advancing further into a meta-Ptolemaic universe, Kepler long remained ensnared in the Ptolemaic system and in fact never found the scientifically correct gate of exit. He pointed the way to that gate, but it was Galileo and especially Newton who entered it.

Tycho Brahe's faith in Ptolemy remained unshaken, but he was not afraid to correct and modify the astronomer's Bible on important points, while Kepler remained completely faithful to the conclusions of the *Almagest*. This fact emerges from other passages in Gans's book besides the ones that we have just examined.

THE PHENOMENON OF PRECESSION:
JOHANNES MULLER'S THEORY

Thus, in chapter 130, for instance, we see that Gans adopted, for the phenomenon of precession, the new figures given by Tycho Brahe, who had drastically altered those provided in the *Almagest*. In chapter 219, similarly, we see Tycho Brahe correcting the figures for the moon's distance from the earth given by both Ptolemy and Copernicus.

Gans always reacted to these audacious assertions in the same way. He turned to his colleagues, his fellow-collaborators with Tycho Brahe, and particularly to Johannes Muller who supported these daring new opinions. Muller explained precession by a phenomenon which Gans said was called *motus trepitianus* in Latin and *die zittrige Bewegung* in German. What amazing new vistas now opened out before Gans! In chapter 131 which follows chapter 130 in which we see Johannes Muller supporting the theories of Tycho Brahe, we have the dizzying idea of a progressive radical modification of the heavenly realm with all its bodies. The passage concluding both these chapters bears witness to David Gans's confusion:

With regard to Johannes Muller, I must admit that I am not able to discuss his theory as I have not yet succeeded in understanding it entirely. I shall have to go into it and examine it more carefully than I have done so far. I shall conclude by saying that Johannes Muller's theory with all its astounding consequences is beyond our comprehension. We are still like a lost herd, searching vainly for intellectual security. I have already expressed my opinion in this matter in chapter 25 [the key-chapter]. Here we are confronted with very serious problems, and in order to be able to solve them we humble creatures will no doubt have to wait for many more years.[1]

Yes, poor Gans, you will have to wait the many years which still separate you from Newton, but when he appears, you will have long gone from this world! David Gans felt more reassured with Kepler, or, to be precise, with the Kepler he knew from 1599 to 1613.

Indeed, Kepler, too, proposed new figures (for the distance of the planets from the sun, chapter 108), new facts (the lunar epicycles, chapter 200), and a system of planetary cycles which David Gans described (chapter 241), but in general nothing he heard from Kepler was 'revolutionary' in the sense of what he had heard from Tycho Brahe and Johannes Muller. On the contrary: when, in

---

[1] We should point out that care should be taken not to confuse our Johannes Muller, mathematician to Johann Georg, Elector of Brandenburg, with his famous namesake Johann Muller, called Regiomontanus. The latter, who lived in the fifteenth century (he was born in Königsberg in 1436 and died in Rome in 1476) could have known neither Brahe, nor Kepler, nor Gans. Nevertheless, Freedman (p. 24) mentions seven serious nineteenth-century authors who confused them, and I have found others among our contemporaries (see the bibliography).

The mathematician Johannes Muller referred to by David Gans had already been Tycho Brahe's assistant on the island of Sveen in 1598. He is remembered above all for Kepler's wife's picturesque description of his sudden departure from Prague in a letter to her husband (Kepler, *Werke*, 14, 169, letter 188 of 31 May 1601): 'Der hanss Miller ist den 29 Mai mit seinem frau darvon und haim, der diho Prei hat jm abgeförtigt und hat jm göben was jm hat zugesagt, aber vom Khaiser ist jm Khain, heler nit worten . . .' (Hans Muller went off on 29 May with his wife and his bag and baggage. Tycho [Brahe] paid him compensation and gave him all he promised, but from the Emperor he did not receive a penny). We know that Kepler himself died in Ratisbon in a state of abject poverty. Sick and miserable, he had gone there in an attempt to recover, during a session of the Diet, the twelve thousand florins still owed to him by the Emperor Matthias, successor to Rudolph.

Did this hasty departure put an end to Johannes Muller's career? Dreyer (*Tycho Brahe*, p. 289) seems to suggest this: 'after which he disappeared from the history of science altogether'. This would appear to be too drastic a judgement: Johannes Muller seems to have taken up his position with the Elector of Brandenburg again. In any event, David Gans's account could refer either to an oral discussion between Gans and Muller in Prague or to a discussion by correspondence between Gans and Muller after the latter had left Prague (see the discussion of this problem in Freedman, pp. 28–9). We should like to elucidate this problem in the critical edition of *Neḥmad ve-Na'im*. Whatever the truth of the matter, we should at any rate be conscious of the fact that in David Gans we have a witness to the actions and thought of a late sixteenth-century astronomer worthy of the attention of historians of science.

chapter 218, Gans mentioned certain astronomers who had dared to question the system of spheres and epicycles of Hipparchus, Ptolemy, and Al-Battani, he found Kepler an eloquent and vigorous defender of these ancient and medieval theorists. Gans heard him rail against these 'boors' who dared to rise up against Ptolemy, and who were really only miserable plagiarists of pre-Ptolemaic astronomers of antiquity whose theses and arguments had been completely refuted by Ptolemy. It was probably because he so often heard this refrain of 'We have to stick to Ptolemy' from Kepler that he turned to him first with a problem whose implications, at any rate, were so considerable that David Gans finally felt he had to submit it to Tycho Brahe's whole team as the subject of a colloquy whose proceedings he reported directly in chapter 161 of his book.

THE COLLOQUY OF PRAGUE

'Despite my wish to be brief and concise, I cannot refrain, given the importance of the matter, from dwelling longer on this subject than is my custom.' Having begun in this way, David Gans spreads himself over seven columns—seven exploratory columns in which the problem is stated in four points, each of which adds a new question mark without arriving at a solution. 'Know, dear reader', wrote David Gans, searching for a conclusion which might provide some meagre consolation for his unsatisfied curiosity, 'Know that I have submitted this tangled mesh of problems and perplexities to the scholars of genius who make up the college of astronomers unequalled in science and knowledge assembled by our lord the Emperor Rudolph, may his glory be resplendent! They pondered the problem for several days, debated with me at length, and in the end were not ashamed to admit humbly that they were unable to find any correct or satisfactory solution to the problem.'

What a fascinating spectacle! A scientific colloquy in Prague in the year 1600 at which Tycho Brahe, Johannes Muller, and other astronomers and mathematicians, among the most celebrated of their period, had gathered to consider a problem raised by the modest Jewish scholar David Gans... Perhaps the Emperor Rudolph himself followed the discussions behind a screen! The colloquy ended with an admission of failure. The problem submitted by David Gans was one of those to which, in the year

1600, even men such as Brahe and Kepler were unable to find an answer.

That was quite understandable, for the problem concerned nothing other than the impact on astronomy of the discoveries of the navigators, now a century old. Here we touch upon one of the points of convergence of the discovery of the New World and of the astronomical revolution. It was now not only Copernicus who was in question, but Columbus, Amerigo Vespucci, and Vasco da Gama who entered the battle. They had changed the shape of the earth and, by that very fact, had changed that of the heavens. Even if Copernicus had not overthrown Ptolemy, the great navigators alone would have been enough to do so.

Hence the compelling interest of this chapter 161 of David Gans's *Neḥmad ve-Na'im*. He gathers up, in one crucial astronomical problem, all the questions raised by the cosmographical revolution. Here the importance given by David Gans to the 'geographical revolution' receives its true explanation. It was not only out of mere curiosity that a student of the heavens had also to be a student of the earth: the earth, in the last century, had undergone such drastic changes that they inevitably had a repercussion on the heavens also. If Ptolemy's armour had been pierced on earth, the trace of that wound was discernible in the heavens.

The problem of the prime meridian

The problem itself was certainly not a new one. It was the problem of the prime meridian, or, to use David Gans's terminology, of the point on the earth's surface where the beginning of each day of the week is determined. Ancient and medieval authorities were well aware that this problem was bound up with empirical geographical facts. The larger the inhabited world becomes, the more the sun's hundred and eighty degree revolution is extended, and the human twelve-hour day becomes subject to a pattern of extensibility whose starting and ending-points must be known if this day is to be a truly human measure of time—i.e., valid for the whole of humanity.

This was the problem which David Gans first submitted to Kepler (chapter 99). The answer he received from him was satisfactory as far as it went, but incomplete. It only applied to each day of the week separately. But David Gans, for specifically *Jewish* reasons we shall describe later, required a truly comprehensive explanation, a key which would allow the entire terrestrial globe to be embraced in the movement of the whole week. So he now submitted to Kepler's colleagues, to the whole team in the castle of Benatek, the problem in its *universal* aspect.

From Ptolemy until the fifteenth century, the prime meridian had shifted a few degrees as men had moved westwards into the Atlantic or eastwards to China. However, the fiction was maintained of a sort of 'universal day' as long as the difference—let us say, from the Canaries to China—did not exceed eighteen hours. Did not the long summer days attain this length all over the world? And might one not, through a fictional mathematical transposition, assume a similar though imaginary day in winter?

But now this scheme was wrecked by the discovery of the New World—if one took this discovery seriously, that is, and accepted its exact consequences as described by David Gans at length and in a masterly fashion in the third part of his book of astronomy!

The fatal error

'We have lived until now in a fatal error!' cried David Gans in chapter 161 of his book: 'We, the Jews, no less than the non-Jews!' Our whole system was based on the absurd hypothesis that the southern hemisphere of the terrestrial globe sank into the sea. Obviously, in such a conception, a hundred and eighty degrees would be enough to delimit the human solar day. The nightly course of the sun, the hundred and eighty degrees it turned under the water, could only interest the world of fishes. Should humanity break its head to discover 'how the fishes reckon their days'?

But now that we know with absolute certainty that in the antipodes of our three ancient continents there is an inhabited continent, that the earth does not sink into the sea, and that while it is night between the Canaries and China it is day in New Guinea; now that we know with absolute certainty that there are not three continents but eight, and that in two of these eight, even if they are not yet inhabited, the day does not last for twenty-four hours but for six months, who can now tell us where the day begins which would be valid for all humanity?

Jules Verne on the horizon

As though to colour his question, in chapter 162 which immediately follows that of the 'Colloquy of Prague', David Gans tells us that 'a contender in a round-the-world race would gain or lose a day depending on whether he were going from east to west or in the opposite direction.' Gans was careful to point out that the length of time taken by the journey is of no importance. Whether the journey took many years or only a few would make no difference to the results; it would also not affect an amazing and entirely new hypothesis which Gans now put forward. The hypothesis was this: supposing Reuben, Simeon, and Levi are at a given point of the globe. Reuben travels round the world going westwards; Simeon travels round the world going eastwards, and Levi remains stationary. When the three of them meet again and Levi says: 'Today is Tuesday', Reuben will say 'No, it's Monday', and Simeon will say 'No, it's Wednesday', and between Reuben and Simeon there will quite genuinely be a difference of two days.

Nothing could give a clearer foretaste of the adventures of Jules Verne's Phileas Fogg, and nothing, either, could better suggest the essential insolubility of the problem. For, in the final analysis—as Gans says quite explicitly in chapter 161—everything depends on an absolutely arbitrary choice: '*ein nafkuta ba-davar*' (there is no conclusion to the matter) (49c). The prime meridian has no real physical existence: it can only be defined by an arbitrary human decision. The admission of failure with which the Colloquy of Prague ended was the only rational conclusion of a discussion to which no conclusion was possible. But the Brahes and Keplers, Mullers and Ganses were not yet aware of this rationality of incertitude. They merely had a vague presentiment of it which they put forward as a humble admission of ignorance. Very long after their time it began to be understood that the only reasonable solution was an arbitrary one, and for two centuries there was the anarchy of multiple prime meridians until finally, in 1884, an international convention fixed at Greenwich the meridian so passionately sought for by David Gans.

The Jewish aspect of the problem: the absolute Sabbath

But why did David Gans put so much passion into this search? Having understood the arbitrary nature of this problem, we may ask why he so much insisted on looking for an answer that was not imaginary like his basic premises, but real like the physical facts of nature.

For Tycho Brahe or Johannes Kepler such a requirement might have seemed of secondary importance, but not for David Gans, for it must be pointed out that when he illustrated his example with Levi, Reuben, and Simeon, these fellows were Jews just like Gans himself. Now Jews, like Christians, can be perfectly indifferent to the fact that the same solar day can be Tuesday for one person, Monday for another, and Wednesday for a third, but Jews cannot remain unaffected by the 'scandal and absurdity' (49d) of a Sabbath whose twenty-four hours fail to correspond, for all the Jews of the world, to a single solar day.

For the Jewish calendar has a remarkable peculiarity. Unlike the Christian calendar, heir to the Graeco-Roman world, which is based on the solar orbit, and unlike the Muslim calendar which derives from an oriental environment and is based on the lunar orbit, the Jewish calendar throws a bridge, boldly-conceived and equal to every test, between the sun and the moon. And upon these scales in which the months and years are held in equilibrium, the Jews have placed a third element: the week, centred on the Sabbath.

'*Me-erev ad erev*' (Leviticus 23: 32): from one evening to the next. That is how the Jewish day is reckoned, according to the very principle of the creation whereby the evening precedes the morning: 'And there was evening and there was morning, one day' (Genesis 1: 5). The first six days of the week pass in the manner here described, in accordance with the Book of Genesis, and none has a name, for their purpose is to lead towards the seventh day, the seal and completion of the work of God. And the seventh day, preceded by its retinue of six days, constitutes, together with these, the Jewish week.

This is the starting-point of the Jewish system of measuring time. It is simple in its division of days and weeks, and it is immutable because it draws its origins from the account of the creation. It is original in the importance given to evening, to the precedence of night over day. All the Jewish festivals are marked by feverish preparations on the day preceding them, and then, at sunset, with the appearance of the first stars, by a sudden transfiguration, a transition from a state of activity to a state of rest, from the profane to the sacred. Nightfall is solemn, fervent, joyful. The sense of human communion in the synagogue, first of all, and then around the family table, removes from the night its terrifying quality. The evening watch becomes a hymn. And certain nights which introduce an event, like that of the Passover Seder and that of Yom

Kippur whose twenty-four hours are devoted to prayer and fasting, possess a poetic magic to which it is hard to remain indifferent. When the sun rises, it only prolongs this already-created atmosphere to dusk, which comes as a farewell, a parting, but also as the vigorous confrontation with a new day. The normal rhythm of the day is, as it were, reversed by a sequence of three times of prayer stretching from one evening to another: evening prayer, morning prayer and afternoon prayer. It is not the cock-crow which awakens the Jew to his day: already in the evening, the Jew sings the 'psalm of the day', both human and cosmic. Because the days of the week have no names, they escape the mythological or astral influences imposed upon them by their names in the non-Jewish calendars. They are drawn towards the seventh day, the only one to have a name: *Shabbat*, rest—the concentration of human activity in a nucleus of purification, a moment at the heart of things, assimilating past energies and revitalizing them with a new breath.

But the Sabbath is not only weekly: it affects the whole pulsation of time and is expressed in a veritable pyramid of time based on the number seven. Each seventh year is a Sabbatical year in which the earth must rest, debts must be paid, slaves must be freed, and social and agricultural life restored to its proper equilibrium. And after the cycle of seven Sabbatical years—that is, after forty-nine years—there is the fiftieth year, the jubilee year, whose redemptive power is even greater than that of the Sabbatical year. It is the culmination of the Sabbatical years and crowns them by the return of transferred property to its original owner. A man estranged from his inheritance finds himself once more, and regains his true identity.

The Sabbath is thus the measure of a cyclical concept of time which originates with the creation and has its vital points of reference in the moments of 'return' which are so many stages on the road to completion. It is an arbitrary measure, since it is independent of the cycles of nature. Each person and each community chooses its own Sabbath. Are you lost in the desert or in the polar regions without contact with other Jews, and have you forgotten what day of the week it is? Well, you will have to decide on a first day for yourself, and then the seventh day will be your Sabbath. David Gans was one of the first Jewish scholars to sense and fear this relativity of the Sabbath, which contains within it the risk of its disintegration.

The medieval Jewish scholars had foreseen this risk, and in order to avoid it they attempted to introduce a stable element into this arbitrariness, a sort of standard, but a standard not in the dimension of time but in that of space. It was the Sabbath of the Holy Land, Erez Israel, Palestine. It was as though that Sabbath alone was regarded as being of metaphysical importance, and just as the Jews of the whole world turned their eyes towards Jerusalem at the hour of prayer, so the Jewish soul was said to be turned towards the Jerusalem Sabbath whose twenty-four hours constitute the absolute Sabbath in just the same way as the ordinances of the Sabbatical year and the jubilee year apply exclusively within the frontiers of the Holy Land.

However, this theory, so admirably expounded on the basis of purely astronomical arguments by the twelfth-century poet-philosopher Judah Halevi, had been refuted—also through astronomical arguments—by Isaac Israeli two centuries later. Two centuries later still, the maritime discoveries added important empirical considerations to the mathematical considerations, and the idea of the centrality of Erez Israel, if it still preserved its value in the world of metaphysical symbolism, no longer worked in the purely physical context of a world transformed by the cosmographical and astronomical revolutions.

We have seen that David Gans did not evade the issue: he raised it in his book, long before the 'Colloquy of Prague', in chapters 89 to 91, in connection with the question of the choice of a new prime meridian. But we have also seen that—unfaithful in this as in other things to the comprehensively metaphysical vision of his Master the Maharal—he introduced the Holy Land into profane geography, thus divesting Erez Israel of its magnetic power and simultaneously passing on the problem of the Sabbath, under the more general guise of the problem of measuring the day, to his non-Jewish masters of astronomy in Prague. The de-sacralization of the Holy Land had automatically led to a de-sacralization of the Sabbath which now only became a twenty-four hour day like any other.

Chapters 99 and 152 are revealing on this point. In chapter 99, Gans, talking to Kepler, strongly insisted on the great difference between the Christian calendar with its pagan origins, in which the very names of the days of the week show them to be placed under the astrological influence of the planets (*Sonntag, Montag, Dienstag,* etc.) and the Jewish calendar with its anonymous weekdays which are like arrows pointing towards the Sabbath. But as against this, in chapter 152 Gans specifically states that the Sabbath cannot be used as a standard. Owing to the difference in longitudes between the Sabbath of Jerusalem and that of Prague, there is an unbridgeable difference of an hour. The Sabbath is thus relegated to the category of natural measurements of time, and if the Jewish week escapes the irrational magic of astronomy, it becomes captive to the rigours of scientific astronomy. If one were to recover the sense of the sacredness of the Sabbath and consequently of Erez Israel, a solution to David Gans's serious problem had to be found; but if the Maharal could only offer him a metaphysical key, the professional astronomers—Tycho Brahe, Kepler, Muller—were unable to offer him a physical key. So one can understand David Gans's disappointment when he had to conclude his long chapter on a question mark.

Let us, at any rate, once more admire David Gans's courage, his confidence in tomorrows rich in promises which today is not yet able to fulfil. The failure of the Colloquy of Prague discouraged him no more than the many failures of Tycho and Kepler discouraged them on their difficult path. Like his teachers and colleagues, David Gans had a naïve and limitless faith in science. Whatever it did not know today, it was sure to discover tomorrow. And without betraying any shame or blushing on account of Jewish or non-Jewish science, lost for the moment in the same cul-de-sac, David Gans also continued on his path. Did not Christopher Columbus, Amerigo Vespucci, Vasco da Gama have to make two, three, and four expeditions before they were able to offer up the earth to humanity so that they could grasp it in their hands? One day, owing to the ceaseless expeditions of the navigators of the heavenly vault, mankind would also have within its hands the totality of the sky.

5

Meeting at the summit: Tycho Brahe and the Maharal of Prague

WHILE awaiting that blessed moment, however, whose key will perhaps be provided by the Messiah, one ought nevertheless to take one's bearings. Does not the Talmud often indicate the existence of a problem insoluble in the present by referring it to the prophet Elijah, herald of the Messiah? We feel that it is the logic of the Talmud, of the rabbinical idea of *teku*, so full of humility but also of confidence, which inspired the general character of the conclusion of Gans's book.

THE CONCLUSION OF *NEḤMAD VE-NA'IM*: THE SYSTEM OF TYCHO BRAHE

This conclusion, kept by as a sort of tasty morsel for the end, began with the enthusiastic description of the observatory at Benatek which we have quoted,[1] and with a recollection of the wonderful hours which David Gans spent working in that observatory. The real aim of this autobiographical narrative, however, was a scientific one: to give as brief and clear an account as possible of Tycho Brahe's astronomical revolution.

David Gans's book ends with this brief account, consisting of four points, some of which had already been made earlier in the book, particularly in chapters twenty-five and a hundred and sixty-three. These are:

(1) Tycho Brahe demonstrated that the spheres are immobile, while the stars move (this is what is stated in the 'key chapter', 25, which Gans refers to through the mention of chapter 16 which introduces it).

(2) Brahe demonstrated that in the course of time the sun had deviated from the regular curve of eclipses (this fact was discovered

---

[1] See above III. 2.

through the meticulous researches of Tycho Brahe at Uraniborg, see Dreyer, pp. 357 ff.).

(3) Brahe provided irrefutable evidence that the courses of Mars, Mercury and Venus were dependent on the orbits of the other planets.

(4) According to Brahe, the earth is not the centre of the spheres of the five principal planets: Saturn, Jupiter, Mars, Mercury, and Venus. The earth is only the centre of the solar sphere and the lunar sphere. The centre of the spheres of the five other planets is the sun itself. The sun is situated in the midst of these planets which surround it with their circles like a king enthroned among his servants. These planetary circles are unchanging in their distance from the sun, and together they form a perpetual heliocentric system.

David Gans pointed out that, prior to Tycho Brahe, no astronomer had conceived such a system, geo- and helio-centric (earth-centred and sun-centred) at the same time; and he drew attention to the difficulty, not so much of the system itself, but of representing it in diagrams. At this point, however, his pen betrayed him. Not having the creative and suggestive power of Tycho Brahe, he was content to refer the reader to Tycho Brahe's own works. David Gans possessed these works, and he invited the reader to visit him to consult them. He was sure that the reader, like himself, would be amazed by the convincing clarity of Tycho Brahe's figures, and that, if he gave them a moment of careful consideration, he would understand them and be impressed by their magnificent logic. No astronomer before Tycho Brahe, he declared, had ever thought of such a system!

We think that if, in the end, at this provisional ending-point of his journey, David Gans put his money on Tycho Brahe, it was not only because of his personal fascination with this astronomer. Something else also influenced his choice, and it was this: if, *before* Tycho Brahe, no one had thought of such a system, at the same time as he did and in that same city of Prague where David Gans had been his pupil, David Gans's other Teacher, the great Maharal, had conceived an astronomical system which in the final analysis was quite similar to Tycho Brahe's.

This system was expounded by the Maharal in the sixth 'well' of his *Be'er ha-Golah*. Thus far, we have only examined the influence on David Gans of the methodology of these pages: we are now about to consider the probable influence of their content.

We do not put forward this final hypothesis without a certain apprehension. The astronomical parts of *Be'er ha-Golah* are so cryptic that one hardly dares strip them of their mystical content (as we shall attempt to do) for fear of running the risk of profaning them.

And yet, we—together with Kariv, Kleinberger, Dreyfus, and Gross—are among those who have attempted to demonstrate that there was a key to the Maharal's 'theology'. Would his astronomy, then, which forms an integral part of his theology, lie outside the general rules of his system?

A little earlier, when we were dealing exclusively with questions of method and we came upon the remarkable passage in which the Maharal confronted without fear the astronomical revolution brought about by Copernicus, we saw man portrayed as the central Adam, situated in the middle, exposed to the caprices of physical causality and finality. Man, seen in that light, is the symbol of variability. Here, however, is this same man, still in the middle, but now he represents the element of permanence between the inferior and the superior.

The Maharal, however, did not maintain that the opposition between the inferior and the superior depended exclusively on this contrast between variability and permanence. There was also another polarity which, on a number of occasions, the Maharal brought to our attention: namely, that between the earth below and the sun above. The round earth is in the centre of the lower universe. The sun reigns in the upper universe, separated from all the elements in the lower universe. Being the sovereign of the upper universe, it is its very essence to be separated from these elements.

Now, we see that this, with the difference of a few words, was the phrase used by Pliny, and it corresponds to Copernicus's vision of the distancing of the sun from the other planets: a Pythagorean type of heliocentrism which was antithetically inserted here into the Ptolemaic geocentrism. According to this conception, man on earth and the sun in the heavens share the sovereignty of the universe between them.

This construction represents a typically Maharalian tension of opposites. Does not the Maharal constantly repeat that man is not only the sovereign of the lower world, but also a participant in the upper world? Upper and lower are no longer two different self-contained categories, like Aristotle's sublunary and superlunary worlds. A central point, an *emza* binds them together: hence their bifocal structure. The sun is the heart of the upper world: the earth is the heart of the lower world.

Philosophically, that means that the metaphysical overlaps with the physical and everything belongs to both categories simultaneously. Methodologically, it implies a mixture of reason and mysticism, a comprehensive view embracing the universe in a vision derived from both faith and science.

Looked at in a simpler way, however, from a purely astronomical point of view this tension is resolved by a compromise, a *hashlamah*, as the Maharal would term it, between heliocentrism and geocentrism. Was not this the very compromise reached by Tycho Brahe in his desperate bid to combine Copernicus and Ptolemy? The planets revolving around the sun and the sun and its attendants revolving around the earth: that would appear to be the strictly 'physical' aspect of the Maharal's 'metaphysical' system. The tangible sign of the sun's double function is its visibility by day and its disappearance at night, and likewise its warmth in summer and its feebleness in winter. All this may be observed in the very nature of the universe, but, here as elsewhere, the physical manifestation is but the indication of a supernatural truth which the Jewish sages expounded in their particular astronomy. Thus, the physical contrast between a visible sun by day and a sun which is invisible by night, a hot southern sun and a cooler northern sun, is amplified and extended to the limits in which the finite blends into the infinite by the contrast between a sovereign sun and a sovereign earth, disputing the empire of the creation between them and each one claiming its part. For a merely physical observer on his little spot of earth it looks as if the entire system of spheres revolves around this planet, but for the true man, the Adam who embraces both the upper and lower worlds, who is as well able to reach the dizzy heights as to descend into the depths of the void—for him, a living creature before the living creator, there is a division in the cosmos, a polarity appears: the sun and spheres revolve around the earth, but, at the same time, the spheres revolve around the sun.

THE IRRATIONAL OBSESSIONS OF THE MAHARAL AND KEPLER

This grandiose vision was expressed in a highly symbolic language, each element of which could ultimately be translated into scientific laws and propositions. Whether they are true or false is beside the point. What is of overriding importance, however, is that the Maharal was the only Jewish thinker to have been inspired by that 'irrational obsession' (Koestler) so characteristic of the outlook of his contemporaries, Tycho Brahe and Johannes Kepler, which gave rise, in their case, by an internal process, to their scientific theories.

We should recall Kepler's persistent fascination with what he called the 'geometry of the *Kabbalah*'. He spoke about it in a letter sent from Prague on the twelfth of May 1608 to Joachim Tankius, the professor of anatomy and surgery at Leipzig (*Werke*, 16: 158,letter 493). It is worth quoting here, while we are examining the spiritual interrelationship of the Maharal, Tycho, and Kepler:

Ludo quippe et ego Symbolis, et opusculum institui, Cabalam Geometricam, quae est de Ideis rerum Naturalium in Geometria: sed ita ludo, ut me ludere non obliviscar. Nihil enim probatur Symbolis, nihil abstrusi eruitur in Naturali philosophia, per Symbolas geometricas, tantum ante nota accomodantur.

[I, too, sometimes play with symbols. I began to write a little work called 'The Geometrical *Kabbalah*'. In it, I expressed ideas on natural phenomena in geometrical form. In any case, I play in such a way that I never forget that for me this is no more than a game. In natural philosophy, the things which are hidden cannot be discovered by means of geometrical symbols, and they can only be related to previously known ideas.]

These few lines characteristically reveal the coexistence in Kepler of 'two souls': one, rational, deductive, mathematical, and the other, mystical, inductive, meta-scientific. This latter soul sought and found encouragement in the methodology of Jewish mysticism: *Kabbalah*, geometry (which must be understood here as *gematria*, a Hebrew term denoting the science of the mystical significance of numbers and letters: we have already pointed out that Kepler knew Hebrew), and symbolism.

That year 1608 was the one in which Kepler finished his

Astronomia Nova which appeared the following year. The Maharal's *Be'er ha-Golah* had already appeared in 1600, but the Maharal was still alive and the two writers could have met one another in Prague. Kepler was still a follower of Tycho.

Of course (this is a very important point) Kepler insisted that the symbolism of the *Kabbalah* was for him only a game. That was the great fundamental difference between Kepler and the Maharal. What for the one was only a game—and he never forgot it—for the other was a deeply serious truth. But, over and above the difference of conception of two minds for one of whom the *Kabbalah* was a recreational exercise and for the other of whom it was a form of philosophical reflection, there was the meeting of these two minds in the world of the *Kabbalah* and its various forms of expression.

In the Maharal, the scientific aspect of his theory was not very clearly expressed, no doubt because that was not his main point of interest. It was enough for him to be intimate with the 'secret' of the creation, without feeling the need or possessing the faculty to describe this secret in mathematical terms. Yet, for all that, we nevertheless repeat that the account of it he provides in these few pages clearly recalls the system of Tycho Brahe.

In David Gans, precisely, we have a witness to the similarity of the Maharal's conception and Tycho Brahe's theory. His introduction to the seventh part of *Neḥmad ve-Na'im* and the 'final conclusion' of his book permit us to support our hypothesis with the opinion of someone who was very close to both these men, one Jewish and the other not, who illumined Prague with their brilliance around the year 1600.

DAVID GANS'S SYSTEM: IMPRESSION OF THE SPIRITUAL
ENCOUNTER OF THE MAHARAL AND TYCHO BRAHE

In chapter 163 of his book, the first of the seventh part dealing with the description of the motions of the planets, David Gans explained why he began his description with an account of the sun's orbit, although the solar sphere was only the fourth among the seven celestial spheres.

The reason he gave (an idea literally taken from the Maharal) was that the number four was the middle number of the seven: it was *emẓayi* (in the middle). The other spheres therefore depend upon the solar sphere, since the centre supports the whole and makes it comprehensible. This central, mediating position of the sun, said Gans, was compared by the sages to that of a king surrounded by his servants who carry out their tasks in accordance with the orders which he gives them. Gans did not say who these 'sages' were. They were clearly ancients, particularly Pliny and the Pythagoreans, whom Gans regarded as the precursors of Copernicus. But the term 'sage' also suggests the Maharal, for two reasons: namely, that the metaphor of the sun-as-king actually appears, as we have seen, in his *Be'er ha-Golah*, and that, in addition, the idea, expressed in *Be'er ha-Golah*, of a sun separated from all other elements, in the total context of the Maharal's cosmology (see our *Puits de l'Exil*) indicates his metaphysical conception of the function of the middle. That which is in the middle is separated, *nivdal*, metaphysical, or, in the case of the sun, meta-terrestrial. The ideas expressed by David Gans and his use of the Maharal's terminology clearly suggest that in this passage it was his Jewish Teacher whom he had in mind.[2]

Immediately afterwards, he specifically mentioned his non-Jewish teacher: 'And in the opinion of the great investigator Tycho Brahe, the central position of the sun is the (astronomical) centre of five (of the seven) planets: an idea which no scholar before him had ever expressed, and an admirable conception concerning which I shall say a few words as a final conclusion to this book.' A conclusion which, as we have seen, culminates in an account of Tycho Brahe's system in terms common to the terminology of Tycho Brahe and the Maharal. Thus, David Gans was the living witness to the similarity, if not the identity, of the astronomical theories of the Maharal and of Tycho Brahe.

Perhaps the mysterious dialogue between Rudolph of Habsburg and the Maharal in 1592 concerned nothing else than this new revelation of the heavens. Beyond the curtain which shielded the Emperor from the Maharal, another curtain arose, dazzling Rudolph with the vision of the cosmos which it suddenly revealed. Tycho Brahe was not in Prague yet, nor was Johannes Kepler, and perhaps the Emperor Rudolph first heard about the 'astronomical revolution'

[2] I do not find the metaphor of the sun as a king surrounded by servants 'banal', as Koyré would have it (p. 103). All the writers who recall Copernicus or his teachings in the late sixteenth or early seventeenth centuries are implicitly referring to Copernicus when they describe the sun as a king surrounded by servants, and this applies equally to the Maharal and David Gans. In the case of Delmedigo, his reference to Copernicus in his book *Elim* (p. 300) is a translation of Copernicus's phrase into Hebrew.

not from his 'imperial mathematicians' but from the venerable aged
rabbi who was much preoccupied with *Kabbalah* and mysticism as
with science and rational knowledge.

In his novel *Tycho Brahe in Search of God*, Max Brod made the
astronomer meet the rabbi at the precise moment of the audience
of 1592. Tycho Brahe entered the Hradschin Palace and crossed
the majestic figure of the eminent Rabbi Loeb at the very instant
when he had just left the chamber where the Emperor had been
listening to him. Tycho Brahe, for his part, had the feeling that this
old Jew held the key to the secret which he, the non-Jew, was
pained at being unable to discover. This scene is of course
fictitious, since the meeting between the Maharal and Rudolf took
place in 1592, and at that date Tycho Brahe was not yet in Prague,
where he settled only in 1599.[3] And yet the scene does have an
element of truth in it: the truth of the spiritual encounter of the
Maharal and of Tycho Brahe. It represented a real moment in the
history of astronomy in its transition from a medieval to a modern
outlook, and it is not the least merit of David Gans's book that it
offers a living impression of that moment.

[3] Was there a meeting between the Maharal and Tycho Brahe between 1599 and
1600? We do not know, and we probably never will. What is quite certain is that the
stories associating the Maharal with Tycho Brahe in L. Weisel's *Sippurim* (Prague,
Pascheles, 1847), like the myth of the golem, are fictional, and F. Thieberger (p. 82) is
right to mention them in the part of his book entitled 'The Legend'.

APPENDIX

Copernicus in Hebrew literature from the end of the sixteenth to the end of the eighteenth century

WE are planning to make a detailed study of the place of Copernicus in Jewish and Hebrew literature in the seventeenth and eighteenth centuries. The subject is not only interesting in itself, but it has a bearing on the question of religious tolerance, of which it was one of the chief indicators during that period. In these few pages, however, we shall limit ourselves to stating a few salient facts which only yield their full significance when set against the background of the evolution of Copernicanism in non-Jewish European thought. Without over-simplification, we can state first of all that:

(1) In the realm of science, Copernicus's hypothesis was accepted, until about the end of the eighteenth century, only by a few outstanding thinkers such as Kepler, Galileo, Newton, Laplace, and Herschel. Most learned astronomers, while paying lip-service to Copernicus, continued to base their work on the Ptolemaic system. It was the physicists who forced them to come to terms with the Copernican revolution.

(2) In the realm of theology, the opposition to Copernicus remained persistent and often violent until the beginning of the nineteenth century. The Catholics took his book off the Index only in 1832. The Protestants changed their attitude a little sooner because the development of biblical criticism in the eighteenth century deprived the anti-Copernican arguments from Holy Scripture of much of their authority.

The Jewish attitude was especially interesting in that although, scientifically, they resembled the others (all the Jewish astronomical works which mentioned Copernicus were based on Ptolemy), they nevertheless displayed a remarkable theological tolerance.

As we have seen in this book, the tone was set by David Gans and the Maharal. These two inhabitants of Prague were shortly followed by the celebrated Joseph Solomon Delmedigo (1591–1655), known as *Yashar* of Candia, where he was born (this title was made up of the first letters in Hebrew: Joseph Solomon Rofe = physician). After many vicissitudes which took him through Europe, Asia, and Africa, Delmedigo finally joined David Gans and the Maharal in the Jewish cemetery in Prague. We have pointed out that G. Alter associates him with David Gans in his *Two Renaissance Astronomers*, which we have often referred to in this book. Several of Delmedigo's works were about astronomy: one of them, *Elim*, was published by Menasseh ben Israel in Amsterdam in 1629, sixteen years after David Gans's death (and more than a century before *Neḥmad ve-Na'im* was published), during Kepler's lifetime, and in the very year when Galileo's trial began in Rome.

In *Elim* (and in his later works gathered together under the general title *Elim* in the Odessa edition (1864), from which we have taken our references) Delmedigo very feelingly recalled that in Padua, about 1613—the year of David Gans's death—the great Galileo was his 'Rabbi'. Galileo several times allowed his young Jewish student to make a few observations with the use of the famous telescope which he had constructed in 1609 (*Elim*, pp. 301 and 417).

I invite the reader to linger for a few moments over this image of two Jewish astronomers with a few years between them scanning the heavens at the beginning of the seventeenth century—one in Tycho Brahe's observatory in Prague and the other in Galileo's in Padua. Hats off to those philosemitic Christians, Tycho and Galileo, and a low bow, skullcap on head, before these believing and strictly observant Jews who had the courage to take time off from their religious practices to devote to experiments in an observatory!

Delmedigo was clearly introduced by Galileo to the Copernican system, which he explained and sometimes praised on a number of occasions (pp. 300, 304, 315). In practical terms, however, he did not turn his back on Ptolemy. His attitude to the astronomical revolution is summed up in a short observation on page 315: 'The two great luminaries, Ptolemy and Copernicus, are agreed on this point . . .'. When they disagree, however, Ptolemy is given preference over Copernicus.

Never, on the other hand, does Delmedigo invoke any argument of a religious or theological nature against Copernicus. If his system as a whole was based on Ptolemy's, that is because (as we have said) nobody escaped Ptolemy's dominance at that period, yet on certain points of detail Delmedigo was categorical: Copernicus's proofs are convincing, he said, 'and anyone who will not accept them can only be classed as a perfect imbecile' (p. 304).

For the next references to Copernicus after the Maharal, Gans, and Delmedigo, we have to wait until the eighteenth century. There we find a number of relevant works, and we begin by giving their dates of publication: 1707, 1714, 1720, 1756, 1765, 1777, 1779, 1785, and 1791. This is an interesting collection, to which, however, we can devote only a few brief lines.

With the exception of the two earliest works, which we shall speak about in a moment, all the works on this list remained in the tradition of the pioneers of the sixteenth and seventeenth centuries: that is to say, they were theologically positive towards Copernicus, even if they had practical reservations.

Sefer Yeshuah be-Yisrael by Jonathan ben Joseph of Rozhany (Frankfurt-on-Main, 1720) was a great compendium, displaying much erudition on the writer's part. Through Delmedigo, to whom he often referred, he knew of Galileo and Copernicus and appreciated their value. His book has a more specific interest for us, however, because Jonathan included in it the glosses to Abraham bar Ḥiyya's *Ẓurat ha-Areẓ* written in 1587 by Samson ben Beẓalel, who was none other than the youngest of the three brothers of the Maharal (see I,4 above). Thus, we see that astronomy was studied not only in the School of the Maharal, but in his closest family circle. We have already pointed this out in connection with his son-in-law Isaac Cohen (see I,5 above); we now also have an indication with regard to his brother Samson.

One finds the same positive attitude to Copernicus in *Neẓaḥ Yisrael* by Israel ben Moses Halevi of Zamosc (Frankfurt-on-Oder, 1741) and *Ammudei Shamayim* by Baruch ben Jacob Schick, also called Baruch Shklover (Berlin, 1777)—in *Yaarot Dvash*, by Jonathan Eibeschutz (Karlsruhe, 1779), and in *Givat ha-Moreh* by Solomon Maimon (Berlin, 1791). If I mention these different works in the same breath, it is because they are all directly connected with Moses Mendelssohn, who, as we said, settled in Berlin in 1743, at the same time as Rabbi Joel Sachs, editor of David Gans's *Neḥmad ve-Na'im*. Israel of Zamosc was Mendelssohn's teacher of mathematics in Berlin, while Baruch Schick is known to have acted as a liaison between Mendelssohn's circle and the School of the Gaon Elijah of Vilna. Finally, Solomon Maimon is sufficiently well known for us not to have to stress the importance of this disciple of Mendelssohn. His book, published in 1791, was the latest in date of those presented here. In this work, Copernicanism is treated with the most remarkable tolerance and enlightenment.

This, however, cannot be said of the first two of these works of the eighteenth century: Tobias Cohn's *Ma'aseh Tuviyyah*, published in Venice in 1707 (there was a second edition in Jessnitz in 1721, at the very press where David Gans's *Neḥmad ve-Na'im* was published only twenty-two years later!), and David Nieto's *Matteh Dan, Kuzari Sheni*, published in London in 1714 (reprinted, London, 1958). These were the only Hebrew works—the only ones—in which one finds a violent anti-Copernican stand.

Tobias ben Moses Cohn (1652–1729), the author of *Ma'aseh Tuviyyah*, was a many-sided figure who in many respects recalls Joseph Solomon Delmedigo. Both men were physicians, and had obtained their diplomas in Padua; both men had experienced many vicissitudes. Born in Metz, where his father, Rabbi Moses Hacohen Narol had the honour of receiving King Louis XIV with great pomp when he visited the Metz synagogue in September 1657 (see A. Cahen, 'Le Rabbinat de Metz pendant la période française', *REJ*, 14 (1883), pp. 220–4), Tobias Cohn studied first in Cracow and then in Frankfurt-on-Oder, where he received a stipend from the Elector of Brandenburg. Then, having completed his medical studies in Padua, he settled in Turkey and went to die in Jerusalem. Both men, finally, were humanists in the widest sense of the term. Versed in religious subjects, they were also interested in all the secular sciences, and Cohn's *Ma'aseh Tuviyyah* dealt with theology, astronomy, cosmography, and botany as well as—naturally—medicine. In this latter subject, his approach was a very modern one. He was one of the first doctors to accept Harvey's theory of the circulation of the blood, and consequently did not hesitate to criticize Galen and hence Maimonides. He attacked superstitions, quack physicians, belief in amulets . . .

But in astronomy, on the other hand, our worthy Tobias Cohn was the only Jewish writer, the *only* one, to abuse Copernicus, calling him the 'first-born of Satan'. He condemned his system on biblical grounds.

Here I deliberately say 'biblical' and not 'rabbinical'. This distinction is an important one, as we have pointed out, and we shall see how Cohn, in putting forward his own argument, was caught in his own snare.

First of all, we should admire the clarity of the astronomical exposition in *Ma'aseh Tuviyyah* (second part, pp. 48b–66a). After explaining what he called the old system, he introduced the representatives of the 'new' system, headed by Hipparchus and Ptolemy and followed by Copernicus and Tycho Brahe (50a–52b). One sees that Cohn perfectly understood the connection between Copernicus and Hipparchus, and also Tycho Brahe's attempt to reconcile Copernicus with Ptolemy. The systems of Copernicus and Tycho Brahe were illustrated by two very clear diagrams.

Then came the refutation of the 'firstborn of Satan'—in other words, Copernicus. But if Cohn supported his refutation with an appeal to common sense, Galilei (*sic*), and, finally, the Bible, through intellectual honesty he added an important marginal note (52b) when attempting to prove the falsity of the Copernican system of the movement of the earth by means of a verse in Ecclesiastes (1: 4): 'The earth is ever at rest'. 'A remark from the author', he wrote. 'I am afraid that doubters may base their objections on a text in *Midrash Bereshit Rabba* (5: 7) in which our Teachers, the Rabbis, of blessed memory, teach that if the earth is called *erez* in Hebrew, it is because it ran (in Hebrew, *razta*) before the creator to do His bidding. I must admit that I find it difficult to provide an answer to that objection.'

Thus, Cohn (who could obviously not have been acquainted with *Nehmad ve-Na'im*, which was published only in 1743), tripped up over the very problem which David Gans had been able to solve through his conversations with Tycho Brahe. In Judaism, as we have seen, the theological objections to the Ptolemaic system were not based on the Bible but the Talmud. The Talmudic rabbis spoke a 'Copernican' language, and Tycho approved of their views. It was owing to this very approval that David Gans felt free to praise Copernicus.

Cohn found himself in an impasse. Perhaps his attitude is partly to be explained by the fact that in Venice in 1707 one could no doubt still hear the echo of the stormy appearance in Jewish history of Shabbetai Zevi in 1666. With the advent of Shabbataianism, there began a witch-hunt such as had never been known in Judaism before. One of its most illustrious victims, Moses Haim Luzatto, was born in Padua in 1707, the very year when Cohn published his book—the only one, we repeat, in which a crude anti-Copernican expression issued from a Jewish pen. The Venetian Rabbinate, which gave its warm approval to Cohn's book, did not distinguish itself in the Luzatto affair by its dignity or tolerance. It did not hesitate to hurl prohibitions at him twenty years later, smelling out Shabbataianism in him, just as Cohn may have sniffed it out among the followers of Copernicus in 1707.

Most ironic of all: Cohn's book bore, in addition to the approval of the Venetian Rabbinate, a very warm recommendation from Rabbi David Oppenheim of Prague, the very one who then had in his library the only still-existing copy of David Gans's *Magen David*, in which Gans wrote enthusiastically about the so-called 'firstborn of Satan', alias Copernicus. True enough, there were thousands of volumes in David Oppenheim's library, and perhaps the worthy rabbi did not have the time or the opportunity to read the little twelve-page work called *Magen David* whose point of view about Copernicus was at the opposite extreme from that expressed in the hundred and fifty-eight double pages of the *Ma'aseh Tuviyyah* which he praised in his *Haskamah*.

David Nieto (1654–1728), a Doctor of Medicine of Padua like Tobias Cohn, came from the same Venetian milieu. He had been a *dayyan* at Leghorn before becoming *Haham* of the Sephardi congregation in London, and his book *Esh Dat* made a frontal attack on the Shabbataian heresy. This book came out in 1715, one year before *Matteh Dan*, a dialogue modelled on that of Judah Halevi's *Kuzari*, in which the writer was able to broaden his scope and consider most of the theological, philosophical, and scientific problems of the period. Astronomy was dealt with in the fourth dialogue, where Copernicus's hypothesis was summarily refuted in paragraphs 130–4 by a reference to the classic verse in the Book of Joshua. On the other hand, in the following paragraphs David Nieto readily acknowledged that the stars were inhabited, and he was happy to be able to support this modern concept of the plurality of worlds with rabbinical texts. The tone of the dialogue is much more moderate than that of the pages of Tobias Cohn: Copernicus himself is not insulted; his doctrine is not suspected of being diabolical. The phrase used by David Nieto was a stereotyped formula, and was part of the normal usage of a language respectful, despite everything, of the opinions of others, even when one disagreed with them: *pigul hu, lo yerazeh* ('it is a sacrifice which would not be acceptable in the Temple') (p. 59a, b of the *editio princeps*. Recent edition: D. Nieto, *Ha-Kuzari ha-Sheni* (1958), J. L. Maimon, C. Roth).

When Moses Hayyim Luzatto had to leave Italy—and before he went to the Holy Land, where he died on his arrival in 1747—in 1736 he came to Amsterdam, where he found a moment of peace and quiet in the tolerant atmosphere of the Jewish community.

It was similarly in Amsterdam that the *Sefer Tekhunat ha-Shamayim* by Raphael Halevi of Hanover (1685–1779) appeared, in which the astronomical revolution was approached with a combination of disarming naïvety and remarkable intellectual honesty. In that book, we find once more the serene atmosphere of Prague in 1600.

With the warm recommendation of the two Chief Rabbis of Amsterdam —the Ashkenazi and the Sephardi—Raphael Halevi, in ninety-five short chapters (thirty-two double pages) expounded the astronomical ideas necessary to the fixing of the Jewish calendar. These ideas were based on those of the *Code* of Maimonides (whose name figures on the title-page before that of Raphael Halevi himself), and were consequently drawn entirely from the Ptolemaic system.

However, when we reach the conclusion of the work, the last chapter, no. 96, the logical sequence which the book had followed until then is suddenly broken. In some twenty lines, complete with diagram, the Copernican system is explained in this chapter, and Raphael Halevi says:

So far, up to the end of chapter ninety-five, we have followed the opinion of the ancients, but now in our time the great astronomer Copernicus has discovered another way of describing the cosmos; it is this system, which is called the new astronomy, which places the sun in the centre of the cosmos . . . the third sphere being that of the earth which rotates around the sun in three hundred and sixty-five and a quarter days . . . and each of these planets, in addition to its rotation around the sun, also rotates on its own axis, the earth taking twenty-four hours . . . something which clearly also involves a rotation of the moon around the earth . . .

It is interesting to see the judgement which Raphael Halevi now passes on this 'new astronomy' which completely contradicts the 'old' astronomy on which he had based his book. Here it is, in all its moving simplicity: 'This new system has enormous advantages, but this is not the place to explain them all. We shall limit ourselves to pointing out one advantage of general significance: the new system relieves us of having to imagine the famous diurnal sphere . . . whose existence is incompatible with the requirements of reason . . . May this suffice the novice in astronomy for whom this book is intended.'

Thus, invoking reason and certain elementary didactical principles, Raphael Halevi brought his reader onto the threshold of the new system, encouraging him to admire its general outlines, but without actually entering into it. And he concludes, in a tone which I find equally moving:

And here as a sort of signature to this book, small in scale but rich in content, is the prayer which I address to my pupils and to all my readers: study it carefully, and do not be hasty to accuse me if you come across passages where I take up a position contrary to that of my predecessors. He who fathoms secrets and penetrates the hidden places of the conscience knows and will testify on my behalf that my intention was in no way to diminish the importance of my predecessors. No, our intention was entirely disinterested, in the service of truth and enlightenment, and in the service also of my pupils whom I hope to stimulate and to familiarize with the methods of these noble sciences. May this endeavour gain me the sympathy of God and man . . .

Needless to say, Raphael Halevi, that brave and modest servant of the truth in the age of enlightenment—but also, alas! of anti-enlightenment— has fully gained the sympathy of us twentieth-century readers. Reminiscent as he is of David Gans, that other servant of the truth in the age of the Renaissance, we should honour both of them alike as men who did not recoil from taking risks.

True enough, the work was published without the writer's consent (Steinschneider, p. 726), as he himself said in the second part of his Tables (*Luḥot ha-Ibbur*) published in Hanover in that same year (1756). But we should not conclude from that that Raphael Halevi objected to the contents of his *Sefer Tekhunot ha-Shamayim*. He merely reproached the editor Moses Titkin in a very courteous manner for publishing, without his knowledge, lecture-notes by his pupils. Raphael Halevi was fortunate enough to have had a long lifespan (born in 1685, he died at the age of 94 in 1779). A pupil of Leibniz, he devoted his whole life to teaching (free of charge: like Mendelssohn, he made his living as a book-keeper). In 1726, he wrote an astronomical treatise, *Ḥokhmat Ha-tekhuna*, a manuscript of which is in the Bodleian Library (Neubauer 2063). His greatest work in 1756 was his *Tables*, expressing a completely new approach to an understanding of the Jewish calendar according to the principles of Maimonides, and he had in view an encyclopaedic work which would progress systematically from the physical sciences to metaphysics (Neubauer 2062).

One can therefore understand Raphael Halevi's displeasure when they published notes on his lectures without his knowledge just when he was projecting a great work which never saw the light of day. It was an entirely comprehensible, but purely psychological reaction. We have no reason, then, to suppose that he repudiated the book itself, which has preserved its full documentary value for the historian, and we have no wish in any way to diminish the honour which, we are convinced, is legitimately due to him.

No less deserving of our respect are the two last books we should mention in this account of the Copernican revolution in Hebrew literature in the seventeenth and eighteenth centuries.

A book which appeared in 1765 is particularly dear to me. Its author was Moses Steinhardt (died in 1799), son of the celebrated Rabbi Joseph Steinhardt (1720–76), known for his Responsa, *Zikhron Yosef*. The book appeared in Fuerth in Germany, where Joseph Steinhardt had become rabbi in 1763, but for the previous eight years, from 1755, he had been Chief Rabbi of Lower Alsace, resident in Niedernai. Thus, his son Moses must have breathed the air of Niedernai when he was writing the book which was to be published in Fuerth in 1765. Will the reader please allow me to wax euphoric for a moment as I reflect that in the middle of the eighteenth century, on the paths of the Ehn between Obernai and Niedernai which I trod so often in my youth, the son of the Chief Rabbi of Lower Alsace dreamed . . . of Copernicus.

This was a truly remarkable dream, revealing a genuine obsession with truth and enlightenment, for Moses Steinhardt's book was in no sense a treatise of astronomy. It was a translation into Judeo-German of *The Duties of the Heart* by Baḥya Ibn Paquda, that classic of medieval asceticism.

Moses Steinhardt, however, felt the need to provide the first 'Gateway' of this book of ethics ('The Gateway of Unity') with a commentary, also in Judeo-German, and to justify the inclusion of this commentary in a brief introduction in Hebrew (p. 161) explaining that since this 'Gateway' included a cosmology obviously based on the medieval Ptolemaic system, it needed to be corrected by cross-references to the Copernican system whereby the earth turned both upon its own axis and also around the sun. He added:

I am well aware that if these notes are read by ignoramuses, they will laugh at me and regard me as an idiot. But I boldly affirm that this system of Copernicus is in no way in contradiction with our religion, and even less with reason . . . I therefore firmly maintain my point of view, ready to face any criticisms whatsoever, and I shall be able to give rational and convincing replies. I am also aware, moreover, that among my readers I shall find intelligent men who have been reared upon the knees of Wisdom, and it is to them that I address this translation and commentary.

The book, I repeat, appeared at Fuerth in 1765, two years after the Steinhardts had left Niedernai, with the approval of Rabbi Schwabach of Bavaria, of the Rabbi of Karlsruhe, Baden, and, last but not least, of the writer's father, the *Gaon* Joseph Steinhardt (as he is called on the title-page), Ab-Bet-Din of Fuerth, previously Rabbi of all Lower Alsace, who specifically congratulated his son Moses on having completed the Judeo-German translation of Bahya's book with 'a commentary on the Gateway of Unity in the German-Jewish language which will delight the German philosophers, for he throws light on a great number of astronomical problems concerning the course of the sun, moon, and planets around the terrestrial globe'.

Ah, I knew that the violets and primroses in the fields around Niedernai and Obernai could only inspire a boundless love of enlightenment! I now have a better understanding of where my grandparents, my parents, and their offspring acquired their feeling for light and tolerance.

We shall now close the cycle which opened in Prague in 1612 with a book which appeared, once more in Prague, in 1785.

Shevilei de Raki'a (The Paths of the Heavens) by Elijah ben Hayyim of Hochheim was a quarto-volume of only fifty-seven pages, twenty-five of which were devoted to a trigonometrical exposition, and thirty-two to a brief account of the astronomical conceptions necessary for fixing the Jewish calendar. The writer stated:

Seeing that my intention is to interpret the principles laid down by Maimonides in his *Code*, I cannot relinquish his own [Ptolemaic] cosmological and astrological conceptions, and I cannot take modern conceptions into account even where they seem to me correct. However, I intend to complement this work with another, an algebraic and astronomical treatise based on the system of Copernicus. The work as a whole will be grounded on the ideas of contemporary scholars.

As far as we know, Elijah never wrote (or, at any rate, never published) this complementary work, a modern, Copernican approach to the Jewish calendar as against the old Ptolemaic approach. We should at any rate note with satisfaction that, in 1785, a Jewish writer dealing with a basic Jewish traditional theme felt sufficiently sure of himself to consider bringing it into line with the Copernican system, and that this happened in Prague about two centuries after David Gans, in the same city, had glimpsed the possibility and even the necessity of doing this, although he never took the decisive step which could have brought this about.

The wheel had come full circle. With Elijah of Hochheim, Copernicus had gained full acceptance by the Jews.

We can end this survey with an intriguing incident. In its edition of 1786 (the year of the deaths of Moses Mendelssohn and Frederick II), the Hebrew journal *Ha-me'assef*, founded three years previously by disciples of Mendelssohn, contained a review of Elijah of Hochheim's book (pp. 106–10). *Ha-me'assef* was in the forefront of Jewish enlightenment at that period, and in this review the writer was naturally congratulated for demonstrating the need for a harmonization between Jewish tradition and Copernicus.

He was reproached, however, with employing the Hebrew term *nizoz* (spark) to describe rays of light, instead of the more usual *keren* hitherto used by scholars writing in Hebrew (p. 109). Elijah would thus appear, said the anonymous reviewer of his book (quite possibly the very 'enlightened' David Friedländer) to have fully accepted Newton's theories on the origins of light, theories which were purely hypothetical (we should note in passing that Elijah was an innovator in translation, and he proposed rendering the word logarithm in Hebrew by *magbil*; today, more simply, they say *logaritm*!)

Newton's theories on light dated from the beginning of the eighteenth century (1704). By this time the century had nearly ended, but we should remember that the two thick volumes of *Farbenlehre* in which Goethe attacked Newton's ideas appeared as late as 1810. That is how it is in science. No sooner had an agreement been reached on Copernicus and one began to rejoice over the triumph of reason, than reason became suspicious of Newton, whom, a century later, no one would dare to criticize . . . And so on, until the next challenge. Is this not the relativistic image of scientific evolution which was conceived about the year 1596 by David Gans's old Teacher in Prague—our own Teacher, the Maharal?

Bibliography

INTRODUCTION

This book is a first attempt at a comprehensive study of the work of David Gans and his intellectual environment, both in the Jewish context and in the general context of the world of the end of the sixteenth and the beginning of the seventeenth centuries.

As far as possible, all previous studies have been carefully consulted. However, these, although numerous, are so various and so unequal in quality that to include them all in an analytical bibliography of this kind would mean a wholesale presentation of material not all of which would be of value.

Accordingly, we are presenting a bibliography in which we have endeavoured to separate the wheat from the chaff, giving, however, a degree of importance, otherwise unjustified, to certain works which could mislead the researcher by the sometimes stupefying and always inexplicable absurdity of the statements they contain.

There are a great many such warnings to be found both in the main body of the book and in the notes. Together with those in the bibliography, they indicate a series of errors which is only too characteristic of the way in which, for a long period, people have worked in what I might describe as the wild territories rather than the domains of the vast sphere of Hebrew and Jewish studies.

With regard to the background materials to David Gans's works and period, we have given them only a very limited place in our bibliography, as the sources and studies on which our book is based are generally given in the book itself or in the notes. We have therefore been content simply to provide a few indications and to supply the names of authors: by consulting the index, the reader will easily find within the book itself all the bibliographical information he requires.

On the other hand, we have included a section we have entitled 'David Gans's library'. Rather than an index of writers and works referred to by Gans (Huminer's index for *Zemah David* comprises some major omissions, and, where *Nehmad ve-Na'im* is concerned, everything still remains to be done), does not a list of works which Gans may be presumed to have consulted provide a clearer idea of his Jewish and humanistic culture? There were certain books which he specifically claimed to have read, there were others of which he said he had a second-hand knowledge (mainly through Yossipon, Azariah dei Rossi, and certain Christian historiographers), and there were others, again, which he said he had searched for but did not find. All this constituted an intellectual totality, the half-real, half-imaginary library of David Gans, the world of books in which he moved at ease and felt at home.

There is obviously little point in including in this list the classics of Jewish thought from the Bible to the Kabbalistic works of the sixteenth century (*Zemah David* provides sufficient proof of the breadth of David Gans's general rabbinical culture). In this domain, we shall mention only the specialized works (history, geography, astronomy) which Gans himself brings to our notice.

Apart from that, we have divided David Gans's library into the two main categories which he favoured: Jewish and non-Jewish; where some point of particular interest or curiosity occurs, we have indicated the source in *Zemah David* or *Nehmad ve-Na'im*, and we have indicated, by square brackets, the most recent edition of a book, which is often simply a photostatic reproduction of the edition of the work which David Gans had in front of him. In this way we are able to join him, so to speak, in his reading, peering over his shoulders and over four centuries of time.

PLAN OF THE BIBLIOGRAPHY

I   References to David Gans

A   In the General History of Science and in the History of Thought
B   In works of Jewish Bibliography
C   In the 'Jewish Sciences' (Histories, Encyclopaedias, Studies)
    1 Valid and sometimes excellent notices and references
    2 Banal or completely inaccurate notices
    3 Gans ? Never heard of him

II   General Background

A   The Jews in the Renaissance
B   The thought of the Renaissance
    1 General
    2 Cosmography
    3 Astronomy

III   David Gans's Library

A   Historiography, Chronicles, Cosmography, Geography
    1 Jewish sources
    2 Non-Jewish sources

B Astronomy
  1 Jewish sources
  2 Non-Jewish sources

I REFERENCES TO DAVID GANS

A In the General History of Science and in the History of Thought

Before 1974, the date of the appearance of my book on David Gans in the original French edition, Gans was mentioned in only eight works. We shall give them here in chronological order. In this way one can see how the presence of David Gans, still comparatively strong in the nineteenth century, grew faint in the twentieth century until it almost disappeared from the purview of universal history. It only survived in the area of purely Jewish historiography.

1734 *Universal Lexicon aller Wissenschaften und Künste* (Leipzig), vol. 7. A brief entry on David Gantz [*sic*] by Richard Simon.

1851 *Allgemeine Encyclopädie der Wissenschaften und Künste* by Ersch und Gruber (Leipzig), 53rd part, pp. 366–8. Article Gans (David) by D. Cassel. Three pages giving an excellent, detailed, and accurate account, utilizing all the documentation available at the period. In view of this entry, one is surprised that so many errors have found their way into subsequent presentations of Gans's work.

1852 *Lehrbuch einer allgemeinen Literaturgeschichte aller bekanntem Völker der Welt* by J. G. T. Gräsze (Leipzig). David Gans is briefly mentioned in vol. 4, p. 1281 and in vol. 5, pp. 1132–3.

1871 *Zeitschrift für Mathematik und Physick*, ed. Cantor and Schlömilch, 16, 272c. Moritz Steinschneider, '*Kopernikus nach dem Urteile des David Gans*'. A very short page, complementing Steinschneider's entry on Gans in his Cat. Bodl. It should be pointed out that *Bibliotheca Mathematica* (Leipzig), ed. E. G. Eneström, had published Steinschneider's important *Die Mathematik bei den Juden* in 1899, but this first part, beginning with the Talmud, only extended as far as 1500. The reference to David Gans is to be found in the second part which extends from 1551 to 1840, but that part, which appeared in 1905, was published not in *Bibliotheca Mathematica* which was universal in character (and which had ceased publication) but in the specialized review of Jewish studies *MGWJ* (Nf, 13, 193–204, 300–14, 581–605).

1877 S. Gunther, *Studien zur Geschichte der mathematischen und physischen Geographie* (Halle), pp. 114–15 and 118. These mention Gans's account of the Pythagorean sources of Copernicus and of Gans's dialogue with Tycho Brahe in *Neḥmad ve-Na'im*. (The writer wrongly gives 1623 as the date of Gans's death.)

1878 *Allgemeine Deutsche Biographie* (Leipzig), 8, 360–1: Gans (David): a correct but uninteresting entry by N. Brull, who did more significant work on David Gans.

1890 Dreyer, J. L. E.: *Tycho Brahe. A Picture of Scientific Life and Work in the XVI Century* (New York) (Reprint, New York, 1963). 'The historian David Ganz' (*sic*) is mentioned on p. 303 among Tycho Brahe's collaborators in Prague, but his work is not listed in the bibliography of books by contemporaries mentioning the work of Tycho Brahe, although this 'Bibliographical Summary' (pp. 392–6) is described as 'a complete chronological catalogue of books and memoirs containing biographical details or investigations of Tycho's scientific work. . .' Nevertheless, Dreyer was the only Tycho Brahe scholar to do David Gans the honour of including him in one or more of his publications.

1931 Zinner, Ernst, *Die Geschichte der Sternkunde* (Berlin), pp. 427: David Gans's description of Tycho Brahe's astronomical clock. This writer ignored Gans in his *Geschichte und Bibliographie der astronomischen Literatur in Deutschland zur Zeit der Renaissance* (Stuttgart, 1941, 1964²) where a mention of Gans's anti-astrological attitude would have been appropriate (p. 239 ff.). A cruelly ironical detail: in referring to Gans, Zinner called him 'Rabbi David Gans' in his book of 1931, thus stressing Gans's Judaism and his rank in the rabbinic hierarchy. Two years later, Zinner was an enthusiastic adherent of the ideology of the Third Reich.

1976 *Encyclopaedia Universalis* (Paris), see Gans, David. A rather substantial entry written by myself. After the appearance of my book in 1974, the editors of the *Encyclopaedia Universalis*, who had previously approached me for an article on the Maharal of Prague, asked me to contribute this entry on David Gans, who thus, after a century of neglect, made his re-entry into the encyclopaedias of universal history.

B   *In works of Jewish Bibliography*

Apart from the works of Steinschneider who with much competence, though sometimes gropingly, occasionally dwells upon *Ẓemaḥ David* and *Neḥmad ve-Na'im*, there are simple entries in Bartolocci, Buxtorf, Furst, Plantavitius, Wolf, Zedner, and, in Hebrew, in Ben Jacob, Friedberg, and Michael. For details, see index.

C   *In the 'Jewish Sciences' (Histories, Encyclopaedias, Studies)*

Twelve serious monographs have been devoted so far to David Gans:
Alter, Jiri (George), *Two Renaissance Astronomers: David Gans, Joseph Delmedigo*, Rozpravy Ceskoslovenske Akademie, Ved, 68, II (Prague, 1958).
Breuer, Mordechai: 'Megamatav shel Ẓemaḥ David le-Rabbi David Gans', *Hamayan*, 5, 2 (1975), pp. 52–62.

—— *David Gans, Ẓemaḥ David, A Chronicle of Jewish and World History* (Jerusalem, 1983), preface, pp. 1–33.

Huminer, Chaim, *Ẓemaḥ David shel David Gans* (Jerusalem, 1962), preface, pp. 11–47.

Neher, André, 'David Gans', *RHPR*, 4 (1972), pp. 407–13.

—— 'Homer Hadash al David Ganz ke-token', *Tarbiz*, 45, 1–2 (1976), pp. 138–47.

—— 'Tevuna u-mistika bi-tfisa ha-astronomit shel ha-Maharal mi-prag', *Da'at*, 2–3 (1978–9), pp. 139–46.

—— 'Copernicus in the Hebraic Literature from the Sixteenth to the Eighteenth Century', *Journal of the History of Ideas*, xxxviii, 2 (1977), pp. 211–26.

—— 'Gans, David' in *Encyclopaedia Universalis* (1976), vol. 5.

Sedinova, Jirina, 'Non-Jewish Sources in the Chronicle by David Gans Tsemah David', *JB*, viii, 1 (1972), pp. 3–15.

—— 'Czech History as Reflected in the Historical World by David Gans', *JB*, viii, 2 (1972), pp. 74–83.

As for the rest, one has to find one's way between sometimes short but excellent notices, banal or completely inaccurate ones, and, above all, a no man's land in which one searches vainly for the name of David Gans when everything—the subject, the context, the period. etc.—seems to call for it.

Here we shall examine the three categories I have mentioned, confining ourselves, for the last two, to a few typical examples.

1 Valid and sometimes excellent notices and references

These may be found:

(a) in the works of Alter, Breuer, Freedman, Huminer, Neher, Sedinova, Steinschneider. See index.

(b) in works or studies in which Gans is usually mentioned as a historian and in which there is sometimes a clear allusion to his work as an astronomer. See index: Baron, Ben Sasson, Brull, Cohen David, Munk, Stoszel. To which one can add:

Baron, Salo Wittmayer, *A Social and Religious History of the Jews*, vol. xiii (New York, 1969).

Basnage, Jacques, *Histoire des Juifs* (Amsterdam, 1716) (Gans used as an occasional source).

Cohen-Yashar, Yohanan, 'Rabbi Yehuda Halevi veqav shinuy ha-taarik', *Meḥqarim begeografia shel Ereẓ Israël*, 9 (1976).

Goetschel, Roland, *Meïr Ibn Gabbay, Le Discours de la Kabbale Espagnole* (Louvain, 1981).

Kahane, Abraham, *Sifrut Ha-Historia Ha-Israelit* (Warsaw, 1922), ii. 178–93.

Kleinberger, A. F., *The Educational Theory of the Maharal of Prague* (Hebrew) (Jerusalem, 1962).

Levi, Zeev, *Ben Yefet le-Shem, On the Relationship between Jewish and General Philosophy* (Hebrew) (Tel Aviv, 1982).

Mallin, Shlomo, *The Book of Divine Power by the Maharal of Prague* (Jerusalem, 1979).

Ozar, Israel, *A Hebrew Encyclopaedia*, ed. J. D. Eisenstein (New York, 1909), article 'Gans', iii. 233–4 by Shlomo Berman (excellent).

The Jewish Encyclopaedia (New York–London, 1903), v, article 'Gans' by I. Broyde (see below).

Waxman, Meyer, *History of Jewish Literature* (New York, 1960), ii. 324–5 (see below).

Winter, J. and Wunsche: *Die Jüdische Literatur seit Abschluss des Kanons* (Berlin, 1897), iii. 323, 708.

Yerushalmi, Y. H., *Zakhor, Jewish History and Memory* (Seattle, 1982).

Zinberg, Israel, *Die Geschichte fun der Literatur bei Yiden* (Vilna, 1935), v. 58–64 (see below).

(c)   in the vast (and generally excellent) literature concerned with the Jewish community in Prague and Bohemia.

See index: Horowitz, Kisch, Muneles, Scholem, Suler, Thieberger. To which one can add:

Bondy, G., and Dvorsky, F, *Zur Geschichte der Juden in Böhmen, Mähren und Schlesien, Von 906 bis 1620* (1906).

Freudenthal, Max, *Aus der Heimat Mendelssohns* (Berlin, 1900), pp. 222 ff., 264, excellent on the printing-press at Jessnitz where *Neḥmad ve-Na'im* was published in 1743.

Klemperer, Gutmann, 'The Rabbis of Prague', *HJ*, xii (1950), pp. 33–66; xiii (1951), pp. 55–82.

Kohut, A., *Der Alte Prager Friedhof* (1897).

Lieben, Koppelmann, and Hock, Simon, *Gal-Ed*, Grabsteininschriften des Prager israelitischen alten Friedhofs mit biographischen Notizen (Prague, 1856). On David Gans, see pp. 10–12.

Lion, J., and Lukas, J., *Das Prager Ghetto* (Prague, 1959).

—— *The Old Prague Jewish Cemetery* (Prague, 1960).

Muneles, Otto, *Bibliographical Survey of Jewish Prague* (Prague, 1952).

—— *Prague Ghetto in the Renaissance Period* (Prague, 1965) (excellent), p. 85, read 'Magen David' for 'Ahabad David'.

—— 'Zur Prosopographie der Prager Juden im 15. und 16. Jahrhundert,' *JB*, ii, 2 (1966), pp. 64–96.

Schurer, Oskar, *Prag* (Vienna–Leipzig, 1930).

Selbstwehr, Special issue for 1917, *Das jüdische Prag*. Contributions by nearly all the great Prague Jews of the twentieth century. On p. 40 ff. Professor Ladislas Salun (non-Jewish) explained his motivations in erecting the statue of the Maharal at the City Hall in Prague in 1912: a young girl gives the old man a deadly rose (i.e., a new age has ousted the old one).

The complete list of journals:
Jahrbuch der Gesellschaft für Geschichte der Juden in der Cechoslovakischen Republik (*JGGJC*) (Prague 1928–39), and *Judaica Bohemiae* (*JB*), (Prague, publication of the State Jewish Museum from 1965 onwards).
In *JB*, apart from Muneles and Sedinova (see index), see particularly: iv, 1 (1968), pp. 3–19: Krejki, Karel, *Les légendes juives pragoises*. iv, 1 (1968), pp. 20–63: Herman, Jan, *Die wirschaftliche Beätigung und die Berufe der Prager Juden vor ihrer Ausweisung im Jahre 1541*. v, 1 (1969), pp. 30–70: Herman, Jan, *La Communauté juive de Prague et sa structure au commencement des temps modernes (Ire moitié du XVIe siècle)*.

See also the studies devoted to the Maharal by myself and the scholars of my Strasbourg University Department (all now in Israel like myself):
Dreyfus, Théodore, *Dieu parle aux hommes* (Études Maharaliennes, Paris, 1969).

Gross, Benjamin, *Le messianisme juif* (Études Maharaliennes, Paris, 1969).
Neher, André, *Le Puits de l'Exil: la théologie dialectique du Maharal de Prague* (Paris, 1966).
—— 'Jewish Religious Thought', in *Religions and the Promise of the Twentieth Century, Readings in the History of Mankind* (Unesco, New York, 1965), pp. 128–55.
—— 'Michel-Ange et le Maharal de Prague, Essai sur la parenté de leur œuvre créatrice, *RHPR*, 4 (1975), pp. 535–42.
—— 'The View of Time and History in Jewish Culture', in *Cultures and Time*, (Unesco, Paris, 1976), pp. 149–68.
—— 'Le Sionisme du Maharal de Prague d'après Martin Buber,' *Revue Internationale de Philosophie*, 126 (1978), pp. 526–35.
Neher-Bernheim, Renée, *Histoire juive—Faits et Documents—de la Renaissance à nos jours* (Paris, 1974), vol. i.

2   Banal or completely inaccurate notices
Clichés and errors accumulate and are duly passed on from one scholar to another.

(a) Among the clichés, there is the idea that David Gans was the first Jew *in the Ashkenazi world* to take up secular studies (astronomy, history, mathematics, etc.), but to accept such a notion would mean overlooking the Rema, the Maharal, Jaffe, and many other 'Ashkenazi' Jews who were Gans's authorities and consequently his predecessors. The following is a list of authors who are guilty of this misapprehension:

Jost, J. M., *Geschichte der Israeliten seit der Zeit der Maccabäer bis auf unsere Tage* (Berlin, 1828), viii 194: 'Eigentliche Gelehrte Juden von höherer Bildung als das rabbinische Fach zuliess gab es wohl in Deutschland damals gar nicht.'

Zunz, Leopold, *Gesammelte Schriften* (Berlin, 1875), i. 185–6. 'David Gans ist der erste deutsche Jude jener Epoche der für Geschichte, für Erd und Himmelskunde Sinn hatte und fähig war.' One should add that Zunz described *Neḥmad ve-Na'im* as follows: 'Eine Anleitung zur mathematischen Geographie'. A strange formula for an astronomical treatise!

Cassel, David, *Lehrbuch der jüdischen Geschichte und Literatur* (1st edition, Frankfurt-on-Main, 1868, 2nd edition, *ibid.*, 1896), pp. 478–9: 'Der erste deutsche Jude . . .' In these two pages, Cassel gave the date of Gans's death as 1618 and seemed to have completely forgotten the remarkable pages on Gans he had written in Ersch and Gruber's *Allgemeine Encyclopädie* which we praised above.

Graetz, Heinrich, *Geschichte der Juden* (3rd edition, Leipzig, 1891), lx. 442–3. An almost caricatural sketch of David Gans. Graetz contrasts his enlightenment to his obscurantist milieu, minimizes his importance as a historiographer, and devotes only two lines to his astronomical works which, he says, he wrote 'naturally' (*sic*) in the Hebrew language!

Dubnow, Simon, *Weltgeschichte des jüdischen Völkes* (Berlin, 1927), translated from the Russian by Aron Steinberg, vi, 278–80 and 456. A very superficial sketch, beginning with the false statement 'Als *einziger* Repräsentant des weltlichen Wissens tritt uns in diesem Reiche des Rabbinismus und der Kabbala David Gans entgegen . . .', and dealing with Gans primarily as a historiographer. Neither Dubnow nor Graetz drew attention to the fact that Gans was the first Hebrew writer to mention Copernicus.

Karpeles, Gustav, *Geschichte der jüdischen Literatur* (Berlin, 1886), ii. 990–1. 'Der erste deutsche Jude . . .' He gave the date of his death as 1618: many other errors. He mistranslated *Zemaḥ David* as 'der *Stolz* David's'.

He said: 'Gans war ein Freund des hohen Rabbi Löw und weiss in seiner Chronik von dessen Audienz *mancherlei* zu erzählen . . .' Karpeles must have read between the lines of *Zemaḥ David*, for Gans made it perfectly plain there that he did not wish to say anything about that audience!

Encyclopaedia Judaica (Berlin, 1931), vii, article 'GANS (AWSA)' (S. A. Horodetsky). 'Gans, der als erster deutscher Jude, in einer Umgebung, in der halachische Judentum herrscht, gründliche profanwissenschaftliche Studien trieb . . .'

Enzyclopaedia le-Toldot Gedolei Yisrael, ed. Mordechai Margoliut (Tel Aviv, Jerusalem, undated) ii, col. 355–8 (Akiba Posner): 'The first Ashkenazi . . .'.

(*b*) Among the errors, the commonest is a confusion beween the astronomer Johannes Muller, contemporary with David Gans, and his fifteenth-century namesake, generally known as Regiomontanus (see index).

In 1937, Freedman (p. 24) drew up a list of scholarly writers who fell into the trap:

Kohut, *Geschichte der deutschen Juden*, p. 568.

Karpeles, *Geschichte der jüdischen Literatur* (see above).

Wininger, *Grosse Jüdische National-Biographie*, article Gans, ii. 386.

Encyclopaedia Judaica (see previously).

The Jewish Encyclopedia (New York–London, 1903), v, article Gans (by I. Broyde). (Apart from this, the article is full of substance).

Grunwald, *Illustrierter Israelitischer Volks Kalender für das Jahr 5650* (1890), 'Rabbi David Gans', p. 118.

—— *Mitteilungen des Vereins für Geschichte der Deutschen in Böhmen*, pp. 27, 279.

Zinberg, *Die Geschichte der Literatur bei Yiden* (in Yiddish) (Vilna, 1935), v, 60. (Apart from this, pages 58–64 are excellent.)

    In 1937, he could have added to this list the article 'Astronomy' by Joseph Jacobs in *The Jewish Encyclopedia* (1902), ii, the article 'Astronomie' in *Encyclopaedia Judaica* (1929), iii (by B. Suler who at any rate did justice to the Rema, the Maharal, and Jaffe), and the article 'Gans' in *Jüdisches Lexikon* (Berlin, 1928), ii, 892.

    At the time of writing, I am sorry to have to add to this impressive list an over-hasty statement by J. Babelon (q.v.), and, especially:

Roth, Cecil, *The Jews in the Renaissance* (Philadelphia, 1959), p. 235.

Encyclopedia Judaica (Jerusalem, 1971), vii, article 'Gans' (name of writer not given). This would be a good article if it did not hand on this gross confusion between the two Mullers. And yet the bibliography mentions the work of G. Alter who protested strongly against precisely this error!

    The writer of the article 'Astronomy' (iii) in the same encyclopaedia (Arthur Beer) was more careful, however. Where Gans was concerned, he did not mention Johannes Muller at all. The presentation of Gans in this article as an astronomer is correct, but the article also claims that there is no evidence that the Maharal was anything but an astrologer. Dare I ask Mr Arthur Beer if he has read what the Maharal has to say about astrology in *Netivot Olam*?

    While we are on the subject, it is worth looking at the article 'Astrology' in the old, but still valid *Jewish Encyclopedia* (1902, ii). The writer (and what a writer! None other than Kaufmann Kohler) stated that the astronomer and historian David Gans was the last important Jewish adherent of astrology. In making this assertion, he based himself on *Ẓemaḥ David* and completely overlooked the chapters rejecting astrology in *Neḥmad ve-Na'im*.

    (*c*)   Another major error that is sometimes made is in connection with David Gans's attitude to the Copernican revolution.

Here the prize goes to:

Feldman, W. M., *Rabbinical Mathematics and Astronomy* (London, 1931). In this very serious and well-documented work with a foreword by Professor A. Fraenkel of the Hebrew University of Jerusalem, one reads, in the chapter entitled 'The Ptolemaic and Copernican Systems' (pp. 70–3):

'The Copernican system met with very determined opposition, and the Christian Church *as well as the Jewish Rabbis* [my italics] denounced it as heretical because the Bible said that the earth was fixed and the sun was moving . . .' As evidence of the 'vehement' Jewish intolerance, the writer mentioned Rabbi Tubia Katz (see Tuvia in our index). He mentioned neither the Maharal, nor Delmedigo, nor David Gans, although his *Naim Venehmad* (*sic*) was included (p. xiv) among the seventeen works in the 'List of Works Frequently Consulted'. This list did not include Delmedigo's *Elim*. As for *Neḥmad ve-Na'im*, I fear that the word 'frequently' as used in this context was more than a little hyperbolical.

On the other hand, I have no wish to pick a quarrel with my learned late colleague, H. H. Ben-Sasson, writer of the article Gans (AWSA) in *Ha-Encyclopedia Ha-Ivrit* (in Hebrew). At the end of the article one finds the surprising statement: 'In *Neḥmad ve-Na'im* one finds the first description of the Copernican system in Hebrew, but Gans rejected it *because of the Talmudic tradition* (*sic*). We have amply demonstrated, for our part, that, on the contrary, the Talmudic tradition would rather have had the effect of inducing Gans to accept the Copernican system were it not for the Ptolemaic scientific objections of Tycho Brahe and Kepler who were still attached to the Ptolemaic system at that period.

There is probably a misprint here, and *talmudit* (Talmudic) should read *talmit* (Ptolemaic), the term correctly used by Zobel and Leibovits in reference to David Gans in the article *Astronomia* in the same encyclopaedia (iv, 821).

The pages on David Gans in:

Waxman, Meyer, *History of Jewish Literature* (New York, 1960), ii (pp. 324 ff.) are excellent, apart from the fact that Gans's opposition to the Copernican system, partly—and correctly—attributed to the influence of Tycho Brahe, was also said to be caused 'partly by the piety of the author who could not accept the view of Copernic since it contradicts Biblical passages', which is quite untrue.

3   Gans? Never heard of him!

Two typical examples:

The Legacy of Israel, ed. I. Abrahams, E. R. Bevan, and Charles Singer (Oxford, 1928).

This work, at once scholarly and apologetic, attempting to give an account of all those Jews who have made a contribution to universal civilization, honoured neither David Gans nor the Maharal with a mention.

One of the collaborators (F. C. Burkitt) ended his study of 'the debt of Christianity to Judaism' with the following dogmatic assertion which contradicts every line of our book: 'In less than a century, the discoveries of

Copernicus and Galileo showed once and for all the vanity of ancient speculations of that kind, whether they were due to a *cosmologist* of the second or the fourteenth centuries. The *Zohar* is now only a curiosity for scholars . . .'. No! The discoveries of Copernicus and Galileo, on the contrary, gave new life to the *Zohar*, and it was largely owing to its influence and that of the *Kabbalah* in general that the Jews and many non-Jews (Kepler, Bruno, Böhme) came to accept the ideas of Copernicus.

F. Secret (*Les Kabbalistes Chrétiens de la Renaissance*, p. 358) rightly pointed out a similar error of understanding in the otherwise remarkable work of J. L. Blau, *The Christian Interpretation of the Cabala in the Renaissance* (New York, 1944).

The Jews, Their History, Culture and Religion, ed. Louis Finkelstein (3rd edition, New York, 2 vols., 1960). No mention of David Gans in the index or in the work itself which is a kind of up-to-date sequel to the *Legacy of Israel*.

II GENERAL BACKGROUND

A The Jews in the Renaissance

Abrahams, Israel, Bevan, E. R., and Singer, Charles, *The Legacy of Israel* (Oxford, 1928) (see above).

Baer, Fritz, *A History of the Jews in Christian Spain*, 2 vols. (Philadelphia, 1961–6).

Barzillay, Isaac, *Yoseph Shlomo Delmedigo (Yashar of Candia): His life, Works and Time* (Leiden, 1974).

Ben-Sasson, Hayim-Hillel, 'Dor Golei Sefarad al Azmo', *Zion* xxvi, (1961), pp. 23–64.

—— 'Galut u-Geulah be-Enav shel Dor Golei Sefarad', *Sefer Yovel le Yizhak Baer* (Jerusalem, 1961), pp. 216–27.

—— 'The Reformation in Contemporary Jewish Eyes', *The Israel Academy of Sciences and Humanities Proceedings*, iv (12) (Jerusalem, 1970), pp. 249–55.

Ben-Sasson, Yona, *Hamaarekhet ha-Hagutit be-mishnato shel ha-Rema* (Hebr. Univ. stencil, Jerusalem, 1972).

Blau, J. L., *The Christian Interpretation of the Cabala in the Renaissance* (New York, 1944).

Bonfil, Reuven, *Ha-Rabbanut be-Italia bitekufat ha-Renaissance* (Jerusalem, 1979).

Brod, Max, *Tycho Brahes Weg Zu Gott* (Leipzig, 1915).

Carlebach, Joseph, *Levi ben Gerson als Mathematiker* (Berlin, 1910).

Chouraqui, Saadia, *Mone Mispar*, ed. Gad B. Sarfati (Ramat-Gan, 1973).

Cohn, Berthold, *Der Almanach Perpetuum des Abraham Zakuto* (Strasbourg, 1918).

Franck, Adolphe, *Dictionnaire des Sciences Philosophiques* (Paris, 1885).

—— *La Kabbale* (Paris, 1843) (*The Kabbala*, (London, 1926)).

Gandz, Salomon, *Studies in Hebrew Astronomy and Mathematics* (New York, 1970).

Goldstein, Baruk Rafaēl, 'Al terumato shel ha-Ralbag le-Astronomia', *The Israel Academy of Sciences and Humanities Proceedings*, iv. (Jerusalem, 1971), pp. 174–85.

Guttmann, Yizḥak, *Philosophies of Judaism* (New York, 1964).

Hyamson, Albert M., 'The Lost Tribes and the Influences of the Search for them on the Return of the Jews to England', *JQR*, xv (1903), pp. 640–76.

Katz, Jacob, *Exclusiveness and Tolerance: Jewish–Gentile Relations in Medieval and Modern Times* (New York, 1962).

Kayserling, Meyer, *Studia Sephardica: Texts and Studies in the History and Literature of Spanish and Portuguese Jewry; Biblioteca Espanola-Portuguesa-Judaica* and other studies in Ibero-Jewish bibliography by this author and by I. S. da Silva-Rosa, with a bibliography of Kayserling Publications by M. Weisz selected with Prolegomena by Yosef Hayim Yerushalmi (New York 1971).

Loeb, Isidore, 'Joseph Hacohen et les chroniqueurs juifs,' *REJ*, xvi, 31 (1888).

Neher, André, *Le Puits de l'Exil: La théologie dialectique du Maharal de Prague* (Paris, 1966).

—— 'Michel-Ange et le Maharal de Prague, Essai sur la parenté de leur œuvre créatrice', *RHPR*, 4 (1975), pp. 535–42.

Neubauer, A., 'Where are the ten Tribes?', *JQR*, i (1889).

Renan-Neubauer, *Les Écrivains juifs français du XIVᵉ siècle* (Paris, 1893).

Revah, I. S., see Nahon, Gérard, 'Les Sephardim, les Marranes, les Inquisitions péninsulaires et leurs archives dans les travaux récents de I. S. Revah', *REJ*, 132 (1973), pp. 5–48.

Roth, Cecil, *The Jews in the Renaissance* (Philadelphia, 1959).

Ruderman, David B., *The World of a Renaissance Jew: The Life and Thought of Abraham ben Mordecai Farissol* (Cincinnati, 1981).

Silber, Mendel, *American Hebrew Literature* (New Orleans, 1928).

Simonson, Shlomo, *Toldot Hayehudim be-Duksut Mantua*, 2 vols. (Tel Aviv–Jerusalem, 1962–4).

Touati, Charlie, *La pensée philosophique et théologique de Gersonide* (Paris, 1974).

Usque, Samuel, *A consolation for the tribulations of Israel* (Philadelphia, 1965) (edit. princeps, Spanish, Ferrara, 1553).

Weil, Gérard E., *Elie Levita, Humaniste et Masorète* (Leiden, 1963).

Wolf, Lucien, *Menasseh ben Israel's Mission to Oliver Cromwell* (London, 1901) (including *The Hope of Israel*, by Menasseh ben Israel (London, 1650)).

Zarfati, Gad Ben-Ami, 'Yashar mi-Qandia: ha-Talmid ha-Yehudi shel Galileo', *Maḥanayim*, 126 (1972), pp. 168–71. (Ibid., pp. 152–9, Erlich, Israel, 'Gedolei Yisrael ke-astronomim u-ke-astrologim'.)

B *The thought of the Renaissance*

1 General

Cassirer, Ernst, *Das Erkenntnisproblem in der Philosophie und Wissenschaft der neueren Zeit* (Berlin, 1911).

Delumeau, Jean, *La civilisation de la Renaissance* (Paris, 1973).

Duhem, Pierre, *Le système du monde*, tome 5 (Paris, 1913).

Evans, R. J. W., *Rudolf II and his World* (Oxford, 1973).

Febvre, Lucien, *Au coeur religieux du XVIᵉ siècle* (Paris, 1957).

Markish, Simon, *Erasme et les Juifs* (Geneva, 1979).

Rice, E. F., *The Renaissance Idea of Wisdom* (Cambridge, 1958).

Secret, F., *Les Kabbalistes chrétiens de la Renaissance* (Paris, 1964).

Servier, Jean, *Histoire de l'Utopie* (Paris, 1967).

2 Cosmography

Babelon, Jean, *L'Amérique des Conquistadores* (Paris, 1947).

Coote, C. H., *The voyage from Lisbon to India 1505–6, being an account and Journal by Albericus Vespuccius* (London, 1894).

Lafaye, Jacques, *Quetzalcoatl et Guadalupe; La formation de la conscience nationale au Mexique* (Paris, 1974).

Peschel, Oscar, *Geschichte der Erdkunde bis auf A. V. Humboldt und Carl Ritter* (Munich, 1865).

3 Astronomy

Cohn, Berthold, 'Vokabularium astronomish-mathematischer Fachausdrücke', *Jarhbuch Jud. Lit. Ges.*, xvii.

Deissmann, Adolf, *Johann Kepler und die Bibel: Ein Beitrag zur Geschichte der Schrift-Autorität* (Marburg, 1894).

Delambre, J. B., *Histoire de l'astronomie moderne* (Paris, 1821).

Dreyer, J. L. E., *A History of Astronomy: History of the Planetary System* (2nd edn., New York, 1930).

Gade, J. A., *The Life and Times of Tycho Brahe* (New York, 1947).

Galileo Galilei, *Le Opere*, 20 vols., Edizione Nazionale (Florence, 1890–1909).

Galileo, *Man of Science*, ed. Ernam McMullin (New York–London, 1967).

Gunther, Ludwig, *Kepler und die Theologie* (Giessen, 1905).

Gunther, S., *Die Lehre von der Erdrundung bei den Arabern und Hebräern* (1877).

Gusdorf, Georges, *La révolution Galiléenne*, 2 vols. (Paris, 1969).

Hasner, Josef von, *Tycho Brahe und J. Kepler in Prag* (Prague, 1872).

Heisenberg, Werner, *Physik und Philosophie* (Stuttgart, 1959).

Helmleben, Johannes, *Galilei* (Hamburg, 1970).

—— *Kepler* (Hamburg, 1971).

Journal for the History of Astronomy, ed. M. A. Hoskin (Churchill College, Cambridge).

Koestler, Arthur, *The Sleepwalkers* (London, 1958).

Koyré, Alexandre, *From the Closed World to the Infinite Universe* (London, 1962).

Kuhn, Thomas S., *The Copernican Revolution* (Cambridge, 1957).

Langford, Jerome J., *Galileo, Science and the Church* (Michigan Press, 1971).

Samburski, Samuel (ed.), *Hamaḥshavah ha-Fisikalit be-Hithavutah* (Jerusalem, 1972).

—— 'Kepler in Hegel's eyes', *Proceedings of the Israel Academy of Sciences and Humanities*, v, 3 (Jerusalem, 1971).

—— 'Copernicus in the Perspective of our generation,' *Proceedings of the Israel Academy of Sciences and Humanities*, v, 11 (Jerusalem, 1976).

Schwarzschild, Steven and Henry: *Raphael Levi Hannover and Moses Wolff*, Leo Baeck Institute, Y.B. XXIX, 1984, pp. 229–58.

III   DAVID GANS'S LIBRARY

A   Historiography, Chronicles, Cosmography, Geography

1   Jewish Sources

Seder Olam (Mantua, 1514; Venice, 1545; Basle, 1580).

Yossipon (Mantua, 1476–9) (Huminer, Jerusalem, 1972).

Benjamin of Tudela, *Massaot*, (Constantinople, 1543; Ferrara, 1556) (London 1907, reprint 1964).

Farissol, Abraham, *Iggeret Orḥot Olam* (Ferrara, 1524; Venice, 1587).

Zacuto, Abraham, *Sefer ha-Yuḥasin* (Constantinople, 1566; Cracow, 1580).

Joselmann of Rosheim, Diary MS (ed. Krakauer, *REJ*, xvi (1888)). *Sefer Hammiknah* MS (ed. Hava Fraenkel-Goldschmidt, Mekiẓei Nirdamim (Jerusalem, 1970).

Ha-Kohen, Joseph ben Joshua, *Sefer Divrēi Hayamim* (Sabionetta, 1554). *Emek Habakha*, MS (1575) (ed. Litteris (Vienna 1852) Transl. by Harry S. May, *The Vale of Tears* (The Hague, 1971). *Massiv Gevulot Ammim*, MS (1557), see index.

Gedaliah ibn-Yaḥya, *Shalshelet ha-Kabbalah* (Venice, 1587; Cracow, 1590).

Azariah dei Rossi (Min Ha-Adomim), *Meor Enayim* (Mantua, 1595) (reprint ed. Cassel, Makor (Jerusalem, 1970)).

2   Non-Jewish Sources

The Historians of Antiquity (mentioned by Azariah dei Rossi).

Cosmas (de Prague), *Chronica Boemorum*, MS (Migne, *Patrol. Latina*, 166).

Eisenberg, Jacob, *Croneck der Sassen* (Mainz, 1492).

Christopher Columbus, *His Life, by his son Fernando Columbus* (Venice, 1571).

Amerigo Vespucci, *Mundus Novus*, see index.

Magellan, *Account of his Travels by Antonio Pigafetta* (Ramusio, 1540).

Boemus, Joan, *Omnium gentium mores leges et ritus* (Augsburg, 1520).

De Gomara, Francisco Lopez, *Historia general de las Indias* (Anvers, 1554).

Apianus, Peter, *Cosmographia* (Landshut, 1524).

Munster, Sebastian, *Cosmographia* (Basle, from 1541 to 1588), see index.

Mercator, Gerardus, *Terrae Santae descriptio* (Louvain, 1537). *Mappamunda* (Louvain, 1538). *Chronologia* . . . *ab initio mundi ad annum Domini 1568 ex eclipsibus et observationibus astronomicis* (Duisburg, 1568). *Nova et aucta orbis terrae descriptio ad usum navigantium accommodata* (Duisburg, 1568), see index.

Ortelius, Abraham, *Theatrum Orbis Terrarum* (Antwerp, 1550; 25th edn. 1598), see index.

Caesius, Georg, *Catalogus* . . . *omnium cometarum secundum seriem annorum a diluvio conspectorum* . . . *ad 1579* (Nuremberg, 1579).

Buenting, Heinrich, *Itinerarium Sacrae Scripturae* (Wittenberg and Helmstedt, 1581; Magdeburg, 1585, 1592) see index.

Rattel, Heinrich, *Schlesische und der weitberümpten Stadt Bretzlaw General Chronica* (1585, folio, 1587).

Spangenberg, Cyriak, *Sächssische Chronica* (Frankfurt O/M, 1585).

Faustus, Laurentius, *Chronologia auch Anatomia* (Leipzig, 1586).

Boregk, Martin, *Behmische Chronika* (Wittemberg, 1587).

Golzius, Hubert, *Keyserische Chronik* (Frankfurt O/M, 1588).

B *Astronomy*

1 Jewish sources

Abraham bar Ḥiyya, *Sefer Zurat HaArez* (1130), Latin translation by Sebastian Munster (Basle, 1546) (*Sefer Po'al HaShem* (Bnei Brak, 1968), vol. 1).

Zeraḥiah ben Isaac Ha-Levi Gerondi (1150), *Sefer Ha-Ma'or* (Venice Talmud, 1552).

Isaac Israeli, *Yesod Olam*, MS 1330 (1st edn. Berlin, 1777, 2nd edn. Berlin, 1848; recent edn. in *Sefer Poal Hashem* (Bnei Brak, 1968), vol. ii).

Levi ben Gerson (Gersonides, Ralbag), *see* index.

Moses Isserles (Rema), *see* index.

Judah Loew ben Bezalel (*Maharal*), *see* index.

Mordecai Jaffe, *see* index.

Eliezer Ashkenazi, *see* index.

Alphonsine and Pedrine Tables, *see* index.

Tables of Abraham Zacuto (facsimile reproduction by Berthold Cohn (Munich, 1915).

The published version of *Neḥmad ve-Na'im* refers to 'the great astronomer and astrologer' Abraham ben Ḥayyim (*NN* 8a). Alter distinguished him from

Abraham bar Ḥiyya (p. 23), but he was unable to discover any such figure in the history of Jewish astronomy. In reality, it was, in fact, Abraham bar Ḥiyya: his name appears clearly in the Geneva manuscript. If he was mentioned twice within a few lines, it is not surprising, since Gans, on the same page, referred to Isaac Israeli in the same way.

2 Non-Jewish sources

With the exception of Euclid, Aristotle, and Copernicus whom he had read, Gans found the names of the ancient and Arab writers he mentioned in the epilogue to *Neḥmad ve-Na'im* (see the index) in the works of the Rema, Azariah dei Rossi, and Tycho Brahe.

Nicholas Copernicus, *De Revolutionibus Orbium Coelestium*, Libri VI (Nuremberg, 1543) (Anastatic impression, Brussels, 1966).

Astronomia Teutsch (Frankfurt, 1571).

Tycho Brahe: The 'conclusion of conclusions' of *Neḥmad ve-Na'im* shows that Gans possessed all the works of Tycho Brahe which were published during his lifetime, which would amount to practically all Brahe's works. Gans culled a mass of information and names of writers from these works. (*Tychonis Brahe Dani Opera Omnia*, ed. J. L. E. Dreyer (Copenhagen, 1913–29), 15 vols.)

Johannes Kepler: Until 1613, the year of Gans's death, Kepler had published only ten works, of which Gans could have had a serious knowledge only of *Mysterium Cosmographicum* (Tübingen, 1596), and possibly *Astronomia Nova* (1609). I say possibly because, in the normal way, if Gans had read *Astronomia Nova*, he would have mentioned Galileo, which he did not. Gans knew Kepler only in the first tentative phase of his researches, although he could have seen him working, in Tycho Brahe's lifetime, on the first drafts of the *Rodolphine Tables*, although they were not finally published until 1627. It was with these *New Tables* in view that Gans translated the *Tables of Pedro* from Hebrew into German for Tycho and Kepler. (Johannes Kepler: *Gesammelte Werke*, ed. Max Caspar (Munich, 1949–59), 18 vols.)

Index